MW01193354

TAPROOTS OF TENNESSEE

TAPROOTS

of

TENNESSEE

Historic Sites and Timeless Recipes

Lynne Drysdale Patterson

Photography by Jeffrey Stoner

With a Foreword by Minoa Uffelman

THE UNIVERSITY OF TENNESSEE PRESS
Knoxville

Copyright © 2019 by The University of Tennessee Press / Knoxville.
All Rights Reserved. Manufactured in the United States of America.
First Edition.

Photographs reproduced and distributed by permission. © 2018
Jeffrey Stoner. Unauthorized reproduction prohibited. All rights reserved.

LIBRARY OF CONGRESS CATALOGING-IN-PUBLICATION DATA

Names: Patterson, Lynne Drysdale, author. |
Stoner, Jeffrey, 1953–photographer.
Title: Taproots of Tennessee: historic sites and timeless recipes /
Lynne Drysdale Patterson; photography by Jeffrey Stoner; with a fore-
word by Minoa Uffelman.
Description: First edition. | Knoxville: The University of Tennessee Press,
[2019] | Includes index. |
Identifiers: LCCN 2019003532 (print) | LCCN 2019004058 (ebook) |
ISBN 9781621905127 (Kindle) | ISBN 9781621905134 (pdf) |
ISBN 9781621905110 (pbk.)
Subjects: LCSH: Cooking, American—Southern style. | Cooking—
Tennessee. | Tennessee—History. | Tennessee—Pictorial works. |
LCGFT: Cookbooks.
Classification: LCC TX715.2.S68 (ebook) | LCC TX715.2.S68 P384 2019
(print) | DDC 641.59768—dc23
LC record available at https://lccn.loc.gov/2019003532

Contents

Illustrations

Foreword

Taproots of Tennessee: Historic Sites and Timeless Recipes takes those of us who love Tennessee and delicious food on a fascinating journey through the history of the Tennessee Historical Commission's seventeen state historic sites and their foodways. The lives and times of Tennessee's great frontier statesmen and women seem to come alive as Lynne Drysdale Patterson chronicles these trailblazers and how they impacted the Volunteer State's history. While the breadth and variety of foods indicate that our Tennessee ancestors enjoyed many of the same foods we do today, how we obtain and prepare our food could not be more different. Contemplating change in the way Americans eat is essential to understanding history.

Discussions of food are extremely popular with our global public. Millions watch the Food Network which provides twenty-four hours of programming about cooking, baking, and eating. Exploring food traditions from around the world demonstrates that to understand what people eat one must understand their culture. The historical and academic study of foodways is also robust. Living history museums grow heirloom vegetables and raise heritage breeds of livestock. To understand the history of food one must have knowledge of labor systems, settlement patterns, land distribution, government policies, technology, and markets. Communities were formed around food production for survival and economy, and food was used ritually and religiously.

Unlike our ancestors, most Americans are disconnected from the agricultural world. Supermarkets offer a cornucopia of choices. And fast food is ever-present. Those dining with General Daniel Smith and his family at Rock Castle, or with the Tipton or Haynes families during the late-eighteenth century, however, could never have imagined the conveniences of today. Before early settlers prepared a meal, trees had to be felled, logs would be split into kindling in order to provide heat for cooking, and water would be hauled in buckets from a nearby spring to kitchens and hearths. By the early-twentieth century, water flowed from a faucet with the turn of a wrist. Electric lights illuminated work spaces. And cooks could adjust oven temperatures with the twist of a dial.

The state historic sites themselves reflect the settlement patterns of Tennessee. The earliest sites were settled by English, Scotch-Irish, and French Huguenots who crossed the mountains before Tennessee became a state in 1796. During the days of American settlement, foods and foodway traditions from Europe, Africa, and Native America combined to create the food featured in this book. These settlers would have brought cookbooks from England or wider Europe or owned some of the early cookbooks published in the colonies. The first settlers who crossed the Appalachian Mountains from Virginia and Carolina were primarily Scotch-Irish Presbyterians. They would have eaten in a way we now call locally sourced. They might have brought with them some provisions they knew would not be available, such as sugar, tea, and coffee. But their diet—indeed their survival—depended on plants and animals indigenous to the area. Early Tennesseans ate a great deal of wild game. Early accounts discuss the merits of bear meat. There was an abundance of buffalo and deer, as well as squirrel, rabbit, opossum, raccoon, and other animals modern Americans generally no longer eat. Households having sure-shot hunters enjoyed all manner of birds including wild turkey, quail, and pigeon. Streams, creeks, rivers, and lakes provided fish: brim, blue gill, crappie, catfish, and even freshwater shellfish and turtles were consumed.

As the nineteenth century progressed, Tennesseans established towns and chartered counties. People produced cash crops such as tobacco and cotton that were integrated into the global markets, although slave labor was the engine of the economy particularly after the invention of the cotton gin. Farmers also planted diversified crops to feed their families and the community. Vegetable gardens produced potatoes, squash, tomatoes, pumpkins, melons, beans, peas, turnips, cabbage, and carrots.

As Tennessee was settled, the heart of the community was the country store. A visit to the store meant seeing neighbors, hearing gossip, and perhaps buying a newspaper. Merchants would stock the food products Tennesseans could not grow. Stores sold tools and other necessities, such as fabrics. The store also might house the post office. Store owners provided necessary credit to customers until harvest-time when cash crops could be sold, and they often bought eggs from women, an important source of income for rural families.

Before the days of refrigeration Tennesseans preserved meat with salt, smoke, and by "drying." Root vegetables, such as potatoes and turnips, and other dry goods would be stored in a root cellar or equally dry, cool place. Tennesseans built spring houses on cold running streams to store dairy products, keeping them cool in summer and from freezing in the winter.

As a chapter from *Taproots of Tennessee* reveals, wealthy southerners' elegant dining rooms served complicated dishes to please a discerning pallet. Sarah Polk, wife of President James K. Polk, took her kitchen management skills and Tennessee charm—and enslaved cook—to the White House. The state dinners she oversaw were legendary. One guest from Connecticut recorded in her diary a four-hour dinner in which 150 courses were served "in the French style."

Moreover, Tennesseans have always loved desserts. Baking without the benefit of ovens set at a steady and reliable temperature meant cooks had to be skilled in managing the fire with the appropriate wood—stoking it as needed. Tennesseans cultivated apples, pears and peach orchards, and ate indigenous fruits and berries, like strawberries, blueberries, blackcurrants, and blackberries. The native pawpaw, with its sweet flavor, is often eaten raw but is also used in a variety of desserts and ice cream. Approaching more modern times, citrus fruit would have been imported, and oranges at Christmas would have been a treat in Tennessee well into the twentieth century.

One of the most enduring stereotypes of Tennesseans is that we eat a hearty diet of corn and pork. Indeed, corn would have been a staple in most Tennessee households. This indigenous crop was new to European settlers but soon became essential for survival. It is also efficient to grow and easy to process. Corn takes about six weeks to grow—from planting to eating—and can be consumed in a variety of ways. Fresh corn could be eaten straight from the cobb, or the kernels could be cut from the cob and made into corn pudding, creamed corn, or served hot and buttered in a bowl. Dried corn was ground into cornmeal for bread and grits. Corn was even distilled into whiskey and enjoyed for social occasions or used for medicinal purposes.

Pork was important to Tennesseans' diets as well. Pigs were inexpensive to raise and could be efficiently turned into edible meat. A piglet born in the spring would be ready for slaughter in the fall after the first freeze. Cold weather was essential in preventing spoilage, and every part of the pig was eaten or turned into a food product: bacon, sausage, tenderloin, ribs, pork bellies, pork roast, fatback, and ham hocks. Eating "high on the hog," meant the hams and shoulders were prized sections.

Poultry was also valuable and would have been kept on large, wealthy, farmsteads and by small family homesteads. Chickens, turkeys, ducks, and guineas regularly graced southern tables, but perhaps a more important feature of having poultry would have been egg production, which was important for cooking as well as selling and bartering. Rural Tennesseans, even into the mid-twentieth century, would have had to fight off wild carnivores such as coyotes and foxes that would kill and eat their chickens. And when gathering eggs, settlers were mindful of snakes that might be in the nest trying to eat the eggs.

Dairy products were vital to Tennesseans as well, but not all families had productive milk cows. Part of the daily routine was milking cows and making butter and its by-product, buttermilk. Until refrigeration, milk was drunk warm and initially stored in wooden containers until crockery became available. And when a dairy cow was at the end of her lactation, she would most likely be slaughtered for meat and hide.

Finally, foraging supplemented the settler's diets with a variety of foods. The woods provided nuts, berries, persimmons, wild grapes called muscadine, wild onions called ramps, and especially greens—a standard in southern diets. Africans ate numerous kinds of greens and brought with them the skills necessary to prepare them. Poke salat was common, along with collard greens, and both would have been seasoned with pork fat and trimmings. Pot "likker," a liquid left over after boiling the greens in ham hock seasonings, was relished by Tennesseans. Forest and orchard apples and peaches were baked in pies and cakes and turned into cider. People dug sassafras roots, dried them, and used them to make tea, and alcoholic punches and teas can be traced back to corn mash. Of course, the ubiquitous iced tea served on southern tables could not be until ice was available later in the nineteenth century.

The U.S. government was actively involved in improving American agriculture. The Land Grant College Act of 1862, or the Morrill Act, provided grants of land to finance colleges specializing in agriculture and the mechanical arts. University of Tennessee, Knoxville, is Tennessee's land grand university. Smith-Lever in 1914 established extension services, and a myriad of federal and state efforts changed agriculture dramatically at the turn of the twentieth century. Agricultural productivity skyrocketed to almost unimaginable levels because of the improved varieties of crops and animals. Additionally, federal agricultural agents worked with local farmers to educate and improve farming practices. Female home demonstration agents worked with farm women to improve their lives, teaching them safe canning practices, and establishing 4-H Clubs for children. The Smith-Hughes Act of 1917 provided federal funds for vocational education in agriculture, trades, industry, and homemaking. Improved insecticides, herbicides, and new fertilizers plus selective breeding of animals contributed to the stunning new revolution as well. During the New Deal, the Tennessee Valley Authority (TVA) brought inexpensive electricity to rural Tennesseans. In 1940, a farmer could produce enough food to feed ten people. In the twenty-first-century the number has increased tenfold.

Tennessee's varied history can be traced through its people and culture. In this distinctive work, Lynne Drysdale Patterson honors Tennessee's founding fathers and mothers, and offers her repertoire of recipes from over two centuries of southern food history, with updated recipes for today's cooks.

Minoa Uffelman
Austin Peay State University

Preface

Taproots of Tennessee: Historic Sites and Timeless Recipes weaves the history of Tennessee's seventeen state-owned historic sites into a collection of period foods with updated recipes for the twenty-first-century food enthusiast.

My aim in writing this book is to breathe life into the accounts of Tennessee's early settlers and contemporary residents while sharing details about their homesteads, families, crops and cookery, schoolhouses, stagecoach stops, and religious life. This book evolved, in part, from my award-winning song "Trails of Tennessee." The song idea was birthed during a Donelson-Hermitage Chamber of Commerce luncheon in 2010. Watching a Discover Tennessee Trails and Byways video presentation with my Nashville-native husband, Bruce, I was captivated by images of ancient Native American trails lacing the landscape "shaped like an old boot" (as described by Harriette Simpson Arnow in her timeless tome *Seedtime on the Cumberland*).

As the video rolled, Tennessee's grand divisions—East, Middle, and West, with their rugged terrain and trails trodden into rural, scenic back roads and winding highways—made a lasting impression on me. Like any songwriter worth her salt, I began jotting lines and song ideas on the back of a brochure. I wanted to travel these byways leading into Tennessee's small historic towns. And for me, as a member of General Daniel Smiths Rock Castle Chapter and Fort Nashborough Chapters of the Tennessee Society Daughters of the American Revolution, Tennessee's state historic sites proved the perfect place to learn about the lives of the men and women who traversed these territories and staked their famous claims. I left the luncheon that day inspired to travel these trails, the fruit of which became this book.

Driving across beautiful Tennessee with its undulating hills and pasturelands is its own reward. I can imagine a time, not so very long ago, when rivers were "highways" and farming was not just an occupation but a way of life.

Arriving at each state historic site, I sensed that the members of these families had simply stepped away—perhaps to the garden or nearby spring—and would return at any moment. And in touring each site, I was delighted to be greeted by gracious, welcoming, and well-informed executive directors and staff, eager to share the lives and times of its former residents and their significant contributions to American history.

I consider cooking to be a creative art form much like music and writing. As a bona fide "foodie," I explored each state historic site, digging deeper into Tennessee's treasured landmarks. Thus, recipes in this book are derived from historic resources, cookbooks, and prized recipes (or "receipts," as they were called prior to and throughout the eighteenth and nineteenth centuries) from food historians, family members and friends, and includes updated measurements and ingredients to suit current baking standards. A beautifully handwritten recipe for orange pudding from Carter House State Historic Site was given to me by Kristi Farrow and the Battle of Franklin Trust (BOFT). Paging through the Wynne Family Papers file at the Tennessee State Library and Archives while researching Wynnewood State Historic Site, I was elated to find a faded, handwritten gingerbread recipe scrawled on a scrap of paper with baking instructions using a large, cast-iron skillet. I made their recipe—tweaking it a bit—employing my mother's spectacular, fourteen-inch, antique, cast-iron skillet.

After learning from each site director what these families planted and harvested on their acreage, the animals they kept in their barnyards and pastures or shot out of the sky, and what they baked, fried, and sipped, I organized period menus—to which I add my occasionally humorous and always informative recipe notes—with updated recipes readers can prepare in their own kitchens, as I do.

Understandably, Rock Castle State Historic Site in Sumner County is one of my favorites. General Daniel Smith constructed his fashionable Middle Tennessee mansion in 1784 from solid limestone—named Tennessee's State Rock in 1979—quarried on site. At the behest of his childhood friend President Thomas Jefferson, General Smith surveyed, mapped, and named each of Tennessee's forty-eight counties and presided over them as sheriff for the next thirteen years. In learning that Smith sowed wheat, grew peaches in the small orchard he planted on his 3,140-acre plantation, and bedded a substantial kitchen garden (refurbished today by the Sumner County Master Gardeners), I developed a relevant menu, including a recipe for peach brandy pound cake using whole wheat flour and natural peach brandy—a libation Smith and his neighbor and in-law, General Andrew Jackson, perhaps sipped from General Smith's still.

Traveling south from Nashville, I found the President James K. Polk Ancestral Home and Museum in Columbia resting in genteel composure as a testament to a man of high moral integrity who, at the age of forty-nine, became the youngest president to enter the White House (1845–49). James Knox Polk, our eleventh president, entered politics shortly after graduating from the University of North Carolina and returning to his father Samuel's house built in 1816. As he moved through Tennessee's political circles to the highest office in the land, cuisine served to President Polk and his wife, First Lady Sarah Childress Polk, was prepared by well-known and sought-after French chef de cuisine Honoré Julien—President Jefferson's chef—who stayed in Washington after Jefferson's presidency to open a catering business. Chef Julien passed down his culinary expertise to his son, Auguste, who catered many of the Polk's presidential banquets.

According to Adrian Miller in his 2017 award-winning book, *The President's Kitchen Cabinet: The Story of African Americans Who Fed Our First Families From the Washingtons to the Obamas,* President Polk preferred small meals of simpler, familiar fare—ham and cornbread made by Coakley, their enslaved servant, whom they brought to Washington, D.C., from their home in Nashville. Coakley kept the stoves stoked with firewood, oftentimes sleeping in the kitchen to do so, assuring the president and First Lady a hot breakfast, lunch, and supper. My menu from one of President Polk's White House banquets includes recipes of a selection of French fare said to have been served.

As a result of President Polk extending America's territory by more than one third, a Native American trail (now Interstate 40) leads westward to Henning and the boyhood home of Alex Haley, 1976 Pulitzer Prize–winning author of *Roots: The Saga of an American Family.* The classic bungalow-style home built by Haley's grandfather, Will Palmer, remains much as it was when his grandmother, Cynthia Palmer, regaled young Alex from their front porch swing with stories of his ancestor, the enslaved African Kunte Kinte. Sunday meals were no small matter at the Palmer house. The local pastor and many of the family's friends and neighbors walked from church to the Palmer home to partake of Grandmother Cynthia's bountiful offerings heaped on their formal dining room table.

Rather than an exhaustive study on the lives and times of each site's inhabitants, this book presents a condensed, albeit insightful, portrait of Tennessee's pioneering families, their place in our state's history, and the foods that sustained them. I'm inviting you, the reader, to travel these trails, these scenic back roads and byways, to our remarkable state historic sites and to experience the great taste that is truly Tennessee.

I wish to thank my editors, Jessica R. Everson and Eva Marie Everson of Pen in Hand Edits, who were there even as I began preparing my manuscript in 2012 for publication.

I wish to express my gratitude to former University of Tennessee Press acquisitions editor Kerry Webb, for her initial interest in this book.

My sincere thanks and deep appreciation to Thomas G. Wells, acquisitions editor at the University of Tennessee Press, for recognizing the merit of the book as I continued my research. Special thanks to the press staff—including Jon Boggs, Editorial Assistant; Linsey Perry, Marketing Assistant; Kelly Gray, Senior Designer; and Tom Post, Publicist—for their skilled and professional "midwifery" in helping birth this book.

Many thanks to former Tennessee state representative Tony Shipley and his wife, Susan, for introducing me to the brilliant photography of Jeffrey Stoner.

My deep appreciation and thanks to Jeffrey Stoner for accepting my invitation to provide photographs of each state historic site for this book. Mr. Stoner's professionalism, timing, and instincts employed in producing each image makes them—as always—one of a kind.

I extend special thanks to the executive directors and staff at each of the seventeen state historic sites, without whose knowledge and understanding of Tennessee's early settlers and contemporary residents this book would not be complete: Richard Griffin, Alex Haley Home Museum and Interpretive Center State Historic Site, Henning; Kristi Farrow, Joanna Stephens, and Eric A. Jacobson, Battle of Franklin Trust (BOFT) Carter House State Historic Site, Franklin; Anna G'Fellers-Mason, and Deborah Montanti, the Chester Inn State Historic Site, Heritage Alliance of

Northeast Tennessee and Southwest Virginia, Jonesborough; Mr. and Mrs. Lowell Fayna and Mr. David Wyllie, Cragfont State Historic Site, Castalian Springs; Ken Rush, Ducktown Museum and Burra Burra Mine State Historic Site, Ducktown; Michele Anderson, the Governor Frank G. Clement Museum and Hotel Halbrook State Historic Site, Dickson; Rick Hendrix, Hawthorne Hill State Historic Site in Castalian Springs; John Holtzapple, Tom Price, curator, President James K. Polk Ancestral Home and Museum, Columbia; John Gammon, Marble Springs State Historic Site, Knoxville; Allison Hoskins, Rock Castle State Historic Site; Gary Walrath, Rocky Mount State Historic Site, Piney Flats; Jennifer Bauer, park ranger, Tennessee State Parks–Sycamore Shoals State Historic Area, Sabine Hill State Historic Site, Elizabethton; Ed Corlew, Sam Davis State Historic Site, Pulaski; Bob and Mary Bell, Sam Houston Schoolhouse State Historic Site, Maryville; the late Juanita Sandra "Sandy" Tracy, Sparta Rock House State Historic Site, chapter regent, Tennessee Society Daughters of the American Revolution; Penny McLaughlin (retired), Tipton-Haynes State Historic Site, Johnson City; and Rick Hendrix, Wynnewood State Historic Site, Castalian Springs.

I wish to express special thanks and gratitude to the staff at the Tennessee State Library and Archives for their inestimable guidance and assistance in researching this book. The Tennessee Agricultural Census of 1850—an invaluable chronicle from the TSLA—is a treasured resource from which I gleaned animal husbandry and gardening facts on which to base my menus.

For their special interest in this book, I wish to thank Tennessee state representative Terri Lynn Weaver, the Honorable Beth Harwell, speaker of the Tennessee House of Representatives; Jody Patrick Sliger, community development director at the Tennessee Department of Economic and Community Development; Ruth Dyal, executive director, Upper Cumberland Tourism Association; Linda Witt, Tennessee Society Daughters of the American Revolution, Rock House State Historic Site Chapter; Guy Zimmerman, certified arborist, State of Tennessee; and Lee Anne Faust, residential horticulture, University of Tennessee Extension, Sumner County.

I am grateful to Dr. Carole Stanford Bucy, professor of history at Volunteer State Community College and Davidson County historian, for *Housekeeper's Manual of Practical Receipts* by the Ladies of Moore Memorial Presbyterian Church in downtown Nashville, renamed Westminster Presbyterian Church in 1871.

My deep appreciation goes to Lucy Kennerly Gump for her East Tennessee State University 1989 master's thesis, "Possessions and Patterns of Living in Washington County: The 20 Years Before Tennessee Statehood, 1777–1796."

I extend my sincere gratitude to James Thweatt, archivist in Special Collections at the Eskind Biomedical Library at Vanderbilt University, for his help and guidance in researching historical recipes in the History of Nutrition Collection.

Many thanks to Sheri Castle, writer, cook, raconteur, for professionally indexing the recipes.

Finally, my love, admiration, and deepest appreciation forever belong to my brilliant, handsome, husband, Bruce. Not only did Bruce support my idea for this book, he encouraged me every step of the way; traveling with me to each site, and embracing his role as "taste-tester-in-chief." His devotion to me knows no bounds. Most importantly, every day he shows me how marvelous it is to be married to a man who loves the Lord with all his heart, mind, soul, and strength and his neighbor as himself; and many days he brings me roses.

Chapter 1

ROCKY MOUNT STATE HISTORIC SITE

◆————————————————————————————◆

Built ca. 1772
Piney Flats, Tennessee

Taproots

We fear the tyranny of the Indians less than
that of the British!

—William Cobb, 1770,
"Rocky Mount and the Masengills,"
Rocky Mount Historical Association

Rocky Mount, also known as the Cobb-Massengill House, is one of the oldest, most well-preserved log structures in Tennessee. The handsome, weather-boarded "living museum" was constructed around 1772 of hewn-logs—presumably, white oak—from the surrounding forest. Rocky Mount served as the temporary capital of the Southwest Territory (the area south of the Ohio River now recognized as Tennessee) from 1790 to 1792, and it is known as the first government site west of the Allegheny Mountains.

William Cobb was a successful farmer, surveyor, and one of Tennessee's earliest settlers; and he served as one of North Carolina's first county magistrates. Cobb's brother-in-law, Henry Massengill Sr., who married Cobb's sister, Mary, had already settled in nearby Boone's Creek in 1769. William received land— "a most valuable commodity"—from his father, Benjamin Cobb, so it seemed natural that William, now in his early forties, would follow Henry and Mary into this new wilderness land.

In 1770, William Cobb and his wife Barsheba brought their family, along with sixteen to twenty other families, out of the relative safety and security of eastern North Carolina. They traveled over the Allegheny Mountains and into the wilderness territory of the Cherokees. This area, known as "the Fork" or the Watauga Settlement, lay between the confluence of the Watauga and Holston Rivers—tributaries of the Tennessee River. Before long, William Cobb built his spacious log home, known as Rocky Mount, on the side of a limestone embankment.

The large, detached kitchen was designed for entertaining dignitaries and guests on a grand scale. Note the beehive oven (left) used for baking bread, pies, cakes, and crackers.

Frontier log structures needed some kind of "notching" at the corners to hold each log in place and keep the structure stable. Seven styles of "corner notching" are identified as being used in constructing frontier log structures. These include the dovetail, half-dovetail, saddle, V-notch, square, diamond, and half diamond. The majority of the notching on both the main house and the dining room are of a V-notch configuration, although slightly modified.

Although furnished with trappings considered extravagant for its time

In the rear of the Cobbs' two-story residence, family and guests would walk through a "dog trot" or breezeway into the spacious dining room.

and place, William Cobb designed his house for practical functionality, and it was geared towards hospitality rather than the desire to simply impress. The stairway leading to the second floor is wood paneled, and the handrails are fashioned from solid walnut. A rustic pine mantle adorns the large stone fireplace that warms a large living area. Original glass windows add a touch of elegance to each room—the perfect temporary abode for American statesman, land speculator, and signer of the United States Constitution William Blount.

Blount was appointed by President George Washington as the first governor of the Southwest Territory. Governor Blount set up his office at Rocky Mount until he relocated Tennessee's capital to Knoxville in March 1792. Earlier in his political career, Blount sponsored a bill establishing the city of Nashville, the state's future capital, in what was then

In back of the detached kitchen lies a cold-frame greenhouse in which garden vegetables and herbs were planted after the last frost.

the site of French Lick, or the Cumberland Settlements—known today as Fort Nashborough—founded by James Robertson and John Donelson. Donelson, aboard his flatboat, the *Adventure,* had maneuvered thirty flatboats to the site from the mouth of the Holston River in 1780.

In his invaluable publication *The Annals of Tennessee to the End of the Eighteenth Century,* Dr. J. G. M. Ramsey stated, "Mr. Cobb . . . was no stranger to comfort or taste nor unaccustomed to what, in that day, was called 'style.' Like the old Carolina-Virginia gentlemen, he entertained elegantly, with profusion rather than plenty, without ceremony and without grudging. His equipage was simple and unpretending."

The Cobb hospitality was praised in one of Governor Blount's journal entries soon after his arrival. Governor Blount wrote, "On the 11th instant, I was received with every mark of attention and gladness that I could have wished. I am very well accommodated with a Room with Glass Windows, Fireplace, etc., at this place."

A stagecoach road was built from Abingdon, Virginia, to Jonesborough, North Carolina (now Tennessee), in 1776–77. The road ran in front of Rocky Mount, which became a stop on the route. Indeed, Cobb's distinguished hospitality was enjoyed by notables including Daniel Boone, John Sevier, Daniel Smith, William Campbell, and Richard Henderson. Andrew Jackson is said to have lodged at Rocky Mount for six weeks while waiting to be admitted to the bar and practice law in nearby Jonesborough.

Eventually, William Cobb moved his family west to Grainger County (named for Mary Grainger, Governor Blount's wife's maiden name) in 1775, and Rocky Mount was passed to Harold "Hal" Massengill Jr., who married Cobb's daughter, Penelope. Several generations later, during the 1800s, the Massengill family added weatherboarding to the log exterior. They wanted to please their daughters, who wished to impress their would-be suitors.

Rocky Mount was owned and preserved through four generations of Massengills. The buildings and property remained in the Massengill family until the mid-1950's, and it was at this time that one of the descendants, realizing the historical significance of his ancestral home, began negotiations with the State of Tennessee to purchase Rocky Mount. Restorations by the Tennessee Historical Commission and the Rocky Mount Historical Association began shortly thereafter. In 1962, beautiful Rocky Mount State Historic Site was open to the public. Rocky Mount was added to the National Register of Historic Places on February 26, 1970.

ADDRESS AND CONTACT INFORMATION
Rocky Mount State Historic Site
200 Hyder Hill Road
Piney Flats, TN 37686
(423) 538-7396

Timeless Recipes

He kept his horse, his dogs, his rifles, even his traps,
for the use, comfort, and entertainment of his guests.

—Dr. J. G. M. Ramsey, *Annals of Tennessee
to the End of the Eighteenth Century* (1853)

The Cobb family kitchen stands separate from the main house. In the eighteenth and nineteenth centuries, a detached kitchen was common for a prosperous pioneer and helped preserve the main structure in the event of a kitchen fire.

The Cobb kitchen houses a brick fireplace, Dutch ovens, skillets, and pots for baking, frying, boiling, and stewing. The nearby Holston and Watauga Rivers were teeming with perch, mullet, catfish, and carp. William Cobb fished the Holston and Watauga Rivers and nearby streams. He may have taken his houseguests fishing as entertainment—a refreshing diversion from work and travel.

William Cobb built an earthen oven for baking bread and a gridiron for barbecuing outside. Pork, beef, lamb, turkey, chicken, squirrel, duck, pigeon, and venison were staples of the "back country" and could be smoked or "spit-roasted" as part of Cobb's penchant for entertaining guests.

MENU
Bacon and Thyme Biscuits
Pan-Fried Corn Cakes
Duck Egg Sauce
Red and Green Bell Pepper Relish
Cast Iron Pan-Fried Perch with Pan Roasted Vegetables
Sweet Potato Upside-Down Whiskey Cake

BACON AND THYME BISCUITS
There is no written record of the number of hogs foraging the Cobb or Massengill acreage. We can assume, though, that pork—the principal meat during the Colonial period and after the American Revolution—was a staple on the family's table. Hogs are the animal most mentioned in early estate inventories and wills in Washington County and northeastern Tennessee.

Fresh thyme from the Cobb kitchen garden, mingled with bacon and butter layered into biscuit dough, would please the palate of prominent Rocky Mount guests, offering them a tastier bite of everyday victuals.

Ingredients

2 cups all-purpose flour

1 tablespoon baking powder

½ teaspoon baking soda

1 cup buttermilk

3 strips smoked bacon

6 tablespoons salted butter

2 teaspoons thyme, finely chopped

Directions

Preheat the oven to 350°F. Cut the raw bacon into ½-inch pieces. Place the bacon pieces on a baking sheet and cook in the preheated oven for 18 to 20 minutes, until the bacon is cooked through but not crisp. Remove the bacon from the oven and turn the oven up to 375°F . Combine the flour and thyme in a mixing bowl and whisk thoroughly. Cut the butter into the flour mixture with your fingers until the mixture resembles the size of small peas. Add the buttermilk and stir until the flour and butter are evenly moist. Sprinkle flour on your work surface or pastry cloth and then turn the biscuit dough out of the bowl onto the floured surface. Use a rolling pin to roll the dough into a rectangle about ¾ inches thick. Fold the dough in half, bringing the two short ends together. Turn it a half turn and roll it again. Place half the bacon onto the biscuit dough. Repeat the fold technique and roll two more times. Add the rest of the bacon. Turn the dough and roll two more times (a total of four times). On the fourth and final roll, use the pin to roll the dough to a thickness of ½ inch. Cut the biscuits using a 2½ inch round biscuit cutter. The dough should be layered with butter and bacon. Place the biscuits in a 10 inch cast-iron skillet beginning with one biscuit in the center of the skillet and 7 all-around. Bake at 375°F for 18 to 20 minutes or until golden brown. (Yields 8 biscuits.)

PAN-FRIED CORN CAKES

Hogs and corn continue to be Tennessee's leading agricultural industry. Serve these delightful cakes drizzled with duck egg sauce sprinkled with red and green bell pepper relish (recipes to follow).

Ingredients
8 ears (6 cups) of shucked sweet corn
½ cup or more all-purpose flour
1 large egg, lightly beaten
3 scallions, thinly sliced
3 tablespoons fresh, finely minced parsley
1½ teaspoons salt
¼ teaspoon, coarsely ground pepper
Unsalted butter for frying

Directions
Grate 6 ears of corn on the large holes of a box grater placed in a medium bowl. Cut the kernels from the remaining 2 ears with a sharp knife, scraping some of the juice from the cob (called "milk") into the medium bowl. Add the flour, egg, scallions, parsley, salt, and pepper. Stir the mixture until a thick batter forms. Add more flour if the batter seems thin. The batter should have the consistency of thick cake batter. Melt 2 tablespoons of butter in a large cast-iron pan. Working in batches, spoon ¼-cup of batter into the skillet and fry over medium heat until golden brown (about 4 minutes per side). Wipe the pan out and repeat with additional butter and batter. Serve the corn cakes hot.
(Yields 24 servings.)

DUCK EGG SAUCE
According to Lucy Kennerly Gump's research in "Possessions and Patterns of Living in Washington County: The 20 Years Before Tennessee Statehood, 1777–1796," ducks and geese are listed as inventory in estate wills. Domestic fowl provided eggs. Feather beds are listed in estate inventories as well. Cattle are listed as making up 89 percent of Washington and Sullivan County inventories. William Cobb and later the Massengill family likely kept their barnyard full of chickens and ducks and their pastureland peppered with grazing cows that offered up beef, as well as butter, and cream for cooking.

Duck eggs remain rich in calcium, selenium, and vitamin A. Their large, luscious, deep-yellow yolks promise a sumptuous sauce to drizzle over perch, veggies, corn cakes, and biscuits.

Ingredients
4 duck egg yolks (or 5 large chicken egg yolks)
1 cup chicken stock
¼ teaspoon salt
¼ teaspoon fresh lemon juice (or to taste)

Directions
In a small sauce pan, whisk together all ingredients. Place the pan over low heat. Stir constantly until the sauce thickens.
(Yields about 1 cup.)

RED AND GREEN BELL PEPPER RELISH

Fresh cabbage provided frontier families with vitamin C, manganese, and other much-needed nutrients, which helped stave off disease. Green cabbage was planted in the spring and harvested during the summer about eight to ten weeks later. Cabbage could be sliced and fried, boiled and served with meat, made into sauerkraut, or pickled and put up in heavy stone crocks, then stored in the springhouse for use in a slaw or as a condiment. Peppers planted in the spring were harvested two or three months later and served fresh or hung on heavy wire to dry. Garlic and onions were often braided into wreaths for decoration and seasoning.

Ingredients
1½ cups finely shredded green cabbage
3 large red bell peppers cut into ½-inch dice
1 large green bell pepper, cut into ½-inch dice
1 small yellow onion, finely diced
1 celery rib, finely chopped
1 cup white vinegar (or apple cider vinegar, if preferred)
1½ teaspoons kosher salt
1½ teaspoons yellow mustard seeds
¾ teaspoon turmeric
½ teaspoon celery seeds
¼ cup sugar

Directions

In a large stainless-steel stock pot, toss together the shredded cabbage with the bell peppers, onion, and celery. Add the vinegar, salt, mustard seeds, turmeric, celery seeds, and sugar. Stir to combine. Bring the mixture to a boil. Cover. Reduce to low heat and simmer, stirring occasionally until the vegetables just soften (about 20 minutes). Transfer the relish to sterilized glass jars and seal while hot.
(Yields 4 cups.)

CAST IRON PAN–FRIED PERCH
WITH PAN-ROASTED VEGETABLES

Bringing a string of fresh perch from the Holston and Watauga Rivers to serve from fry pan to table would be considered the height of hospitality in the Cobb or Massengill home. Seasonal vegetables would have been grown on their property. Herbs from kitchen gardens were often tied into small bundles and hung upside down to dry for use during winter months.

Pan frying with today's Lodge cast-iron skillet is much like using the old-fashioned, cast-iron "spider," minus the legs and direct heat over coals—although this dish still makes perfect campfire cuisine.

Ingredients:
4 six- to seven-ounce perch fillets
Salt and pepper to taste
2 tablespoons corn oil
2 tablespoons unsalted butter
8 small carrots, halved lengthwise
8 small zucchini squashes, halved lengthwise
8 small yellow squashes, halved lengthwise
4 small white onions, peeled and halved
½ pound asparagus spears, trimmed and halved crosswise
2 sprigs fresh thyme
½ cup vegetable or chicken stock

Directions
Heat a large cast-iron skillet over medium high heat. Season the perch with salt and pepper. Add the corn oil to the skillet. Fry the perch until golden

brown, 3 to 4 minutes per side. Remove from the pan and set aside on a warm platter. Add the butter and carrot to the skillet; cook 2 minutes, stirring occasionally. Add the onion, zucchini, and yellow squash; cook 2 more minutes. Add the asparagus, thyme, and broth. Simmer until the broth evaporates (about 3 to 5 minutes). Season lightly with salt and pepper. Return the perch to the skillet, warm, and serve immediately. (Yields 4 servings.)

SWEET POTATO UPSIDE-DOWN WHISKY CAKE

The 1775–96 tax records on stills reveal important information about the distilling industry in Washington County. William Cobb is recorded as having the second-largest-capacity still, producing 187 gallons yearly. Cobb is also noted for his rye whiskey and apple and peach brandy. He also produced corn whiskey. Corn whiskey was distilled for drinking and was used for flavor in recipes and as a standard rate to pay taxes. Corn could be made into cakes, pies, and puddings as well as roasted, boiled, fried, or dried for use in soups or stews during winter months.

Maple sugar, another sweetener produced west of the Alleghenies, was also used to pay taxes. In nearby Jonesborough, families boiled maple sugar in quantities of a thousand pounds. Then, as now, pure maple syrup is prized condiment. Forty gallons of sap makes just one gallon of syrup. Honey was sometimes used as a substitute for sugar or sold as a means of paying taxes.

Sweet potatoes were planted in the spring and harvested in the fall. They were hearth roasted, served buttered as a side dish, in casseroles, or served as dessert. The modern-day recipe for this old-fashioned cake uses self-rising flour rather than pearl ash (potassium carbonate) and sour cream instead of "clabber" (clotted sour milk).

Ingredients
1 cup maple syrup, divided
2 tablespoons Jack Daniels Whiskey or pure corn whiskey (moonshine), divided, (for non-alcoholic, substitute with apple cider)
2 tablespoons salted butter
2½ cups peeled, thinly sliced sweet potato (2 medium-size)
1¾ cups self-rising flour

¾ cup sugar
½ teaspoon salt
¼ cup whole milk
9 tablespoons butter, melted
3 large eggs, lightly beaten
¾ cup sour cream

Directions
Preheat the oven to 350°F. In a 10-inch cast-iron skillet, combine ½ cup of maple syrup with 2 tablespoons of butter and one tablespoon of whisky (or substitute). Bring to a boil over medium heat; cook for 1 minute. Remove from the heat. Layer the thinly sliced sweet potatoes in the bottom of the skillet, overlapping slightly. In a large bowl, sift together the flour and sugar. Add ¼ cup of maple syrup, along with the milk, melted butter, eggs, and sour cream. Beat with a mixer at low speed until smooth. Gently spread the mixture over the sweet potato slices. Place the skillet in the oven and bake the cake for approximately 45 minutes until the cake is set and golden brown. Let stand for 5 minutes. Carefully invert the cake onto a flat serving platter. Mix the remaining tablespoon of whiskey with the remaining ¼ cup of maple syrup and drizzle over the cake. (Yields 8–10 servings.)

The Massengill House of Worship

I marched with Shelby in 1779. While I was away
Tories came, abused my family, destroyed my property
and burned the House of Worship to the ground.
This first day of June, 1779

—From the journal of Henry Massengill Sr.,
Watauga District

New Bethel Presbyterian Church, located in the tiny hamlet of Piney Flats, is rooted and grounded in the Massengill House of Worship. It's the oldest Presbyterian congregation in Tennessee and was founded by the Reverend Dr. Joseph Rhea, a Presbyterian pastor from Ireland. Upon moving from Taneytown (Taw-nee-town), Maryland, Reverend Rhea served as chaplain in a 1776 Tennessee military campaign. During his service, Rhea fell in love with Tennessee's rolling hills and rich bottomland. He returned to Maryland and inspired his congregation to move with him to Tennessee. Unfortunately, Reverend Rhea died before he reached his earthly destination. His family, however, and many of his congregants made Tennessee their home.

In April 1777, Reverend Charles Cummings, a Presbyterian minister from the Wolf Hills Settlement in Abingdon, Virginia, and Reverend Jonathan Mulky, a Baptist minister and pioneer preacher from Virginia, came to the Watauga Settlement to preach. Reverend Cummings stayed for three days and was welcomed "with great joy, for our souls were hungering and thirsting for spiritual nourishment," as Henry Massengill Sr. noted in his journal. Encouraged by Cummings and Mulky, Massengill urged the settlers to build a house of worship. He even supplied the logs, boards, and all the timber needed to build the large church-like building "with a section of benches in the back, for the Massengill and Cobb negroes numbering at this time 151 souls," continued Massengill, "so the slaves can come out and be refreshed body and soul."

The Massengill House of Worship was completed in July 1779. Reverend Cummings, from the Hanover Presbytery in Virginia and licensed to preach on April 18, 1767, was one of the first ministers to bring the hymns of Isaac Watts—recognized today as "The Father of Hymnody"—to the Holston Watauga region. Some Presbyterians were suspicious of Watts, who was a Nonconformist. They worried about the theology of his psalms and hymns.

Watts's psalms—which he paraphrased from the Scriptures—were salted with the spirit of the New Testament. Watts wanted to improve Presbyterian and Congregational singing with his works, *The Psalms of David; Imitated in the Language of the New Testament, and Applied to the Christian State of Worship of 1719* and *Divine and Moral Songs for Children.* From this perspective, Watts wrote the popular Christmas carol "Joy to the World" from Psalm 98 and "O, God, Our Help in Ages Past" from Psalm 70. Surely these hymns were balm for the hearts and souls of slaves and settlers in their wilderness communities.

Cummings continued his life of service as pastor of Sinking Spring and Ebbing Spring Presbyterian Church back in Abingdon, Virginia, where he served until his death in 1812.

Samuel Doak, recognized as Tennessee's first Christian minister and evangelist, is said to have taken over that congregation and to have preached in the auspicious Massengill House of Worship. In 1782, five years after the Massengill House of Worship burned to the ground, Reverend Doak began a new church in nearby Sullivan County, naming it New Bethel Presbyterian Church. This church continues today with local people of faith.

There is evidence that the renowned Methodist minister Bishop Francis Asbury visited the Cobb-Massengill House. The first Methodist conference was held in Tennessee—the Southwest Territory at the time—on April 2, 1793, with several families at Nelson's Chapel.

For this congregational gathering, "dinner on the ground" would have included not "loaves and fishes," as was the first dinner on the ground, but a hearty stew, bread, a vegetable of some sort, and, of course, dessert.

MENU
Massengill Family Punch
Cornbread with Cheddar Cheese, Bacon, and Kale
Kale and Butternut Squash Salad with Cornbread Croutons
    and Warm Bacon Vinaigrette
Brunswick Stew
Scripture Cake with Burnt Jeremiah Syrup

MASSENGILL FAMILY PUNCH
Massengill Family Punch would not have been served after the Sunday worship services. This original recipe, however, standing alone as one served to family and houseguests, has been handed down through generations.

Ingredients
1-quart apple cider
¼ pound sugar
1 cup sherry—medium dry
Juice of one lemon
Grated nutmeg to taste
¼ cup brandy
1 medium cucumber, thinly sliced

Directions

Combine the cider, sugar, sherry, lemon, and nutmeg in a punchbowl and refrigerate. When ready to serve, add the brandy. Float the cucumber slices on top.

(Yields 10 servings.)

CORNBREAD WITH CHEDDAR CHEESE, BACON, AND KALE

The Massengill women were responsible for caring for all aspects of the household. They likely supervised their enslaved workers who ground corn into meal, milked cows, fetched the milk, made butter and cheese, and prepared food to serve after church.

This cheddar-cheesy cornbread with kale, served in thick, crisp, hot wedges, is enough to make anyone shout "hallelujah!" Collards or another green may be substituted for kale.

Ingredients

2 slices bacon, chopped

1½ cup chopped kale, firmly packed

½ teaspoon dried sage

2 cups self-rising cornmeal

¼ teaspoon ground black pepper

1⅓ cup buttermilk

2 large eggs, lightly beaten

3 tablespoons vegetable oil, divided

¾ cup shredded cheddar cheese

Directions

Preheat the oven to 375°F. In a 10-inch cast-iron skillet, fry bacon over medium heat until crisp. Set the bacon aside, reserving the rendered fat in the skillet. Add the kale and sage to the rendered fat; cook until the kale wilts, approximately 1 minute. Remove from the heat. Remove the kale mixture from the skillet and set aside. In a medium bowl, stir together the cornmeal, pepper, buttermilk, eggs, and 1 tablespoon of oil. Stir in the kale mixture, bacon, and cheese. Add the

Tidbits:
To achieve a lighter texture, this recipe employs self-rising cornmeal.

remaining oil to the skillet; heat over medium heat until hot. Remove from the heat. Pour the cornmeal mixture into the hot oil. The mixture will sizzle. Smooth the top with the back of a spoon (do not stir). Bake until a toothpick inserted into the center comes out clean, approximately 20 minutes. Allow the cornbread to cool in the skillet 10 minutes on a sturdy wire rack.

(Yields 8 slices.)

KALE AND BUTTERNUT SQUASH SALAD WITH CORNBREAD CROUTONS AND WARM BACON VINAIGRETTE

Crouton is a seventeenth-century French word derived from the Latin *crusta,* meaning "shell." Thus, the outside of a loaf of bread is called the "crust"—a lofty position for the humble husk.

On the frontier, corn was king. Cornbread could be crumbled on top of food, as it sometimes is today. But why crumble it when you can crown your freshly made salad with these corn and bread gems?

Lacinato kale, listed among the plants Thomas Jefferson recorded in his 1777 garden journal at Monticello, could have been grown in the Massengill vegetable plot.

Ingredients
Salad
4 cups (1-inch cubes) day-old cornbread
5 cloves garlic, smashed
3 tablespoons plus 1 teaspoon extra-virgin olive oil
½ teaspoon kosher salt, divided
5 slices of bacon cut into 1-inch pieces
2 cups (1-inch cubes) peeled butternut squash
1 bunch Lacinato kale, thinly sliced (about 8 cups, packed)
1 apple (Granny Smith or Macintosh), cored and thinly sliced

Vinaigrette
½ cup red wine vinegar
½ cup thinly sliced red onion

5 tablespoons rendered bacon fat
2 teaspoons Dijon mustard
½ teaspoon kosher salt
¼ teaspoon freshly cracked black pepper

Directions

To Prepare Croutons and Bacon: Preheat the oven to 350°F. In a large bowl, gently toss together the cornbread cubes, garlic, 3 tablespoons of olive oil, and ¼ teaspoon of salt until well combined. Spread the mixture on a rimmed baking sheet and bake until the croutons are browned and crisp, approximately 30 minutes. Set aside. In a large cast-iron skillet, fry the bacon over medium-high heat for about 8 minutes, turning as needed, until crisp. Remove the bacon with a slotted spoon, reserving the rendered bacon fat for the vinaigrette.

To Prepare Butternut Squash: Increase the oven temperature to 425°F. On another rimmed baking sheet, toss cubes of squash together with the remaining 1 teaspoon of olive oil and ¼ teaspoon of salt. Bake until the squash is tender and beginning to brown, approximately 30 minutes. Set aside and allow to cool.
(Yields 10–12 servings.)

To Prepare Vinaigrette: In a small saucepan, simmer ½ cup of red wine vinegar until it is steaming hot, approximately 1 minute. Add the sliced red onion to the hot vinegar. Remove from the heat and let stand for 30 minutes. Remove the onion and combine the warm vinegar mixture with the bacon fat, mustard, ½ teaspoon of salt, and pepper. Stir the mustard, salt, and pepper into the warm vinegar mixture. Whisk the vinegar mixture into the warm bacon fat. Set aside.

Putting the Salad Together: In a large bowl, combine the croutons, squash, onion, kale, apple, and reserved chopped bacon. Pour the warm bacon vinaigrette over the salad; gently toss to combine. Serve immediately.
(Yields 10–12 servings.)

BRUNSWICK STEW

Congregants at the Massengill House of Worship likely lingered after their church services, their hearts and souls warmed and filled with the spiritual food that never perishes. What better way to satisfy their bellies than with mouth-watering, Virginia-based Brunswick stew, simmered all day in a large, black cast-iron Dutch oven.

Reverends Cummings and Mulky hailed from Virginia. Brunswick stew—from Brunswick County, Virginia—is a tomato-based stew originally made with squirrel. Chicken makes a delicious alternative.

Ingredients
1 four-pound chicken, cut into serving pieces
2 teaspoons salt
Paprika to taste
3 tablespoons unsalted butter
2 medium onions, sliced
1 medium green pepper, diced
3 cups chicken broth
2 cups canned tomatoes, undrained
2 tablespoons chopped parsley
½ teaspoon Tabasco sauce
1 tablespoon Worcestershire sauce
2 cups whole-kernel corn
2 cups lima beans
1 pound russet potatoes, peeled and quartered

Directions
Season the chicken pieces with 1 teaspoon of the salt and paprika. Heat the butter in a Dutch oven and brown the chicken pieces on all sides. Add the onions and green pepper and cook until the onions are transparent. Add the chicken stock, tomatoes with their liquid, parsley, remaining teaspoon of salt, Tabasco sauce, and Worcestershire sauce. Bring to a boil. Cover, reduce the heat, and simmer for 30 minutes. Add the corn and lima beans and cook 20 minutes longer. Meanwhile, in a medium-sized saucepan, boil the potatoes until they are tender. Mash the potatoes

or use a ricer. Stir the mashed potatoes into the stew. Cook 10 minutes longer. Serve in flat soup plates.
(Yields 4–6 servings.)

SCRIPTURE CAKE WITH BURNT JEREMIAH SYRUP

Scripture cake is said to have been popular as far back as the late 1700s in England and Ireland. Also known as "Bible Cake" and "Old Testament Cake," it is said to have been a favorite of the effervescent Dolley Madison, wife of James Madison, fourth president of the United States.

Scripture cake became popular on Tennessee's frontier and beyond as a delicious way to teach young girls to bake and memorize Bible verses. Perhaps this satisfying sweet was offered at the Massengill House of Worship.

Ingredients
Scripture Cake
¾ cup butter (Judges 5:25)
1½ cup sugar (Jeremiah 6:20)
5 eggs, separated (Isaiah 10:14)
3 cups sifted flour (Leviticus 24:5)
3 teaspoons salt (2 Kings 2:20)
3 teaspoons baking powder (Amos 4:5)
1 teaspoon cinnamon (Exodus 30:23)
¼ teaspoon each nutmeg, ginger, allspice (2 Chronicles 9:9)
½ cup milk (Judges 4:19)
¾ cup nuts (Genesis 43:11) (chopped pistachio and slivered almonds)
¾ cup finely chopped figs (Jeremiah 24:5)
¾ cup raisins (2 Samuel 16:1)
Slivered almonds for garnish (Genesis 43:11)

Burnt Jeremiah Syrup
1½ cups sugar (Jeremiah 6:20)
½ cup water (Genesis 24:45)
¼ cup butter (Genesis 18:8)

Directions

For the Cake: Preheat the oven to 325°F. Butter and dust with flour a 10-inch Bundt pan. In a 4-quart bowl (or the bowl on an electric stand mixer), beat the butter and sugar until light and fluffy. Beat in the egg yolks—one at a time—mixing well after each addition. Sift together the flour, salt, baking powder, cinnamon, and spices. Beat the flour mixture into the butter and egg mixture—alternating with milk until the flour is just incorporated. Beat the egg whites until stiff and fold them gently into the batter. Fold in the prepared nuts, figs, and raisins. Turn the mixture into the buttered and floured 10-inch Bundt pan. Bake at 325°F for 1 hour until a wooden skewer, or tooth pick inserted into the cake comes out clean. Remove from the oven and place on a wire rack to cool. After 15 minutes, turn the cake out of the pan onto a wire rack to cool completely. (Yields 12–16 servings.)

For the Syrup: In a 2-quart saucepan over low heat, melt the sugar, stirring to prevent sticking. As the sugar melts, stir it continuously until it turns a deep golden brown. Add the water and cook, stirring frequently, until smooth. Remove from the heat. Add the butter and stir until the butter melts. Allow to cool. Drizzle over the cooled cake and garnish with more slivered almonds.
(Yields 2 cups.)

Chapter 2

ROCK CASTLE STATE HISTORIC SITE

◆ ─────────────────────────────── ◆

Built 1784–1795
Hendersonville, Tennessee

Taproots

Your most obedient and very humble servant . . . (the
valediction used in correspondence by polite society)

—Daniel Smith, surveyor, map maker, Revolutionary War general,
and United States senator

Rock Castle is Tennessee's first state-owned historic site. The multilevel
limestone "castle" was designed and constructed by frontier statesman
Daniel Smith, whose military life and political career played a major role
in the growth of Tennessee.

Rock Castle, recognized as the first plantation-type family dwelling
in the state, reflects an architectural style similar to Federal-style homes
"back east." Built by Daniel Smith (1748–1818), with his enslaved African
American workers, Rock Castle took an estimated eight to twelve years
to complete. Smith's travels and the unrelenting attacks from resident
Cherokees account for this long construction period. Smith's home presented an unofficial transition from the customary frontier shelters to the
mansion-type homes of the future. When Rock Castle was completed in
1791, it was considered the finest residence in Middle Tennessee.

Smith built his home from quarried limestone—declared Tennessee's
official state rock in 1979. The two-and-a-half-story main section includes
a half-story L-shaped building projecting from the rear of the house.

The dining room fireplace in Rock Castle. The original woodwork mantel is made from black walnut harvested from the estate.

When the hurriedly constructed stockade-style log home Smith initially built was burned to the ground by Native Americans, the L-shaped building in the rear is said to have served as the kitchen and living quarters for Smith, his wife, Sarah Michie Smith, and their two children, eight-year-old George and five-year-old Mary Ann (nicknamed Polly). Polly, at age fifteen, jumped from the window of her upstairs bedroom into the arms of Samuel Donelson—Andrew Jackson's brother-in-law—and eloped!

Born as a twin in Stafford County, Virginia, in 1748, Daniel Smith was baptized in Elbo Warren Baptist Church days before his twin sister Sarah died. By age ten, Smith was one of eight out of eleven siblings who survived the maladies of their rural surroundings. Before his twentieth birthday, Smith's parents, Henry and Sarah Crosby Smith, sent him westward to Albemarle County, Virginia, to live at Castle Hill, home of the distinguished physician and renowned surveyor-explorer Dr. Thomas

Originally a sitting room, this space became a bedroom
when the staircase leading to the third floor became
a difficult climb for the aging Smiths.

Walker. Life at Castle Hill launched Daniel Smith on a journey that shaped
his destiny.

Trained as a surveyor by Dr. Walker—who mentored a young Thomas
Jefferson and named Tennessee's Cumberland River—Daniel Smith was
commissioned by Governor Thomas Jefferson and the Commonwealth of
Virginia to map out the western portion of the state of North Carolina.
This area—what is now Tennessee—was known as part of the Southwest
Territory (or land southwest of the Ohio River). Smith mapped out and
named the state *Tenasi* (or, Tennessee). Tenasi, a flooded eighteenth-century
Cherokee village, is located in present-day Monroe County, named in honor
of James Monroe, fifth president of the United States.

In the late 1700s, Smith and Walker were joined by Irish immigrant
and legendary Indian fighter Hugh Rogan. Rogan joined the survey party
as a guard while the group marked the boundaries of North Carolina

and Virginia. Rogan and Daniel Smith were among 255 men who signed the Cumberland Compact and spent nearly twenty years helping establish and protect the forts (or "stations," as they were sometimes called) along the Cumberland River. Rogan accrued nearly a thousand acres of fertile farmland in Sumner County near Bledsoe's Creek. His neighbors

Rock Castle State Historic Site. Note the original limestone fence posts and horse-mounting blocks at the entrance.

included James Winchester of Cragfont, Isaac Bledsoe, and William Hall, who would later serve in the Tennessee Senate and, briefly, as governor following Sam Houston's resignation in 1829.

Hugh Rogan is credited with bringing many aspects of Irish culture to early Tennessee, including the Roman Catholic Church. Rogan's two-room limestone cottage, "Rogana" (ca.1800), was used by Rogan, his wife Nancy, their sons Bernard and Francis, and neighboring Catholics for nearly fifty-years as a place to hold services. In 1998, the cottage was dismantled, moved, and reconstructed at Bledsoe's Fort Historical Park.

In 1782, Daniel Smith and his family moved from Suffolk County, Virginia, into the area known today as Sumner County. As payment for work as a surveyor, Smith received a land grant—as did many Revolutionary War soldiers—of approximately 164 acres in the area known as the South Cumberland. Daniel's wife, Sarah Michie Smith, was from Charlottesville, Virginia, outside of Monticello (Italian for "little mountain"), home of the third president, Thomas Jefferson.

Smith developed an interest in Hendersonville, Tennessee—named after Tennessee frontiersman Colonel Richard Henderson—and Middle Tennessee as early as 1780. His interest emerged when he was hired by the Commonwealth of Virginia to survey the area. Today, this area still holds the line that separates Kentucky and Tennessee. Daniel Smith's survey of this border is the first professional map of the area.

Smith became a well-known surveyor, and as he continued working on multiple stages of Rock Castle construction, the state of North Carolina made him an offer to map out a state from the "Western Lands." The General Assembly of North Carolina granted him a license to name the area. Instead of receiving money, Daniel Smith was paid in land. Land records and deeds in the Tennessee State Library and Archives collection include the 1784 North Carolina land grant #56 to Daniel Smith for his service in the American Revolution. According to documents in the state archives, he received 3,140 acres "on the North side of Cumberland River at the mouth of Drakes Creek" in Davidson (now Sumner) County, Tennessee. This property would become the Smith family home, Rock Castle—which by today's standards is the equivalent of half of Sumner County and a pocket of Davidson County. In those days, Smith's acreage nearly touched the Hermitage (at that time, "Hunter's Hill"), home of Andrew Jackson, seventh president of the United States, and his wife, Rachel Donelson Jackson. The Smiths and Jacksons were not only neighbors but friends, and eventually in-laws.

On June 1, 1796, Tennessee was declared the sixteenth state in the Union, and Daniel Smith retired. Upon returning home from a surveying trip, however, he received a letter from Thomas Jefferson urging him to act to ensure Tennessee would remain a "state." The fledgling United States government—while continuing to set up states of the Union—was having difficulty maintaining a law-abiding local government on the frontier. Smith traveled to Knoxville—named for Boston bookseller and President George Washington's secretary of war, Henry Knox—to discuss the matter with Governor William Blount. At the time, Blount served as governor over the Southwest Territory. Smith proposed that he (Smith) would act as interim governor if Blount would govern the forty-eight territories Smith planned to map. Daniel Smith mapped and named each of the forty-eight counties in the newly declared state of Tennessee. He chose a county seat for each territory and for the next thirteen years traveled by horseback to each of these towns to ensure law and order and the success of Tennessee's local and state government.

Smith's wife, Sarah, was displeased to learn of Jefferson's request. Described by her family and friends as a woman of "uncommon strength and courage with a strong sense of humor," she nonetheless expressed dissatisfaction with her husband's absence in a letter to him, a copy of which sits on her writing desk at Rock Castle. "I still find myself under the disagreeable necessity of conversing with you on paper or not at all," she wrote.

Daniel Smith retired in 1809 as a senator on Capitol Hill in Knoxville. He died in 1818; Sarah died in 1831. They are entombed on the property in the family cemetary along with freed slaves, Easter and Alfred Smith and close relatives. Smith family members passed Rock Castle down through four generations, and the plantation and property were once managed by a line of direct descendants, including the Smith and Berry families.

In 1950, the Corps of Engineers claimed eminent domain over the majority of Rock Castle acreage. They noted the need to prevent a pre-dicted one-thousand-year flood. Daniel Smith's limestone quarries were excavated and filled with water from the Cumberland River, now part of Old Hickory Lake. Miss Sarah Crosby Berry, great-granddaughter of Sarah Michie Smith and a 1916 graduate of Peabody College in Nashville, Tennessee, managed the 22,000-acre property. She asked for and received $100,000 for what is now 18 acres and two buildings.

The predicted one-thousand-year flood arrived in May 2010. It was the worst flood in the history of Tennessee, engulfing Nashville and the surrounding communities. It saturated the grounds of Rock Castle, leaving almost three feet of muddy water in the kitchen. The Smiths' springhouse and carriage house disappeared beneath the waters of Old Hickory Lake. (The buildings once used as slave quarters had long since vanished.)

Today, Rock Castle State Historic Site—with its original smokehouse, well-tended kitchen garden, and grounds of the Smith family cemetery— pay homage to Daniel Smith and the trials and triumphs of one of Tennessee's founding frontier families.

Hendersonville, home of Rock Castle, is located in Sumner County, so named by Daniel Smith in honor of Revolutionary War patriot General Jethro Sumner. Davidson County, formed in 1786, was named by Daniel Smith to honor Revolutionary War general William Lee Davidson, and the county seat is Gallatin, so named for Albert Gallatin, United States Secretary of the Treasury under the Jefferson and Madison administrations. Today, modern, upscale homes line the streets surrounding the remaining eighteen acres of beautiful Rock Castle State Historic Site.

ADDRESS AND CONTACT INFORMATION
Rock Castle State Historic Site
139 Rock Castle Lane
Hendersonville, TN 37075
(615) 824-0502
www.historicrockcastle.com

Timeless Recipes

Went about 3 miles lower & killed 6 Buffaloes.
Late before we got them butcher'd: clear
and very cold night.

—Daniel Smith, from his journal, 1780

The walls of Rock Castle's kitchen are of two-feet-deep, hand-quarried limestone. Rough-hewn yellow poplar logs felled on the property still support the kitchen ceiling above the cobblestone floor now trodden smooth. The small open hearth affords the usual cooking accoutrements: a reflector oven, a cast-iron Dutch oven with legs, a cast-iron kettle and fry pan, small hand tongs, the ever-present long-handled fork for meat. A shovel and poker hang on the fireplace. These are the quarters in which the Smith family may have lived for a time while Rock Castle was being built. Much of the construction and plantation management was borne by Sarah since her husband was away on surveying trips for most of their married life.

As a surveyor appointed by his childhood friend and now governor of Virginia Thomas Jefferson, Daniel Smith entered the territory he named "Tenasi" by following old Indian trails "over the mountain" and into river valleys. The area, now recognized as Middle Tennessee, is where the settler wanted to be—on or near the Cumberland River. Middle Tennessee streams carried goods to market. Rivers were, indeed, "highways." Goods that couldn't be walked or taken by buckboard or horseback to a neighboring settlement were sent by flatboats down the river. Springs served as a source of drinking water and water for cooking. In time, a stone springhouse could be built. A springhouse served as refrigerator, cellar, pantry, and milk house during summer months. Forted farms, like the original log stockade Smith built and lived in with his family, were built intentionally encompassing a spring, or to one nearby.

The first pamphlet describing Middle Tennessee was written in 1795 by Smith in an effort to encourage settlers to move to the area. In it, he carefully described rich bottomland and rolling hills—perfect for farming tobacco and flax and for cultivating vegetables. Perhaps some of these seeds were a gift from Monticello, the botanical showpiece and home of his childhood friend Thomas Jefferson.

While there are no written records of exactly what the Smiths fed their family or cooked from their acreage, Rock Castle has been described as a working farm yielding oats, wheat, cotton, tobacco, flax, corn, and timber. As with most pioneers, the Smiths planted a kitchen garden and most likely a vegetable garden. Daniel Smith's still produced a fine peach brandy distilled from trees he cultivated into a small orchard. When he retired at age sixty-one, Smith and his neighbor, Andrew Jackson, perhaps sipped a snifter of peach brandy or savored an occasional slice of fresh pound cake infused with the distillate.

MENU
Peach Tea
Whole Wheat Buttermilk Biscuits
Buffalo Meatloaf
Creamed Collard Greens
Custard Corn Pudding
Pickled Beets and Onions
Peach Brandy Pound Cake

PEACH TEA
Perhaps the Smiths enjoyed a cup of peach tea as their small orchard flourished. Coffee, tea, and chocolate were not produced on the Tennessee frontier but could be imported. Today, flavored tea-bags are popular. If you're a tea purist, however, there is nothing more satisfying than tea flavored with fresh fruit.

Ingredients
Peach Simple Syrup
2 large yellow, ripe peaches, peeled, pitted, and thinly sliced
1 cup water
1 cup sugar

Tea
3 to 4 tea bags
8 cups water

Directions
Place the sliced peaches in a saucepan with water and sugar. Bring the mixture to a boil over medium heat. Reduce the heat and crush the softened peaches into the liquid with the back of a spoon. Turn off the heat, stir to dissolve the sugar, and cover to allow the mixture to cool for a half hour or more. In a 2-quart saucepan or large pot, boil 8 cups of water and remove from the heat. Steep the tea bags no more than 5 minutes and remove from the pot. Let cool and transfer to a large pitcher. Set a sieve over an empty container; place a cheese cloth or thin tea towel over the

sieve. Pour the cooled fruit mixture through the cheese cloth and sieve. This should yield almost 4 cups of syrup. Stir in 1½ cups of the peach syrup into the pitcher of tea. Stir thoroughly. Pour over ice, add a slice of peach, or mint sprig to garnish, and . . . sip!
(Yields 10 servings.)

WHOLE WHEAT BUTTERMILK BISCUITS

Daniel Smith's wheat, freshly harvested and milled, could be fashioned into mighty fine biscuits and breads. Cooks used "clabber," or curdled milk—the liquid left after churning butter out of cream—somewhat like today's buttermilk. Long before baking soda was available, the Smiths' cook may have discovered that adding water to a jar of burned corncob ashes, produced a "raising agent" (alkaline) that helped her biscuits rise. Gently patting, turning, and folding the dough several times produces a flakier biscuit.

Ingredients
1½ cups all purpose flour
½ cup whole wheat flour
1 tablespoon baking powder
½ teaspoon salt
6 tablespoons cold butter, cut into small pieces
1 cup buttermilk (plus more, if needed)

Directions
Preheat the oven to 425°F. Set aside a small bowl of flour to coat the biscuit cutter. Whisk together the all-purpose flour with the whole wheat flour, baking powder, and salt in a medium bowl. Add the butter, toss with your fingers to coat with flour, and quickly pinch, working the butter into the flour using your fingertips to make small flakes. Make a well in the center of the flour mixture and add the buttermilk. Stir to combine until the dough gathers into one large lump. Drizzle in additional drops

Tidbits:
The key to the success of this recipe is not over-kneading the dough. These biscuits are especially good with honey butter. To make honey butter, combine equal amounts of honey and softened, salted butter in a small bowl and whip with a fork until smooth. Add a shake or two of cinnamon, if desired.

of buttermilk, if needed, until the dough comes together. Turn the dough out onto a flat, floured surface and sprinkle with additional all-purpose flour. Roll the dough out to coat with the flour, then pat it into a rough rectangle, about 1 inch thick, and fold it into thirds. Repeat the patting and folding three or four times, then do a final pat of the dough into a 1-inch thickness. Dip a 2½-inch round cutter into the small bowl of flour and cut out the biscuits. Place the biscuits topside up on a heavy, ungreased baking sheet about 1 inch apart. Bake for 14 to 16 minutes until the tops of the biscuits are golden brown.

(Yields about 10 biscuits.)

BUFFALO (BISON) MEATLOAF

During the Revolutionary War era, approximately 40 million buffalo thundered across the plains of North America. From horns to hides to hooves, Native Americans and settlers utilized almost every part of the animal. Buffalo roamed and grazed and were hunted for food across Middle Tennessee's grasslands. Their nutritious meat was roasted and fried, cut into steaks, stewed, baked, ground, and used in a variety of soups and stews. Dr. Thomas Walker spotted a herd of buffalo, "and I believe there was a hundred," he recorded in his journal, a portion of which is included in Samuel Cole Williams's book *Early Travels in the Tennessee Country, 1540–1800.*

Buffalo meat is as high in protein and potassium today as it was on the frontier. Ground fresh and packaged by the pound, my recipe makes one delicious "loaf."

Ingredients
2 pounds ground, grass-fed buffalo (I prefer Maverick Ranch)
1 teaspoon vegetable oil
1 medium onion, finely chopped
¼ cup finely chopped celery
1 cup old-fashioned rolled oats (not quick cooking)
½ cup chili sauce (I prefer Heinz)
1 large egg
1 tablespoon milk

1 tablespoon Worcestershire sauce
2 teaspoons Italian seasoning
2 teaspoons salt
½ teaspoon black pepper

Directions
Preheat the oven to 375°F. Prepare an 8½×4½×2¾-inch loaf pan with nonstick cooking spray. Set aside. Heat the oil in a medium-sized heavy skillet over moderate heat for 1 minute. Add onion and celery. Sauté until tender—about 5 minutes. Transfer the skillet mixture to a large bowl. Add the ground buffalo meat, rolled oats, ½ cup of chili sauce, and remaining ingredients. Mix well with your hands. Pat into the prepared pan and bake uncovered for 30 minutes. Drizzle the remaining 3 tablespoons of chili sauce on top and bake until the meatloaf is set and the juices run clear. The loaf should read 180°F on a meat thermometer. Remove the meatloaf from the oven and let stand in the pan for 15 minutes to allow the meatloaf to set and the juices to settle. Cut into 6 slices. Serve with extra chili sauce, if you like. (Yields 6 servings.)
(Yields approximately 16 medium-sized meatballs.)

> ***Tidbits:***
> *This recipe also makes tasty appetizers. Follow the recipe directions. Form the ground buffalo meat into 2-inch meatballs. Spray the baking sheet with cooking spray. Bake in a 350°F oven for 20 to 25 minutes, longer if necessary, until cooked through. Remove from the oven and let the meatballs cool slightly. Insert decorative Tennessee state flag toothpicks and serve.*

CREAMED COLLARD GREENS

Settlers in Middle Tennessee planted two gardens. A spring garden might yield vegetables such as kale, collards, chard, cabbage, mustard greens, English peas, snap peas, and the like. Settlers brought seeds from home or wrote to relatives and friends "back east" in order to replenish their supply. A cool-season garden may have included root vegetables such as Irish potatoes, sweet potatoes, beets, radishes, and turnips. Summer or warm-season gardens provided heartier vegetables—pumpkins, beans, squash, and the like. Livestock provided dairy.

Rock Castle boasted a basic kitchen garden devoted to herbs used for flavor in cooking. Mint, rosemary, thyme, chives, and tarragon were picked fresh and dried as seasoning. Rosemary and mint were also used as a fragrance to alleviate depression and quell digestive issues.

Collard greens, a member of the cabbage family and rich in vitamin C, added a healthy dimension to a frontier diet just as it does to our modern-day fare.

Ingredients
½ cup unsalted butter, divided
1 cup chopped red bell pepper
½ cup chopped celery
½ cup chopped yellow onion
2 cloves garlic, finely minced
12 cups fresh collards, chopped
¼ cup all-purpose flour
2 cups heavy cream
¼ cup chopped green onion (white and green parts)
2 teaspoons Worcestershire sauce
1 teaspoon salt
¼ teaspoon cayenne pepper
½ cup breadcrumbs

Directions
Preheat the oven to 350°F. Using 2 tablespoons of butter, grease a 9×9-inch baking dish. Set aside. In a large cast-iron skillet, melt 2 tablespoons of butter over medium-high heat. Add the bell pepper, celery, and onion; cook until tender. Add the garlic and chopped collard greens; cook, stirring frequently until just tender (about 5 to 7 minutes). Remove from the heat and set aside. In a medium saucepan, melt 2 tablespoons of butter over medium-heat. Whisk in the flour until smooth. Gradually whisk in the cream. Bring to a boil; reduce the heat to medium-low. Cook, stirring occasionally, until thickened, approximately 5 minutes. Stir the cream mixture into the collard greens mixture. Stir in the green onion, celery salt, Worcestershire sauce, lemon juice salt, and cayenne pepper. Bring the mixture to a boil. Remove from the heat and spoon into the prepared dish.

In a small saucepan, melt 2 tablespoons of butter. Stir in the breadcrumbs. Sprinkle over the greens mixture. Bake until lightly browned and bubbly. (Yields 8 servings.)

CUSTARD CORN PUDDING

Much of the Smiths' summer crops—mainly beans, peas, and corn—could be harvested in early fall and cooked fresh, or dried and stored in their root cellar for use later in the season.

Many eighteenth-century cooks used a "water bath" for custards and cakes. Moisture from the hot water prevents the tops of custards and cakes from splitting. This method remains a popular device with today's cooks and bakers.

Ingredients
4 large ears of fresh corn (or 4 cups frozen corn)
⅓ cup sugar
1 teaspoon salt
1 tablespoon all-purpose flour
2 large eggs, beaten
1 cup whole milk
1 cup heavy cream
3 tablespoons unsalted butter, melted
½ teaspoon freshly grated nutmeg

Directions
Preheat the oven to 350°F. In a large sauce pan, boil 3 cups of water to prepare a "water bath." Butter an 8x8x1½-inch casserole dish and select a second, larger, oven-proof container into which the casserole dish will loosely fit. Prepare the corn by removing the husks and silk. Using a sharp paring knife, cut the top of the kernels off the cob. Use the tines and side of a fork to scrape what remains of the kernels, plus all the juice (called "milk") from the cob. This makes about 4 cups. Place the cut corn into a large mixing bowl, sprinkle in the sugar, salt, and flour and mix well. Whisk the beaten eggs, milk, and cream together and pour, while stirring, into the corn mixture. Blend in the melted butter and nutmeg and spoon the mixture into the buttered casserole dish. Set the casserole

dish into the larger oven-proof container. Pour the boiling water into the larger container until it rises about a ½ inch up the side. Bake for 35 to 40 minutes, or until the center is set and a toothpick, or knife inserted near the center comes out clean.
(Yields 6–8 servings.)

PICKLED BEETS AND ONIONS

The beet, a root vegetable, was likely planted in the Smiths' spring garden. Herbs, on the other hand, were planted in the kitchen garden close to the house. On the early Tennessee frontier, beets were boiled with vinegar and herbs and "put up" in crocks—today's glass jars.

Ingredients
Beets and Onions
4 pounds or 20 small beets
3 medium (white) onions, sliced
3 cups apple cider vinegar
2 cups purified spring water
1 cup organic white sugar
1 cup packed organic light-brown sugar
2 whole cinnamon sticks
2 tablespoons Hain's Iodized Sea Salt
2 tablespoons whole mixed pickling spice (see below)
1 bay leaf

Pickling Spice
2 tablespoons mustard seeds
2 tablespoons whole allspice
2 teaspoons coriander seeds
2 teaspoons whole cloves
1 teaspoon ground ginger
1 teaspoon dried red pepper flakes
1 bay leaf, crumbled
1 cinnamon stick, grated

Directions

For the Beets and Onions: Sterilize 3 quart-sized jars. Cut off all but 2 inches of the beet tops. Wash the beets well and leave whole with the roots attached. In a medium size stock pot, cook the beets in enough boiling water to cover them until just tender (about 20 minutes). Drain. Quickly plunge the beets into cold water; slip the skins off and remove the root ends. Cut the beets into ¼-inch slices. Set aside. In a large sauce pan, stir together the onion slices, vinegar, water, and both sugars. Tie the cinnamon sticks, pickling spice (see ingredients above and directions below), and bay leaf in a cheesecloth bag. Stir the salt and the spice bag into the vinegar, water, and sugar mixture. Heat to boiling; reduce heat. Cover and simmer for 5 minutes. Remove from the heat. Remove the spice bag. Allow the mixture to cool for 5 minutes. Divide the beet slices evenly among hot sterilized jars. Pour the liquid to within ½ inch of the tops of the jars; seal. Process by submerging the jars in a boiling water bath for 30 minutes. (Yields 3 quarts.)

> **Tidbits:**
> When finished with the pickled beets and onions, fill a leftover jar of brine with whole, peeled, hard-boiled eggs. Chill in the marinade for several days.

For the Pickling Spice: Combine all the ingredients. Mix well and store in an airtight container until needed.

PEACH BRANDY POUND CAKE

Daniel Smith furnished Rock Castle with trappings befitting a man of affluence and political stature. Owning and operating a still on one's property was an indication of wealth. Smith's peach orchard afforded him the luxury of producing a fine brandy for sipping and for the occasional special recipe.

The costliest piece of Rock Castle furniture is the family sugar chest. Carved from beautifully inlaid, solid black walnut, the sugar chest housed expensive, highly sought-after sugar imported from Africa. Sugar cane from Africa was imported in cones. One cone of African sugar demanded the hefty market price of two hundred dollars.

To craft a delicious pound cake, the Smiths' cook could open the door to the sugar chest (kept under lock and key) and measure out a portion of the treasured confection. Daniel's prized peach brandy, butter and "clabber" from their butter churn, eggs from their chickens, and freshly harvested wheat ground into flour could be swirled together to satisfy the sweet tooth of family and guests. Flavorings were likely harvested fresh or dried. Confectioners' sugar (powdered), although used in European cookery, was likely unavailable in frontier kitchens.

The original "pound" cake, popular in the 1700s, was made with a pound each of butter, sugar, flour, and eggs mixed in a Dutch oven and slow baked. The cake is making a comeback in the twenty-first-century kitchen. My recipe includes an optional peach glaze.

Ingredients
Cake
3 cups sugar
1 cup butter (2 sticks) softened
6 eggs
3 cups all-purpose flour
¼ teaspoon baking soda
Pinch of salt
8 ounces sour cream
1 tablespoon rum, or 1 ½ teaspoons of rum extract
¼ teaspoon almond extract
1 teaspoon pure vanilla extract
¼ to ½ cup peach brandy, or peach nectar

Peach Glaze (Optional)
2 cups skinless, finely chopped fresh peaches
1½ tablespoons cornstarch
1 cup sugar
1 teaspoon peach brandy, or substitute with ½ teaspoon
     of peach nectar and ¼ teaspoon of brandy extract

Directions
For the Cake: Preheat the oven to 325°F. In a large bowl, with a hand mixer, cream (beat together) the sugar and butter until light and fluffy.

Add eggs one at a time, beating well after each addition. In a medium size bowl, combine the dry ingredients (flour, baking soda, and salt) and add to the creamed mixture alternately with the sour cream, beating well after each addition. Stir in the extracts, rum, and brandy until combined. Pour the batter into a buttered and floured 10 -inch Bundt pan. Bake 1 hour and 15 minutes or until a toothpick comes out clean. Cool in the pan for 15 minutes. Remove the cake from the pan onto a wire rack to cool completely.

(Yields 10–12 servings.)

Tidbits:
Overbaked pound cake equals dry pound cake. Check the cake occasionally for doneness by inserting a wooden skewer or knife into the center of the cake. When the implement comes out clean, the cake is done.

For the Glaze: Combine the peaches, cornstarch, sugar, and brandy in a medium sauce pan. Cook over medium-high heat, stirring constantly until thick (about 1 minute.) Spoon the glaze over each slice of pound cake. Top with a dollop of whipped cream.

Tidbits, Too:
For a simpler peach glaze, combine 1¼ cups of powdered sugar and 6 tablespoons of peach brandy (or substitute with extract recipe above) and drizzle it over the top of the cake.

Chapter 3

TIPTON-HAYNES STATE HISTORIC SITE

◆————————————————————————————————◆

Built 1784
Johnson City, Tennessee

Taproots

Colonel John Tipton was a man of strong conviction
and loyal determination. He was endowed with a high
order of intellect. He possessed a high sense of honor.
He was a personification of loyalty to the State and
Country.

—President Thomas Jefferson,
condolence letter to John Tipton Jr., 1813

O beautiful land of the mountains with thy
sun-painted cliffs how can I ever forget thee!

—Landon Carter Haynes, "Ode to Tennessee" speech, 1872

The Tipton-Haynes State Historic Site in Washington County, Tennessee tells the story of Tennessee history from its early settlement in 1784 to the 1960s. The site offers people of all ages the opportunity to learn about life in the Colonial and Civil War eras and appreciate the skills necessary for farm life during the late 1770s through the 1800s. The site is notable in Tennessee history through its association with two different families who lived there during two different time periods: the Tiptons in the eighteenth and early nineteenth centuries and the Haynes family in the mid-nineteenth century.

THE JOHN TIPTON ERA

Colonel John Tipton, a statesman and central figure in the formation
of the states of Virginia and Tennessee, was born in Baltimore County,
Maryland, on August 15, 1730. When he was seventeen, his family moved
to the Virginia frontier in the Shenandoah Valley. In 1776, while living
in Virginia, Tipton served on committees with Patrick Henry (famous
for his 1775 declaration, "Give me liberty, or give me death!"), George

Tipton-Haynes State
Historic Site.

Mason, and James Madison. He was elected to represent Dunmore County at the Virginia Convention, where they adopted a declaration of rights and a constitution.

Virginia governor Patrick Henry appointed Tipton as the recruiting officer for the Virginia Continental Line, a military unit during the Revolution, in 1779. Five of Tipton's sons from his first marriage served in the Revolutionary War. From 1781 through 1783, Tipton was elected and served as the Shenandoah County sheriff.

Colonel John Tipton's still house.

In 1783, John with his second wife, Martha (his first wife, Mary, died giving birth to their ninth son), purchased plots of land in what is now Washington County, Tennessee, including a one-hundred-acre tract on a branch of Sinking Creek where Tipton and his family would eventually attend Sinking Creek Baptist Church. On May 15, 1784, Colonel Tipton acquired another one-hundred-acre tract from Samuel Henry and built a 25×30-foot cabin (pioneer cabins were typically 16×20 feet) made of hand-hewn logs. Today, John Tipton's one and one-half -story log home, where he lived during the infamous Battle of the State of Franklin (February 29, 1788) is located on the Tipton-Haynes site. The logs are adzed (carved with an 'adz'—an ax-like tool used for dressing timber; pronounced 'adds') with dove-tail joints. The old stone chimney still stands. One of the original cabin walls can be seen as well. The corn crib and the barn have been restored "with materials comparable to that of the original 1850s structure," according to co-director and historian, Wesley Spurgeon.

In 1788, the cabin was located in what was then Washington County, North Carolina. Later the county would be part of the so-called State of Franklin and, finally, Tennessee. The infamous Battle of the State of

The Landon Carter Haynes law office.

The Tipton Place in the Haynes Era.

Franklin—between North Carolina forces led by Tipton and State of Franklin troops commanded by John Sevier, the governor of the three-year old would-be state—took place on the Tipton farm. Tipton would ultimately win this battle and continue working in the halls of what was then the North Carolina government. John Sevier was elected the first governor of Tennessee, which was admitted to the Union as its sixteenth state on June 1, 1796.

After Colonel Tipton's death, John Tipton Jr. inherited the property. Already a successful state legislator and wealthy landowner in Blountville, Tennessee, the younger Tipton expanded his father's cabin in the 1820s, transforming it into a charming Federal-style farmhouse. John Tipton Jr. died in 1831 in Nashville while attending the Nineteenth General Assembly.

Some notable physical features of the Tipton-Haynes site from the Tipton era are the Buffalo Trail, which later became the Jonesborough-Morganton Stage Road. Tradition says that the Cherokees and Daniel Boone camped and took shelter in a cave in this wooded area, which today can still be seen and whose entryway offers an array of native plants and wildflowers. André Michaux, a French botanist, was a guest in the Tipton

Tipton Decorated for Christmastime.

home in 1795 and 1796 and recorded numerous spring wildflowers on the property. Michaux noted that the nearby mountains were covered in "bloodroot, spring beauty, and trout lily."

Colonel John Tipton lived on his property until his death in August 1813. John Tipton Jr., having served on the committee to form the Tennessee State Constitution and elected as the first senator from Washington County, received a personal letter of condolence from President Thomas Jefferson, an excerpt from which opens this chapter.

THE LANDON CARTER HAYNES ERA

The Tipton farmstead experienced a resurgence when David and Rhoda Taylor Haynes bought the property in 1837 from the heirs of John Tipton Jr. for $1,050.00. They gave the property to their son Landon as a wedding present when he married Eleanor Powell in 1839. Of twelve children born to Rhoda and David—seven boys and five girls—Landon Carter Haynes was their first-born.

Landon Carter Haynes was born on December 2, 1816, in Carter County, Tennessee. He was a farmer, slave owner, lawyer, Methodist minister, Confederate senator, and editor of the *Tennessee Sentinel,* a newspaper owned by his brother-in-law Lawson Gifford and published in Jonesborough in the 1840s. Haynes is best remembered, however, for his political career. He was elected to the Tennessee House of Representatives, serving several northeast Tennessee counties, and was Speaker of the House during his third term (1849–51).

Although he lost a bid for Congress in 1859, he was heartened a bit when, that year, the Johnson's Depot post office name was changed to Haynesville in his honor. That name was, however, short-lived: after the Civil War began, Haynes supported the southern cause and represented Tennessee as a Confederate senator from 1862 to 1865. The name Haynesville was changed back to Johnson's Depot by the U.S. government, and the community was eventually incorporated as Johnson City.

Following the war, Haynes's role as a Confederate politician led to the loss of his farm; he also feared retribution from the many Union sympathizers in East Tennessee. He thus relocated his family to Memphis to start anew during Reconstruction. There, he returned to his passion: practicing law. Joining three other lawyers in town, he established the

Office of Haynes, Heath, Lewis & Lee, Attorneys at Law. He continued his practice until his death after a prolonged illness, on February 17, 1875.

Haynes was known and admired as an eloquent orator, a talent evident in his glorious, extemporaneous speech titled "Ode to Tennessee," which he delivered in response to a dubious "toast" offered to him by former Confederate general Nathan Bedford Forrest at a banquet in Jackson, Tennessee, in 1872—the last line of that speech appears at the opening of this chapter.

The farm near Johnson City would eventually return to the Haynes estate when Sarah L. Gifford Simerly (1847–1935), Landon Carter Haynes's niece, purchased the property on May 1, 1882.

Eleanor Powell Haynes

The woman who would become Landon Carter Haynes's wife, Eleanor Powell, was born in Sullivan County, Tennessee, in 1820. Her parents, Dr. Joseph Powell and his wife, Eleanor "Nellie" Wheeler Powell, moved to Carter County, Tennessee, sometime after Eleanor was born. Dr. Powell became a leading physician in Elizabethton, Tennessee. Eleanor's family was made up of prominent members of both the political and academic arenas of northeast Tennessee. Her brothers, uncles, and in-laws included doctors, lawyers, and high-ranking military officers. Eleanor's sister Ann married Colonel John Tipton's grandson, Isaac P. Tipton of Washington County.

Landon and Eleanor Haynes had several children: Robert Walter, Joseph Eugene, Ann Helen, Mary Alice, Landon C. Jr., and David. Robert married Eleanor's second cousin Drucila "Drusie" Cornelia Powell in 1863.

Unfortunately, little is known about the latter life of Eleanor Powell Haynes. After Landon died in 1872, the Federal Census Bureau lists Eleanor as living in Jackson, Tennessee, with her youngest son, David. But the date of her death, as well as the location of her gravesite, is unknown.

BUILDINGS AT THE TIPTON-HAYNES SITE

The Landon Carter Haynes family occupied the Tipton Haynes house from 1839 to 1865. In 1850, Landon and Eleanor Powell Haynes added the Greek revival-style portico to the home and constructed a Greek revival law office beside it, transforming it into what we see today. Additional buildings include a large double-crib barn, smoke house, still house, spring house, pigsty, joinery (wood-working facility), and double-crib corncrib. A reconstructed cabin from the 1800s is used for historic interpretation as the George Haynes cabin. George was one of three enslaved African American workers of Landon. The historic interpretation describes these individuals as they were when George was thirty-five years old; the other two individuals are Charlotte, about sixty years old, and Cornelia, about nine years old.

Surrounding the farmhouse today are cultivated herb, vegetable, and flower gardens containing many of the herbs, and spices presumed to have originally been planted by the Haynes family.

In addition to describing the Tipton and Haynes families, the official web pages of the site also include information about the Taylor family, who were Haynes family in-laws:

> The Taylor family plays an important role in the history of the Tipton-Haynes State Historic Site. The Tipton-Haynes State Historic Site library is dedicated to the Taylor family. In 1816, David Haynes (1788–1868) married Rhoda Taylor (1795–1861). Rhoda was the daughter of Matthew and Rachel Taylor and niece of General Nathaniel Taylor, a hero of the War of 1812. David and Rhoda had several children. Their first child was Landon Carter Haynes (1816–1875), owner of Tipton-Haynes during the 1840s and 1850s. Another child was their daughter Emmaline Haynes (1822–1880). Emmaline married Nathaniel Greene Taylor (1819–1887), the grandson of General Nathaniel Taylor (Sabine Hill). Two of their sons, Bob and Alfred Taylor, served in the United States Senate and House of Representatives and as Governor of Tennessee during the late 1800s and early 1900s. The Taylor Library houses a wide range of research materials. With permission from the site, research within the library is available. Also, certain materials may be loaned upon signing a loan agreement.

Today, the site is managed by the Tipton-Haynes Historical Association.

Address and Contact Information
Tipton-Haynes State Historic Site
2620 South Roan Street
Johnson City, TN 37601
(423) 926-3651
tiptonhaynes@embarqmail.com
www.tipton-haynes.org

Timeless Recipes: The Tipton Era

Tennessee cuisine follows its terrain. The foods of early settlers of East Tennessee hill country had more in common with the mountain folk of North Carolina, Kentucky, and West Virginia. These settlers—English, Scotch-Irish, and French Huguenot—brought with them traditional foods such as corn, potatoes, vegetables, and fruit, along with their cooking methods: pan frying, stewing, smoking, and roasting. The mountains and hollows were replete with wild turkey and deer. Raccoon was readily available, as was rabbit, squirrel, bear, and hogs, prepared in a number of ways that provided food for the winter. Mrs. Tipton learned to make stews from lamb, pork, possum, squirrel, and other wild game.

According to the Tipton-Haynes Historical Association and the Tipton estate inventory, livestock included twenty sheep, thirteen hogs, and two sows with piglets. In an archaeological dig in 2008, eggs shells were discovered, and a possum bone with knife marks was unearthed. We can assume that chickens scratched and pecked in their farmyard. Lucy Kennerly Gump's master's thesis, "Possessions and Patterns of Living in Washington County: The 20 Years Before Tennessee Statehood, 1777–1796," indicates that sheep, pigs, and chickens were used mainly for food, as well as for buying, selling, and trading.

The centerpiece of a typical frontier cabin was the small hearth. The Tipton hearth area was outfitted with fire dogs (known today as andirons, a pair of decorative metal stands used to support logs in an open fire) as well as cast-iron implements and cookware, including trammels (a hook in a fireplace for raising and lowering a kettle), swinging iron cranes used to move pots in and out of the fire, and an assortment of hand-forged tools such as fire pokers, shovels, pot hooks, fireplace tongs, long-handled skimmers, ladles, spoons, and forks—all tools of the trade for the frontier housewife. Cast iron was, in fact, so highly prized that it was passed from generation to generation, as indicated in the Tipton estate inventory.

Today, we might consider the Tiptons' living conditions primitive. Mrs. Tipton's day began early compared to today's standard. Before dawn, like many pioneer housewives, she built, then maintained, the hearth fire, toted heavy wooden buckets (inherited by Elizabeth Tipton, according to estate papers) full of water from the spring to their cabin, and gathered fresh fruit, vegetables, and spices from the kitchen garden for meals—all before preparing breakfast for her family. Breakfast usually consisted of cornmeal mush, scrambled eggs, bacon, hot cakes served with a sweetener such as honey, sorghum, or molasses, and biscuits. Dinner, the main and heaviest meal of the day, was served midday. Supper consisted of dinner-time leftovers.

Comprised of hearty foods in substantial quantities, dinner was served between noon and 3:00 p.m. and was typically a stew with side dishes, the ingredients of which varied with the season. Stew could simmer all day, required little tending (except for the fire), and only one pot. One-pot cooking in a cauldron or Dutch oven, was common in the frontier kitchen. Puddings could be steamed in a fabric bag hung on a hook above the pot of simmering stew.

Martha Tipton's routine consisted mainly of cooking, washing clothes, caring for the children, and spinning, weaving, and sewing their clothing—all amid the constant threat of attacks from native inhabitants. Yet, for their time, Colonel Tipton and his family enjoyed a level of wealth and privilege uncommon for pioneers in Tennessee's wilderness. Their estate papers do not suggest a life of luxury, but touches of graciousness, such as Delft plates, and tea cups with saucers can be found. According to the Encyclopedia Britannica, delftware is earthenware glazed with a thin, opaque coating of tin manufactured in Holland and England.

Most pioneers had at least one apple tree. Colonel Tipton maintained an apple orchard. The apples could be dried, fried, steamed, baked, and made into various cakes and pies, as well as apple sauce; fed as fodder to fatten their livestock; and fermented into cider and apple brandy.

Mrs. Tipton cooked with corn and wheat, purchased either in fifty-pound sacks in Jonesborough or ground by millstones such as the ones seen at the site today. These millstones were donated by Joseph P. Tipton, Colonel John Tipton's great-great-great-great grandson. Dried herbs and even certain flowers such as dandelion greens, for salads and tea, could be roasted and added to coffee. Spices such as cinnamon, nutmeg, and mace were pulled from their well-tended herb garden and used as seasoning.

On a cool fall afternoon at the Tipton home, a substantial "dinner" may have selectively included the following, all of which could be served later as supper.

TIPTON ERA MENU
Roasted Pumpkin Soup
Lamb Stew
Boiled Fresh Turnip Greens
Dilly Skillet-Baked Cornbread
Fried Apples
Cherokee Chestnut Bread
Jonnycakes
Sweet Potato Pudding
Sorghum (Whiskey) Cake
Sassafras Tea

ROASTED PUMPKIN SOUP
Before Colonel John Tipton purchased the land upon which his 1784
cabin stands, parts of northeast Tennessee (then part of North Carolina)
were occupied and farmed by Cherokees. This rich, fertile loam produced
beans, corn, sunflowers, squash, pumpkins, and root vegetables. Tending
their garden, the Tiptons would have picked smaller, sweeter pumpkins
to make pies and soups. Hearth roasting and cooking soups and stews
in a large cast-iron cauldron were among the primary methods used by
housewives on the frontier. Other ways of preparing foods included frying,
boiling, baking, simmering, and braising. Mrs. Tipton used water or broth
for cooking purposes and may have bartered for cream and milk from
a neighbor. Tipton estate papers bear no record of cows as part of their
inventory. Jonesborough, the county seat and Tennessee's oldest town,
was ten miles away by buckboard—a day's journey there and back to a
country store. Ingredients and foods not purchased at the store could be
grown in their large garden.

Imagine Colonel Tipton and his sons coming home for that midday
meal and sitting down to a table laden with rich, hearty pumpkin soup
among other homegrown fare. Surely their hungry bellies were gratified.
With the use of today's immersion blender and other modern-day kitchen
conveniences, yours will be, too.

Ingredients

1 two-pound pumpkin, halved, seeds removed
1 teaspoon salt
¼ teaspoon, plus a pinch, freshly ground black pepper
1 tablespoon olive oil
2 tablespoons butter
2 teaspoons ground cinnamon
1 teaspoon ground allspice
¾ cup chopped yellow onion
½ cup chopped carrot
¼ cup chopped celery
2 tablespoons minced ginger
1 tablespoon minced garlic
3½ cups chicken stock
½ cup heavy cream

Tidbits:
When blending hot liquids, follow these directions: Remove the liquid from the heat and cool for at least 10 minutes. Use an immersion blender or transfer the liquid to a blender or food processor and fill no more than halfway. If using a blender, release one corner of the lid. This prevents the vacuum effect that creates heat explosions. Place a towel over the top of the machine, pulse a few times and then process on high speed until the liquid is smooth.

Directions

Preheat the oven to 400°F. Split the pumpkin in half horizontally and remove the seeds and membranes. Place the pumpkin cut-side up on a prepared baking sheet. Season it with ½ teaspoon of salt and ¼ teaspoon of pepper. Invert the pumpkin to cut-side down and drizzle with 1 tablespoon of olive oil. Place in the oven and roast until the skin is golden brown and the pumpkin is tender (50 to 60 minutes). Remove the pumpkin from the oven and allow it to cool. Once it's cool enough to handle, use a spoon to scoop the pumpkin flesh from its skin and set it aside until ready to use. Set a cast-iron cauldron or Dutch oven over medium heat. Add the remaining 2 tablespoons butter and, when hot, add the cinnamon and allspice and cook, stirring the mixture constantly, for 1 minute. Add the onions, carrots, celery, ginger, and garlic to the pan and sauté, stirring occasionally, until lightly caramelized (3 to 4 minutes). Add the chicken stock and reserved roasted pumpkin and bring the stock to a boil. Reduce to a simmer and cook the soup for 15 to 20 minutes or until the vegetables are soft. Remove the soup from the heat and process with an immersion blender (or in batches in a blender; see "Tidbits" opposite for processing tips) until it's smooth. Season the soup with the remaining ½ teaspoon salt and pinch of pepper. Add the cream to the soup and stir gently to combine. Serve in warm soup bowls with a drizzle of pumpkin oil, if you like. (Yields 6 servings.)

LAMB STEW

Of the twenty or so sheep roaming the Tipton homestead, many were lambs, with a few growing into adult sheep. Lambs, sheep less than a year old with very little fat on them, were used for food. Mutton—the meat of older sheep—had a stronger flavor and was tougher. Sheep provided food as well as wool for clothing. The animal's hard, white, fat was used as "tallow" for making candles.

Cast-iron pots, skillets, and Dutch ovens—basic and important pieces of cooking equipment in the eighteenth-century kitchen and beyond—were listed as part of the Tipton estate inventory. These cast-iron pots and Dutch ovens, filled with lamb and fresh vegetables, simmered directly over the fire in the small fireplace of the Tipton cabin from early morning until noon, when they were served at midday. Lard, bear fat, possum fat, or raccoon fat was used for cooking. Vegetable oil or olive oil is a good modern-day substitute. Mrs. Tipton prepared her vegetables and meat for broth and stock in soups and stews. Lamb stew makes a fine one-pot meal.

Ingredients
2 pounds of lamb shoulder, cut into 1½-inch cubes
3 tablespoons vegetable oil
3 tablespoons all-purpose flour
1¾ cup beef broth, or stock)
½ teaspoon of salt
½ teaspoon pepper
2 medium tomatoes, diced
2 tablespoons butter
2 medium onions, thinly sliced

2 medium carrots, cut into ½-inch pieces
2 large garlic cloves, peeled and thinly sliced
4 small russet potatoes, washed, peeled, and medium diced
½ cup frozen peas
2 small fresh turnips, washed, stalks removed,
    peeled and diced (about 1½ cups)
1 sprig of fresh rosemary
Parsley, to taste

Directions
Brown the meat on all sides in the oil in a heavy, hot skillet. Transfer the browned meat to a Dutch oven or heavy stockpot. Sprinkle the lamb with the flour and add the beef or vegetable stock, salt, pepper, and tomatoes. Bring slowly to a boil, cover, reduce the heat and simmer 1½ hours or until tender. Heat the butter in a skillet; add the onions, carrots, garlic, and turnips and simmer, stirring periodically, until the onions are light brown. Add the browned vegetables, rosemary sprig, and potatoes to the stew. Simmer uncovered until the potatoes are tender, 30 to 40 minutes, stirring occasionally. Twenty minutes before the potatoes are done, add the peas. Remove the rosemary sprig. Serve sprinkled with a small handful of chopped, fresh parsley.
(Yields 6–8 servings)

BOILED FRESH TURNIP GREENS

Early settlers on the Tennessee frontier were resourceful; nothing was wasted. Turnips, for example, like those in my lamb stew recipe, were grown in the Tipton garden patch; they could be peeled, sliced, and then boiled and buttered, much like rutabagas, and served as a side dish. The tops or green leaves of the turnips were washed and trimmed of their tough, thick stems, boiled in water until tender, then served as a nutritious part of a meal. When boiling greens, a ham hock (the lower part of a pig's leg, equivalent to the ankle and calf), fatback (fatty pork), or salt pork (not smoked but aged in salt) would be tossed in the pot for added flavor. Pot likker (or "liquor"), the broth left in the pot after boiling greens with a ham hock or salt pork, is highly prized for its flavor and makes a delicious "sop" for cornbread. You'll need about six times more *fresh* greens than you intend to serve. Greens wilt when boiled and therefore cook down to about half the amount as fresh.

Ingredients
24 ounces, fresh, trimmed, chopped turnip greens
1 ham hock or, small piece salt pork
1½ cups water, salted
1 teaspoon sugar (optional)
Dash of cider vinegar or hot sauce (optional)

Tidbits:
Serve with a dash of vinegar or hot sauce, if desired.

Directions
Cut off and discard the tough stems and discolored leaves from the greens. Wash the greens thoroughly and drain well. Chop them into bite-size pieces and place them in a large pot or Dutch oven with the water. Place the ham hock or salt pork on top of the greens. Cover the pot and bring the water to a rolling boil. (Optional: stir in the sugar for "less bite" to the greens.) Reduce the heat but keep the water boiling for about 30 minutes until the greens begin to get tender. Serve greens in their flavorful "pot likker."
(Yields 4 servings.)

DILLY SKILLET-BAKED CORNBREAD

On the rustic, rural Tennessee frontier, corn was planted around tree stumps and rocks, and could be grown seasonally in a few months. Corn could be dried, ground into meal for bread, boiled into mush, made into whiskey, and fed as fodder to livestock. Corn is one of Tennessee's chief agricultural products and skillet-baked cornbread is a traditional staple of southern rural cuisine. The Tipton boys were in for a treat if one of those skillets was full of fresh hot cornbread batter, known as "pone." Lard (fat) from hogs, groundhogs, bears, or opossum was used in everything from hominy grits to greasing skillets. Mrs. Tipton, like all frontier housewives, melted fat into a heavy iron spider (a three-legged skillet) and placed it in the fire. Batter made from cornmeal and water (or milk, if they had it) was poured directly into the sizzling grease. The mixture was returned to the fire to bake into a dense, very moist cake with a crunchy crust.

This simple recipe using today's self-rising cornmeal is delicious with or without the additional crisp taste of dill weed.

Ingredients
1 egg
1¾ cups buttermilk
5 tablespoons bacon grease (or shortening)
2 cups Martha White self-rising white or yellow cornmeal
1 teaspoons dill weed (optional)

Directions
Preheat the oven to 450°F. Add the bacon grease or shortening to a 10-inch Lodge cast-iron skillet and place in the preheated oven. In a medium bowl, beat the egg and add the remaining ingredients and mix until just combined. The batter should be thick but pourable. Pour the batter into the hot greased skillet. Batter should sizzle when poured into the grease. Bake for 25 to 30 minutes until golden brown.
(Yields 8 servings.)

FRIED APPLES
The apples from Colonel John Tipton's apple orchard provided a variety of sweet sustenance in everything from baked goods to sauces and cider—a fermented alcoholic beverage made from the unfiltered juice of apples. Apples could be peeled, cored, and fried in a mixture of butter and sugar until fragrant and tender.

There is no written record of the variety of apple Colonel Tipton grew in his orchard, but he likely raised Newtown Pippins, a seedling discovered in Newtown, Long Island, in 1759. This apple, credited as the oldest commercially grown native variety in the United States—and Benjamin Franklin's favorite—made its way into East Tennessee as a vital part of early homesteads of the rich and poor. Today, Pippins, considered the best variety for pies, have all but disappeared. The Granny Smith apple, however, offers tangy tartness to a fried-apple side dish when served for breakfast and dinner or when baked in a pie.

Ingredients
4 or 5 medium Granny Smith Apples
5 tablespoons butter
1 cup sugar

Directions
Wash, peel, and then core the apples and slice thinly. Heat 5 tablespoons of butter in a cast-iron skillet. When the butter melts and begins to bubble, add the apple slices and stir over low heat. Cover and simmer over medium-low heat. Stir occasionally until the apples start to cook well and become tender. Remove the cover, add the sugar slowly, and stir thoroughly. Continue to cook the apples uncovered, stirring as needed to prevent sticking. When the sugar develops into a thick consistency and begins to brown, remove the skillet from the heat. Serve immediately. Fried apples, however, may be served hot or cold.
(Yields 4 servings.)

CHEROKEE CHESTNUT BREAD (DUMPLINGS)

On his homestead, Colonel Tipton had access to chestnut and hickory trees tended and harvested by its former inhabitants, the Cherokees. These majestic, giants trees grew to be over one hundred feet tall in the East Tennessee forests of the Appalachian Mountains. For the Tiptons and other pioneer families, chestnuts helped put food on the table and shoes on their feet. Chestnut trees provided food for farm animals and wild game of the forest—bears, passenger pigeons (now extinct), turkeys, squirrels, deer, and raccoon, to name a few—and these animals in turn provided food for the pioneers' tables and "hide" to shod the families' feet. The Tipton pigs were fattened into hogs using chestnuts as fodder. The trees provided a wonderful resource of nourishing golf-ball size nuts for cooking and baking, and solid timber for fence rails and fence posts Additionally, their dense blossoms provide nectar which bees extract to produce Chestnut honey. Chestnuts can be boiled and peeled, roasted, mixed into dressings, and ground into meal and flour.

Tidbits:
For this recipe,
I purchase chestnut
flour from
www.nuts.com.

Roasting chestnuts hasn't changed much through the centuries. Martha Tipton, like

Tidbits, Too:
This recipe can be cooked as a hearty breakfast cereal. Follow the above recipe without forming the dough. I recommend dividing the recipe in half and cooking on the stove top with 4 cups of water or milk. Once cooked to a porridge-like consistency, ladle into a breakfast bowl and drizzle with maple or sorghum syrup.

many housewives on the Tennessee frontier, roasted chestnuts by scoring an "X" on the flat side of the chestnuts with a sharp knife and placing them in a cast-iron skillet directly in her ever-burning fireplace or directly over embers scraped from her fireplace onto the hearth. The pan would be shaken frequently to avoid scorching. Once the shells curled back, the chestnuts were removed from the heat and peeled while warm. This method can be used on stovetops or over a campfire or grill. One of Martha's large cast-iron kettles (as indicated in the Tipton estate inventory papers), full of boiling water and a few large hickory leaves, was all she needed to produce a tasty, nutritious dumpling "bread" that provided for her family's nutritional needs for breakfast, dinner, and supper.

Native Americans made significant contributions to early American cookery by sharing their ways and means of survival with pioneers in the Tennessee wilderness. The Tipton family may have partaken of this pleasing loaf from the grand yield of the American chestnut tree. Sadly, in the early 1930s, a parasitic fungus, brought to the Unites States by the Chinese chestnut tree, produced a blight so devastating that it almost wiped out this magnificent tree. Today, the American Chestnut Foundation in Asheville, North Carolina, has instituted a program to help bring the American chestnut tree back to the forests of East Tennessee; there, chestnuts are available on select small orchards and farms from September through December.

Ingredients
1 cup chestnut flour
1¼ cup honey
1 cup cornmeal
¼ teaspoon salt
¼ teaspoon baking soda
Large hickory leaves or cheese cloth

Directions

Whisk the chestnut flour with the cornmeal, salt, and baking soda until well combined. Add just enough water to make a stiff dough. Knead well. Using a 2-tablespoon cookie scoop, scoop balls of dough from the mixture and place each ball in the center of each hickory leaf or 4x4-inch piece of cheese cloth. Wrap them up and tie with a string. Drop the balls into a pot of boiling water. Cover, reduce heat, and simmer for 45 minutes or until done. (Doneness is determined by the firmness of the dough.) Unwrap and serve immediately.

(Yields 25 dumplings.)

JONNYCAKES

The origin of the word "jonnycake," sometimes spelled "johnnycake," is unknown. But some say it was named for a "journey cake," a type of bread the Pilgrims carried on their journey from England to the New World. The not-so-distant relative "hoe cake" is thought to be named for cornmeal cakes baked or fried over a campfire on the blades of the garden hoes of early settlers. However, the word "hoe" is said to be a colloquialism for the English word "griddle," dating back to at least the 1600s, when baking cakes on boards or griddles was commonplace. At the close of the eighteenth century, pioneer housewives were becoming adept at making many types of bread, Americanizing them from their British contemporaries.

Amelia Simmons wrote the first known American cookbook, *American Cookery*, in 1796 primarily because most British recipes, or "receipts" as they were called through the late 1800s, could not be translated into the dishes that she, as an American, had enjoyed. Simply put, the British did not recognize the New World grain called maize, or corn. In fact, jonnycakes were originally made in England with oatmeal. Eventually, however, corn became the main ingredient, and it grew abundantly in the rich Appalachian Mountain soil.

Mrs. Tipton would have kept most of the following ingredients in her cupboard, barnyard, and garden. Jonnycake was an essential staple that could be eaten with every meal. Amelia Simmons's "receipt" for jonnycakes, with updated ingredients, is as tasty as ever.

Ingredients
1 cup water
4 tablespoons butter, divided
1 cup cornmeal
½ teaspoon salt
½ teaspoon sugar
½ cup milk

Directions
Bring the water and 2 tablespoons of butter to a boil in a saucepan over high heat. Mix the cornmeal, salt, and sugar in a medium-sized bowl and pour the boiling water and butter mixture into the bowl of cornmeal, salt, and sugar. Let the mixture stand for 15 or 20 minutes, just long enough for the liquid to saturate the cornmeal. Add the milk and stir well. Put a 12-inch cast-iron skillet on the stovetop over medium-high heat, or use a large electric griddle. Melt the remaining 2 tablespoons of butter in the skillet or griddle, moving the butter around to coat the pan. When the butter is hot, drop the batter in ¼ cups onto the hot skillet. Use a spatula to form 3-4 inch cakes." Fry about 3 minutes on each side; or, fry until bubbles appear on the uncooked surface of the johnnycake. Flip the cake and fry the flipped side until golden brown. Serve hot, topped with butter, jam, apple butter, or maple syrup.
(Yields 4–6 servings.)

SWEET POTATO PUDDING
Root vegetables were a staple on the Tipton farm and for early settlers who sometimes lived out of their garden. Sweet potatoes flourished in the rich soil of East Tennessee and were part of the fall harvest. Sweet potatoes could be roasted on the hearth, baked in the fire, boiled, mashed, poured into pie crusts and casseroles, made into biscuits, and beaten into puddings, which were hung in a fabric bag to cook over a steaming cauldron of soup or stirred into a stew simmering in the fireplace of the Tipton cabin.

It's uncommon to find open fire pits for cooking in today's homes, and steaming pudding in a fabric bag is equally uncommon in our culture of instant gratification. This recipe using modern-day methods and ingredients, however achieves an equally delectable result.

Ingredients
4 to 5 large sweet potatoes
¼ cup salted butter plus two extra tablespoons for casserole dish
¼ cup sugar
2 eggs
½ cup half and half
1 teaspoon cinnamon
½ teaspoon nutmeg

Tidbits:
A sprinkling of your favorite salty nut works well here.

Directions
Preheat the oven to 350°F. Butter the casserole dish. Peel the potatoes and dice them into 1-inch cubes or smaller. On the stovetop, in a large saucepan, boil the potatoes in lightly salted water until fork tender. Drain thoroughly and mash, preferably by hand with a potato masher, until forming a lumpy mixture. Add the remaining ingredients to the sweet potatoes and mix well. Use a blender or an immersion blender, if you have one, for a creamier pudding. Fold the mixture into a 2-quart buttered casserole dish and smooth the top with the back a of spoon. Bake for 30-35 minutes Serve warm drizzled with sorghum or maple syrup.
(Yields 5 servings.)

SORGHUM (WHISKEY) CAKE

In the short-lived State of Franklin (1784–88), whiskey was listed as "legal tender," meaning it could be used as money. In fact, rye whiskey, peach brandy, and apple brandy could be used to pay Franklin taxes. In 1818, one man remarked, "The necessities of life are bread, meat, and whiskey."

Colonel Tipton's still house, which remains on the property today, afforded him the luxury of making good distilled whiskey, a favorite beverage of men on the early Tennessee frontier and beyond. Many of the ingredients listed in the recipe provided below would have been stored in the Tipton pantry after being harvested from their field (wheat and corn, ground into flour and meal, for example). Although there is no evidence that sorghum was grown on the Tipton property, Tennessee history indicates that sorghum plants were an important food source and principal sweetener across the Appalachian regions of the early East

Tennessee frontier. The sorghum plant, related to the grain millet and a distant cousin to sugarcane, is highly nutritious. Sorghum was also used as fodder for sheep.

Each fall, the Tipton-Haynes State Historic Site hosts its Sorghum and Scutching Festival. "Scutching" is a process through which the useful fibers in plant materials, such as flax, are separated from the useless parts in making clothing. The Tipton men would "scutch" flax or wool, and the women would spin it into clothing. Making sorghum syrup is celebrated at the fall festival the original, old-fashioned way—by horse-drawn milling and processing.

Surely John would part with a jigger or two of his prized whiskey for the reward of Martha's cake. And although Martha didn't have the luxury of using baking powder and baking soda as true "raising agents," which weren't brought to the forefront of baking until the mid-1800s, you can make this recipe using modern ingredients and conveniences.

Ingredients
¼ cup butter, room temperature
½ cup packed brown sugar
½ cup granulated sugar
3 eggs
1 cup all-purpose flour, sifted
½ teaspoon baking powder
¼ teaspoon salt
½ teaspoon cinnamon
½ teaspoon baking soda
¼ cup half and half
½ cup sorghum
¼ cup whiskey (Tennessee's Jack Daniels or preferred brand),
    or substitute liquid with apple juice or cider

Directions
Preheat the oven to 350°F. Beat the butter using a hand mixer at medium speed; gradually add sugars and beat until creamy. Add the eggs, one at a time, beating well after each addition and scraping down the sides of

the bowl. Combine the flour, baking powder, salt, cinnamon, and baking soda. Add these dry ingredients to the egg mixture alternately with the half and half beginning and ending with the dry ingredients. Stop the mixer and add the sorghum. Restart the mixer and slowly add the whiskey, or cider (juice.) Mix until the batter is smooth (about 30 seconds; the batter will be thin). Pour into a greased 9-inch spring-form cake pan. Bake for 35 to 40 minutes, until a wooden pick inserted in the center comes out clean. Drizzle with sorghum syrup.

(Yields 8–10 servings.)

SASSAFRAS TEA

Tea-drinking had a ritual significance in the lives of the eighteenth American settlers, according to Lucy Kennerly Gump's "Possessions and Patterns of Living in Washington County." This is evidenced in the Tipton estate papers, which list a substantial inventory of Delft tea cups and saucers.

Of the many roots, barks, leaves, and twigs found in the beautiful Appalachian woodlands to treat a plethora of "what ails you," the sassafras bush—also known as the "mitten tree" because of its mitten-like shape, having a rounded leaf with a "thumb-like" protrusion—grew abundantly in Washington County and the Tipton meadowlands. Sassafras leaves and twigs, found in sparsely wooded areas and overgrown fields, are consumed by deer in summer and winter and may have been a contributing factor to the sizeable deer population roaming the Tipton-Haynes property. Considered a favorite beverage at mealtime, the roots of the small, shrubby, sassafras tree are dug up in the late winter or at the first sign of spring; they are then cleaned, pounded, and dried for several hours over on open hearth. After simmering in a pot of water and strained through a sieve, sassafras tea is said, when sipped, to "thin the blood and kindle the spirit."

Ingredients
1½ quarts of water
½ cup dried, chopped sassafras roots

Directions

Drop the dried, chopped roots into a pot of boiling water. Cover and simmer for about 20 minutes. Pour the tea through a small strainer to remove any loose bits. Pour the tea into your favorite cup and savor the taste—and the moment.

(Yields 6 servings.)

Timeless Recipes: The Haynes Era

Watch over my house and property and have George
cultivate the land in timothy and corn.

—Landon Haynes, letter to a neighbor, 1863

In the nineteenth century before the Civil War, while Landon Carter Haynes and his family enjoyed their newly acquired homestead, their acreage was likely still rife with wild turkeys, deer, rabbits, raccoons, ducks, and geese. The nearby Watauga River provided trout, bluegill, bass, and catfish. ("Watauga" is said by some to mean "beautiful river," though some dispute this claim.)

As indicated in the quotation above, Landon cultivated Timothy grass on his acreage. He might have used some of it to smoke fish and small game such as quail, rabbit, dove, and even barnyard animals such as chickens. When used in cooking, Timothy grass produces a heady aroma of smoke—a method of food preparation that has found its way back into today's restaurants and home kitchens.

HAYNES ERA MENU
Venison Filet Steaks
Greens
Hot Water Hoe Cakes
Dried Apple Stack Cake
Dried Apple Stack Pie (with Pie Crust Recipe, Instructions for Drying
    Apples, and Recipe for Apple Filling)
Spiced Paw-Paw Fruitcake

VENISON FILET STEAKS

With an abundance of wild game surrounding the Haynes property, deer meat—or venison, as it's commonly called—was a staple on their dinner table and perhaps in their smokehouse. Walking his two-hundred-acre tract, Landon Haynes, with a rifle slung over his shoulder, could easily track and bring home a solid eight-point buck with good mass and long tines. Those deer had plenty of food to eat—nuts to forage and greens to nibble from bushes and trees.

If you're not a hunter, set your sights on a good butcher or a friend who will supply you with venison boned and cut to your specifications. With its low-fat content, however, venison has a tendency to dry out when smoked, unlike its fattier counterparts, pork and beef.

Venison goes well with mashed potatoes, greens, and cornbread. Perhaps Eleanor's cook prepared venison by adding a hearty port to the sauce.

Ingredients

4 venison filet steaks (If the steaks are thick, place them in a zip-lock bag or between two sheets of wax paper and pound them with a wooden rolling pin, meat-tenderizing mallet, or heavy skillet to about ¼ inch thickness.)

3 tablespoons port wine

¾ cup blackberry jelly (or red currant jelly)

3 teaspoons salted butter

1 tablespoon olive oil

Salt and freshly ground black pepper

Directions

Season the venison with salt and pepper and set the meat aside for 30 minutes. Gently warm the port in a small saucepan; dissolve the blackberry jelly into the port and keep warm over low heat. Melt the butter and the oil together in a heavy 12-inch cast-iron skillet until it bubbles. Over medium-high heat, begin cooking the steaks–about 3 to 4 minutes per side. Do not overcook venison as it will become tough. Turn the venison

Tidbits:
The Haynes family certainly didn't have access to the variety of cheeses we have today. But serve the filets with a slice of soft melting cheese, placing it on each filet just before the meat is done. Let it melt in the pan, then spoon the sauce over the meat before serving immediately.

only once. Remove from the skillet when a meat thermometer reaches 165 degrees and immediately spoon the blackberry-and-port mixture over the filets. Venison should be served hot, so it's best to have all other food items, such as the cornbread, greens, and the like, prepared and ready to be served.

(Yields 4 servings.)

GREENS

When Landon Haynes and his enslaved field hand finished clearing the ground from summer crops, they began preparing the soil for a fall harvest. Seeds sown in his large garden patch were typical of most vegetable gardens of that period: kale, collards, mustard, and turnip greens. These vegetables could be boiled, parboiled, or steamed together in one pot. That's why they're called "greens," as in a combination of such. Methods of preparing and cooking greens haven't changed much through the years and are still cooked according to tastes and traditions; the constant is that the amount of greens you wish to serve should measure about six times the amount you boil, parboil, or steam. Greens cook down (wilt) to about half the amount as when fresh.

Ingredients
1 pound kale, center stems (spine) removed, washed and chopped
1 pound mustard greens, washed and chopped
2 teaspoons bacon grease
1 medium onion, peeled and diced
2 cloves garlic, thinly sliced
1 fourteen-ounce can chicken stock
1 large ham hock

Directions
Prepare the kale and mustard greens: Remove the spine (center stems) from the kale, and use only the green leafy part of the mustard green. In a Lodge cast-iron Dutch oven, on your stovetop, heat the bacon grease and add the onion and garlic; stir and simmer for about 5 minutes until tender. Add the can of chicken broth, ham hock, and pepper. Add the kale and mustard greens. Bring the mixture to a boil, stir, cover. Turn the heat

down to a simmer for about an hour until the greens are dark green in color and tender. Remove the hock and drain the excess liquid into a bowl for pot likker. Pick the meat from the hock and add back into the greens. (Yields 8 servings.)

HOT WATER HOE CAKES

Making hot water hoe cakes provided a quick, easy way for the housewife or cook to add a substantial component to a meal. A hot water hoe cake consists of two ingredients: cornmeal and hot water. They're hand-patted into small cakes and fried in hot fat in a cast-iron skillet until they're crispy on the outside and tender like cornbread on the inside. Sometimes known as hot water cornbread, or "corn dodgers," the recipe is similar to the one for jonnycakes but without milk.

Ingredients
2 cups self-rising cornmeal
1 cup boiling water
Vegetable oil for frying

Directions
In a medium bowl pour the boiling water into the cornmeal. Stir until the meal is gradually incorporated and the mixture is completely smooth. Set aside for 15 to 20 minutes until the water is absorbed into the meal. Heat ¼ inch of vegetable oil (it can be flavored with bacon grease) in a 12-inch cast-iron skillet over medium-high heat. While the oil is heating, begin shaping the meal into small cakes. When the oil is hot (about 300°F on a candy thermometer) carefully place the cakes into the oil and press them down slightly with a spatula. Fry until brown on the bottom, then flip them and cook until they are brown on the reverse side.
(Yields 4–6 servings.)

DRIED APPLE STACK CAKE

When Landon Carter Haynes's father, David, gave his son the former Tipton farm, now a two-hundred-acre tract of land (including John Tipton's apple orchard), as a wedding present in 1839, apple stack cake was likely part of the wedding celebration. Since the early 1800s, "stacked" cakes and pies were growing in popularity among Appalachian settlers. And as the community grew, so did the need for baked sweets and treats for various church suppers, weddings, "Dinner on the Grounds" (see "Tidbits"), community singings, and social gatherings.

These edibles were dubbed "stack cake" because the cakes and pies were "stacked" on top of one another for convenience (and for lack of dishware). Stacking was an easy way to carry these delicious gifts to celebrations. Apple stack cake, with its thin pancake-like layers spread with dried applesauce or apple preserves were typically brought to wedding celebrations and presented to the bride and groom from friends and family. And the more friends and family a bride and groom had, the more stacks, or layers on the stack cake. Surely, Landon and Eleanor's cake was stacked to the stars.

Ingredients
Cake
2 cups granulated sugar
1 cup (2 sticks) butter
2 large eggs
1 teaspoon baking soda
3 teaspoons baking powder
6 cups all-purpose flour
2 teaspoons vanilla
½ cup buttermilk

Apple Cider Glaze
1 cup sugar
⅓ to ½ cup apple cider
½ cup (1 stick) butter
1 tablespoon light corn syrup
1 teaspoon vanilla

Directions
For Baking the Cake: Preheat the oven to 400°F. Cream the sugar and butter together. Add the eggs, one at a time, beating well after each. Sift the dry ingredients together and add them to the batter, alternating with the buttermilk and vanilla, until a dough is formed. Roll the dough into a log. Slice

into 6 or 8 uniform pieces. Roll the pieces out on a floured surface using a 9-inch-round cake pan for measurement. Place the dough rounds on lightly greased (quick spritz of cooking oil) cookie sheets or separately in greased cake pans. Bake for about 12 minutes or until the cakes are golden brown. Do not over-bake. Use the dried apple filling recipe in this chapter for the filling.

For Assembling the Cake: Place the first layer on a cake plate and spread with 1 cup of dried applesauce filling (see the recipe below the apple drying tutorial). Repeat with each layer. Do not spread the apple filling on the top layer. Cover the cake lightly with aluminum foil. Let the cake set for 12 hours, allowing the moisture from the apple mixture to soak into the layers. Refrigerate for another 12 to 36 hours before glazing.

For Making the Apple Cider Glaze: Combine the sugar, apple cider, butter, and corn syrup in a small sauce pan over medium- high heat. Bring the mixture to a boil, stirring constantly. Reduce the heat, and simmer for about 4 minutes until the sugar cider mixture thickens. Remove from the heat and stir in the vanilla. Starting at the edge of the cake, pour the hot glaze around the edges of the cake so that it drips down over the layers, tilting the cake plate, if necessary. Pour the remaining glaze over the top of the cake, spreading it with a cake knife. Let it stand overnight.
(Yields 10 servings.)

Tidbits:
"Dinner on the Grounds" is a group of people of all ages gathered together to share food, usually outdoors in conjunction with a church meeting, family gathering, or ceremony. If celebrated in a church setting, Dinner on the Grounds typically takes place after an "all-day singing." Traditional dishes include fried chicken, green beans, potato salad, barbecued pork, pickled ramps, and "leather britches" (dried green beans cooked with hambone, fatback, or bacon). A variety of desserts are enjoyed at the Dinner on the Grounds. Apple stack cake is a traditional offering.

DRIED APPLE STACK PIE

In 1839, when David Haynes purchased the Tipton homestead for his son Landon and Landon's brand-new bride, Eleanor, cooking and baking had come a long way since Martha Tipton stoked, poked, and stirred the embers in the hearth of her 1785 cabin. Southern cookery books were being published across the country and began making their way onto bookshelves and into kitchens. Not the least of these cookbooks came from Martha McCulloch-Williams. A born and bred Tennessean, Ms. McCulloch-Williams was reared on a plantation during the antebellum period (i.e., before the Civil War) and lived there through the war and Reconstruction. After moving to New York in her forties to pursue a successful career in writing, she never forgot her roots. At age sixty-five, she produced from memories of plantation cuisine the delightful cookbook *Dishes and Beverages of the Old South* (1913).

There is, to my knowledge, no record of recipes handed down through either the Haynes family or Eleanor Powell's family. A good pie crust recipe, however, is timeless. Therefore, mine is adapted from Martha McCulloch-Williams's illustrious *Dishes and Beverages of the Old South*. The following is her well-founded "philosophy of pie-crust": "Pie-crust perfection depends on several things—good flour, good fat, good handling, most especially good baking. A good oven, quick, but not scorching, expands the air betwixt the layers of paste, and pops open the flour-grains making them absorb the fat as it melts, thereby growing crisp and 'relishful' instead of hard and tough. Half a pound of shortening and a teaspoon of baking powder to the pound of flour, mixed stiff or soft, according to the consistency of the fat, properly handled and baked makes crust good enough for anybody." This is invaluable information for the serious pie crust maker.

Following the pie crust recipe is a tutorial on drying apples and a recipe for dried apple pie filling, which can be used for the dried apple stack cake (above).

Everyday Pie Crust
Martha McCulloch-Williams considered making pie crust an art form and rightly so. Her "everyday pie crust" directions follow her "philosophy":

> One-pound flour, six ounces shortening—lard or, clarified dripping, pinch salt, half-pint ice water. Mix flour, salt and water to a smooth dough, using a broad knife, roll out thin, spread with a third of the fat, fold in three, roll out again, add another third of fat, roll out again add another

third of fat, roll, add the last fat, roll again, fold and chill for ten minutes before using.

Roll the dough out thinly on a floured board. Use a pie pan as a measure. Roll out the dough and carefully flip over into your pie pan. Trim the edges and crimp using your index finger and thumb, or the handle of a wooden spoon; push the dough out from the inside of the pie pan, then pinch slightly between your thumb and index finger.

A modern recipe using Ms. Martha's timeless method of managing pie crust dough can be found in the following instructions on making dough "circles" for stacks in your pie:

Pie Crust Ingredients
3 cups self-rising flour
2 teaspoons baking soda
1 cup sugar
2 eggs, beaten
½ cup shortening
1 teaspoon vanilla
½ cup buttermilk
½ teaspoon lemon extract or, the zest of one lemon

Pie Crust Directions
Preheat the oven to 375°F. In a medium sized bowl sift together the flour and soda. Add the sugar, beaten eggs, shortening, vanilla, and about ½ cup buttermilk, or enough to make a soft biscuit dough. Knead the dough as you would when making biscuits. Roll out thinly to about an 8-inch circle, using a plate as a template. Trim the dough to fit the round plate. On a cookie sheet, bake the 3 circles (these are your layers) until golden brown. Have about 2 cups of hot, dried apple filling ready. Flavor the filling with the zest of one lemon and spread between each stack (3 layers for each pie).
(Yields an 8-inch 3-layer pie.)

How to Dry Apples
The Haynes family cook and Eleanor Haynes herself likely dried the apples plucked from the orchard. A dried apple mixture spread between the

layers of dried apple stack cake or to fill the perfect pie crust for apple stack pie enhanced a variety of dishes. Drying apples was a way to ensure that there would be plenty for the winter months. Apples were cored, peeled, sliced thinly, and placed in the sun to dry on a wooden plank, a clean sheet on a tin roof, or other flat surfaces. At dusk, the semi-dry apples were gathered and brought inside. This process was repeated the next day.

Before apples can be dried for use in a recipe, however, they had to be *completely* dry in order to be stored in wooden crates in a root cellar to "keep" through the winter without incurring mold or mildew. For use in today's recipes, pack the dried apple slices in gallon-size freezer bags and store in the freezer to be used as needed

Regular store-bought chunky applesauce and even apple butter can be used as filling, but the intensified flavor of dried apples after being revived in water or other liquid (like warm apple cider) produces a deep, savory experience beyond compare. Cinnamon and nutmeg, with a dash of lemon zest, adds depth. Dried apples can also be purchased in packages at the grocery store.

Tidbits:

Regarding quantity:
4 pounds of fresh apples yield 1 pound of dried apples;
1 pound of dried apples equals 4⅓ cups;
4⅓ cups of dried apples yields 8 cups cooked apples.

Dried Apple Filling Ingredients
1 pound dried apple slices (firm,
    tart apples like Newtown Pippins
    or Granny Smith)
Boiling water
1 teaspoon sugar (optional)
¼ teaspoon ground cinnamon, to taste

Tidbits, Too:

As an alternative to adding sugar, you can soak the dried apples in water or orange juice overnight. Drain well and stew over medium-high heat in honey or sorghum before mashing.

Dried Apple Filling Directions
Put the apples in a large, saucepan and cover them with boiling water. Let them soak until tender (about 15 minutes). Add more boiling water, if necessary, to keep the apple slices covered. Drain the apples well and remove from the pan. Using a potato masher, mash the apples into a chunky applesauce consistency (use and immersion blender for a smother consistency) and return the mixture to the pan. Taste the

applesauce and add sugar, if desired. Add the cinnamon. Simmer the applesauce over low heat for about 3 minutes. Remove the thickened applesauce from the heat. The sauce should be just warm for the layers in the apple stack pie and the apple stack cake. (Yields 2 cups.)

SPICED PAWPAW FRUITCAKE

> . . . where oh where, is dear little Nellie?
> Way down yonder in the pawpaw patch . . .
>
> —"The Pawpaw Patch" song

The words and music to "The Pawpaw Patch" song are timeless, and so is the fruit of the pawpaw tree. While the claim that this old folk song was so named for Eleanor "Nellie" Haynes can't be confirmed, there's proof that pawpaw trees provided delicious, nutritious food for the Haynes homestead, as well as for Native Americans, European explorers, and the early settlers of northern Florida, up through East Tennessee and Canada, and west to eastern Nebraska.

A relative of the tropical papaya, pawpaws are said to be the largest edible fruit native to the United States. Sometimes called the "American custard-apple," the beautiful, maroon-colored flowers of the pawpaw appear in the spring and ripen in the fall. Harvest season is from late August to mid-October.

Pawpaws make delicious quick bread, muffins, cake, cookies, and custard pie filling. This recipe for sweet and spicy fruitcake bakes into two loaves and makes about 5½ pounds of fruitcake—a unique offering on the Haynes family's Christmas table, as it can be for yours.

Ingredients
3½ cups all-purpose flour
1 tablespoon baking powder
1 teaspoon salt
½ teaspoon baking soda
2 teaspoons ground cinnamon
2 teaspoons ginger
1 teaspoon nutmeg, freshly ground

1⅓ cup shortening

1½ cups sugar

4 eggs

2 cups pawpaw puree (see "Tidbits" below)

1 cup raisins

1½ cup chopped nuts

3 cups candied fruit

Tidbits:

Pawpaw puree is made by scooping the "custard" out of the center of the pawpaw and, using an immersion blender, pulsing the custard to the consistency of applesauce. Pawpaw's vary in size therefore, the "custard" contents may differ.

Directions

Preheat the oven to 300°F. Grease and flour two 9×5×3½-inch loaf pans. Sift the flour with the baking powder, salt, baking soda, and spices. Cream the shortening and gradually blend in the sugar; beat the mixture until it is light and fluffy. Beat in the eggs, one at a time. Add the flour mixture alternately with pawpaw puree (see "Tidbits" at left). Mix the raisins, nuts, and fruits and stir into the batter. Turn the batter into the greased and floured loaf pans. Bake for about 2 hours. Keep a shallow pan of hot water in the oven underneath the loaf pans throughout the baking time. Store the cooled cakes in a tightly closed container or freeze.

(Yields 2 loaves.)

Chapter 4

SAM HOUSTON SCHOOLHOUSE
STATE HISTORIC SITE

◆————————————————————————————————◆

Built 1794
Maryville, Tennessee

Taproots

While teaching in this one-room schoolhouse
as a boy of 18, I experienced a higher feeling of dignity
and self-satisfaction than from any office or honor
which I have held since.

—Sam Houston circa 1836

Tucked in the foothills of the Great Smoky Mountains lies picturesque Maryville, Tennessee, home of the Sam Houston Schoolhouse. Named for the great statesman and pioneer, this rustic structure is Tennessee's oldest one-room log schoolhouse. Still standing on its original site, the Sam Houston Schoolhouse contains original logs and rests with certain, quaint authority on a shady hillside, providing a perfect place for a picnic.

The schoolhouse was built of hewn poplar in 1794—two years before Tennessee became a state—when North Carolina Revolutionary War veteran Andrew Kennedy and his family settled on a large tract of land along the Little River in what is now Blount County, Tennessee. On Kennedy's property, pioneer and schoolteacher Henry McCulloch constructed a one-room log schoolhouse and became its first teacher, educating his own children, as well as the Kennedy children and those of families in neighboring communities. On one side of the schoolhouse, an

entire log was removed. This would function as a window that could be opened downward on the inside, forming a long shelf that served as desks.

No logical account is given as to why the decision was made to locate the schoolhouse on this somewhat unusual site, more than a half mile from the Little River. Perhaps its proximity to a thirst-quenching spring and its central position in relation to the Kennedy and McCulloch homes were factors in selecting the site. The same spring that daily pumped one

Sam Houston Schoolhouse
State Historic Site in charming
Maryville, Tennessee.

hundred gallons of cool, clean water for the Kennedys, McCullochs, and, eventually, Sam Houston's pupils is alive and bubbling today. When the original community's children were grown and gone, the schoolhouse presumably sat empty until the arrival of the colorful young man of character whose name is now inseparably linked with the one-room log schoolhouse.

Tennessee has spawned its share of American notables, including three presidents of the United States. Among these well-known figures in

School was in session when young Sam Houston
signaled his students to come to class in the rustic
log schoolhouse now bearing his name.

Tennessee history is the controversial Sam Houston. Born in Rockbridge,
Virginia, on March 2, 1793, Samuel Houston was the son of Major Samuel
Houston and Elizabeth Paxton. He was the fifth son of nine children.

Sam's father was a farmer and brigade Inspector, handsome and of
military bearing. When Sam was a young boy, his father taught him to
read, not using a primer but instead the Revolutionary War manual of
arms. When Major Samuel Houston died suddenly in 1807, away from
home, Elizabeth left their homestead on Timber Ridge, Virginia. Accompanied by her husband's brother, she joined members of the Houston
family in Blount County and the small town of Maryville. Known as a
woman of extraordinary accomplishment, Elizabeth reared her children
with manners and good judgment. She is also recognized for helping
establish Presbyterianism in the region.

In 1808, Elizabeth and her five children, with the help of her brother-
in-law, settled on land in Maryville. The land was given to her by the
United States government as a federal land grant for her husband's service
as a Revolutionary War patriot. Sam was fifteen when his older brothers
put him to work as a clerk in a store they had established, but six-foot-
four, handsome Sam—ever the adventurer and dreamer—didn't care for
sweeping floors and weighing potatoes. He soon ran away to live with
the Cherokees at Hiawassee Island on the Hiawassee River. Here, he was

Inside the one-room schoolhouse, Sam Houston taught his students
the three Rs: reading, writing and 'rithmetic.

given the name Ka-lanu—"The Raven"—by the chief of the Cherokee
tribe, Oo-loo-te-ka (which means "John Jolly" in Cherokee). There he
stayed for three years, becoming fluent in their language and learning to
appreciate their culture. As a way of acknowledging Cherokee hospitality,
Sam made occasional trips to Maryville, where he purchased—on credit—
gunpowder, shot, and "little articles of taste and utility" for his Native
American friends and sweethearts. At the end of his three-year stay, he
had incurred a one-hundred-dollar debt to his mother at the family store.

Seeds of honor planted by Elizabeth Houston in Sam's heart as a
boy—dormant though they seemed—began to sprout. After he returned to
Maryville, Sam, in an effort to pay back his debt, took over the one-room
schoolhouse. This amused the townspeople, who spoke in jest about Sam's
degree from "Indian University." True, Sam had not taken advantage of
all the educational opportunities afforded him by his father, but he read
every book he could get his hands on and had memorized all twenty-
four books of Homer's *The Iliad*. Undeterred by ridicule, Sam opened

his school in May 1812, declaring that he would charge eight dollars per student per term for tutelage in the rustic log schoolhouse—a hefty sum in those days. Sam announced that one-third of the eight-dollar tuition could be paid in cash, one-third in corn at thirty-three and a third cents a bushel, and one-third in calico "of variegated colors," from which he was to have shirts made.

Sam's school was a success, with students ranging from six to sixty years of age. His school year began after corn planting in the spring and lasted until harvest and cold weather in the fall. Those split log benches were lined with students, and Sam was forced to turn away applicants.

Years later, an old army comrade reminded Houston of his many accomplishments as they swapped war stories in Texas while crossing Galveston Bay. He had been governor of two states—Tennessee and Texas, a lawyer, a United States congressman, a United States senator, commander-in-chief of an army, president of a republic, and was responsible for annexing said republic, now the state of Texas (where the nation's fourth largest city—Houston—is named for Sam). When the army comrade asked Sam which office had afforded him the greatest pride, Houston replied, "When I was a young man in Tennessee, I kept a country school, being then about eighteen years of age and a strapping fellow." The rest of his memorable quote opens the "Timeless Recipes" section to follow.

The Sam Houston Schoolhouse and the land on which it stands were purchased in the 1940s by the State of Tennessee from Charles Kennedy, a great-great-grandson of Andrew Kennedy. As the story goes, Texas wanted to purchase the log schoolhouse from Tennessee as a monument to their military hero. In the 1950s, Tennessee decided to keep the log house and restore it—maintaining its early rustic grandeur.

Sam Houston died in Huntsville, Texas, on July 26, 1863. The Sam Houston Schoolhouse is part of his Tennessee legacy, and 2019 marks the 207rd year anniversary of the Sam Houston Schoolhouse.

Address and Contact Information
Historic Sam Houston Schoolhouse
3650 Old Sam Houston School Road
Maryville, TN 37804
(865) 983-1550
www.samhoustonhistoricschoolhouse.org

Timeless Recipes

At noon, after the luncheon, which I and my pupils ate
together out of our baskets, I would go into the woods
and cut me a "sour wood" stick, trim it carefully in
circular spirals and thrust one half of it into the fire,
which would turn it blue, leaving the other half white.

—Sam Houston, 1812

Even when Sam Houston was a strapping young man of eighteen years,
his mother, Elizabeth, who started the small family-owned grocery store
in Maryville, Tennessee, likely still fixed his lunch—a basket of simple
provisions to help fortify Sam while he taught his students the rudiments
of reading, writing, and arithmetic.

Tennessee cuisine tells the story of time and place. In the early 1800s,
on the Tennessee Appalachian frontier, Elizabeth Houston would have
packed Sam's lunch basket with perishable items such as fried pies (meat
or sweet), bread of some sort, perhaps the traditional Scotch egg, and a
berry cobbler.

Why not pack a picnic basket, gather your family, friends, and a
blanket and head to the grounds around the Sam Houston Schoolhouse?
Children enjoy *this* schoolhouse so much they don't even realize they're
learning.

MENU
Sea Biscuits
Scotch Egg
Ramp Salad
Potato Hash
Fried Meat Pie
Wild Blackberry Cobbler
Sourwood Honey Shortbread after Wild Blackberry Cobbler

SEA BISCUITS (HARDTACK)
What is known in Tennessee and throughout the Old South as "hardtack"
has its origin in our English heritage and is derived from their recipe for

"sea biscuits." Sea biscuits were generally baked as a sea ration for sailors because pearl ash (pot ash, or potassium carbonate, the forerunner of nineteenth-century baking powder) refined from wood ash, was needed for leavening. The word "biscuit" means "twice cooked"; the Old French word *bescuit* is derived from the Latin words "bis" (twice) and "coquere" or "coctus" (to cook, cooked), hence, "twice-cooked." A "sea biscuit" was practically indestructible, being twice-cooked, and when dunked in a liquid of some sort, would soften to an edible mush. Elizabeth Houston may have tucked one or two of these biscuits in her son's lunch basket.

(An interesting bit of trivia notes: the American champion racehorse, Seabiscuit, was sired by Hard Tack and both were named for this common cracker.)

Ingredients
2 cups whole wheat flour
1 cup all-purpose flour
1 cup plus 2 tablespoons water

Directions
Preheat the oven to 350°F. Combine the flour and water; add an additional tablespoon of water if the dough is too stiff to mix by hand. This dough will be denser than bread dough so be cautious about using modern mixers. They may not fare well under the strain of this stiff dough. The initial water added to the flour will make the dough easier to handle. Knead the dough until smooth. This will take a few minutes. The amount of kneading is less than when you're developing gluten in yeasted bread dough. And the time and effort will be worth it. The dough will become more pliable and easier to knead once the flour has absorbed the water. Divide the dough into 5 pieces. Hand-roll each piece into a round dinner roll until it is a smooth mass. Press the dough down with the palm of your hand until it's about ½ inch thick. If the dough cracks or splits, more kneading is necessary. Make evaporation holes using a toothpick or single skewer. The holes need not go all the way through the dough and should be about ¾ inch apart and cover the entire surface of the biscuit. Place the biscuits on a cookie tray and bake for 1 hour. During the baking process, open the oven door once or twice briefly to allow the water

to evaporate. After an hour, remove the biscuits from the oven and place them on a wire baking rack to cool and dehydrate. Store them in a cool oven or a cool, dry place, and they will last indefinitely. (Yields 12 hardtack or "sea biscuits.")

SCOTCH EGG (BAKED)

Ingredients
1 pound ground pork sausage (ground turkey or ground chicken sausage)
6 hard-boiled eggs, shells removed
7 tablespoons fine dried breadcrumbs
1 egg, beaten
Small bowl of flour

Directions
Preheat the oven to 350°F. Divide the sausage into 6 equal portions. On a lightly breadcrumb-sprinkled surface, pat out each portion to about ⅛-inch thickness. Flour your hands, then lightly dust each hard-boiled egg with flour. Wrap a portion of the sausage around each egg, pressing the edges together to seal. Dip the sausage-coated eggs into the beaten egg, then roll in the breadcrumbs. Pat the breadcrumbs firmly into the sausage. Place the eggs on a baking sheet and bake for about 25 minutes or until golden brown. Let the prepared eggs cool slightly before serving. (Yields 6 servings.)

SCOTCH EGG (FRIED)

Follow the instructions for preparing the Scotch egg (baked). Then, heat 2 cups vegetable oil in a heavy, cast-iron Dutch oven until a breadcrumb sizzles and turns brown when dropped in; the heated oil should be about 300°F. Using a slotted spoon, or modern-day skimmer, carefully place each Scotch egg into the hot oil and deep fry for about 8 to 10 minutes, turning when necessary until the outside is golden brown and the sausage meat is cooked through. Carefully remove the eggs with a skimmer and drain on a paper towel. To ensure the eggs are thoroughly cooked, place in a preheated 350°F oven for about 10 to 15 minutes.

Tidbits:
Serve with a slice of smoked cheddar cheese, pickle, and cold beverage of your choice.

RAMP SALAD

The hills are alive . . . with the smell of wild onions—for the first few weeks in April, that is. And that's a *good* thing. Ramps, or wild leeks, as they're sometimes called, are a welcome sight in the foothills of the Smoky Mountains, signaling the end of a cold, hard winter. Ramps *(Allium tricoccum)* have been growing in and around Maryville, Tennessee, for generations.

Sometimes called "Tennessee truffles" (also, "rampion," the tempting wild onion described in the Grimm brothers' fairytale "Rapunzel"), ramps thrive throughout the cool, musty regions of Appalachia.

A member of the garlic family, ramps have two or three slender, green leaves with a small white bulb attached to a purplish stem. Ramps are high in vitamins C and A and, like their cousin garlic, contain healing properties and are chockfull of minerals.

Sam had to keep his distance from his students, as ramps are known for their strong garlicy taste, hence, odor—unless, of course, his students had ramps in their own lunch baskets. As the legend goes, mountain schoolhouses were known to shut down occasionally during ramp season!

Ramps are typically picked, then washed, rinsed well, and boiled.

Ingredients
1 bunch leaf or, head lettuce
Bulbs and leaves of 1 dozen freshly harvested ramps (wild leeks)
1 cup wild violets, blossoms and leaves
2 cup whole watercress, trimmed and stems removed

Directions
Wash and rinse the ramps well, thoroughly removing any dirt from the leaves and bulbs. Pat dry. Chop the long stems from the water cress. Wash the lettuce and water cress. Carefully rinse the wild violets. Tear the lettuce and water cress into bite-sized pieces. Slice the ramp bulbs thinly. Tear the ramp leaves and toss with whole violets and watercress and lettuce. Serve with a creamy salad dressing or vinaigrette. (Yields 4–6 servings.)

Tidbits:
Ramp salad (without the vinaigrette) tossed in a skillet of fried potato hash, is a tasty side dish.

FRIED POTATO HASH

Potatoes could be stored in the root cellar for months, washed, scrubbed, and then baked, with the skin on, in the coals in the hearth of the Houston home. Dutch oven–style roasted potatoes were washed, scrubbed, sprinkled with salt, cut into quarters, and tossed in the Dutch oven with strips of fatback, or bacon. The "oven" was nestled into the embers. When the lid was closed, embers were placed on top. Periodically, the lid was lifted and the "taters" were stabbed with a long fork called a "skimmer" to check for tenderness. They were served when tender and brown.

Fried as potato cakes, boiled and mashed, or diced to be dished up as hash, the significant spud surely subdued the lunchtime hunger pangs of a young Sam Houston, as they will yours.

Ingredients
3 large baking potatoes (like russets, about 3 pounds)
1 tablespoon vegetable oil (olive oil or bacon grease)
1 tablespoon unsalted butter
1 medium yellow onion (or large, if you prefer)
2 cloves garlic, minced
¼ teaspoon seasoned salt (Lawry's)
¼ teaspoon fresh thyme, chopped
Freshly ground, coarse black pepper to taste

Directions
Place the whole potatoes (skin on) into a Dutch oven, cover with water, and bring to a boil. Lower the heat and simmer until half-cooked and almost tender. Do not overcook. Drain and let sit until the potatoes are cool enough to handle. Slip the skins from the potatoes and cut into a ½-inch dice. Heat the oil and butter in a 12-inch, cast-iron skillet over high heat. Add the onions and cook, stirring for about 2 minutes. Turn the heat down to medium-high. Add the garlic and cook, stirring, for about 20 seconds. Add the diced potato, seasoned salt, thyme leaves, and pepper, shaking the pan occasionally to keep from burning the potatoes. The potatoes

Tidbits:
Cook freshly diced red and green peppers with the onions for an extra bite of hash tang.

will begin to brown and crisp on their underside. Turn the potatoes with a spatula and continue cooking until they are uniformly golden brown. Remove from the pan and serve hot.

(Yields 4–6 servings.)

FRIED MEAT PIE

Most American foods come from across the sea, and the fried pie is no exception. Originally called a "pastie" (pronounced, pass-tee) the meat pie originated in Cornwall, England in thirteenth-century aristocracy. Eventually, the Cornish "pastie" became popular with working people in Cornwall, especially with the tin miners, who found they could take their lunch down into the mine, eat whatever was on the inside of the pastry and—for fear of getting arsenic from their hands onto their food—throw the pastry on the floor of the mine.

Pasties are known by their half-moon shape with a crust (pastry) crimped on the edges and baked. In the Houston home, fried meat pies were made with whatever was left over from yesterday's dinner, stuffed in pastry and fried. But you can make them by design. Imagine a meat pie of ground beef or choice steak (or venison or lamb), onions, and herbs and spices, all wrapped in a flaky dough-pocket and fried until golden brown.

To make pasties, roll out the dough in a circle, place the meat concoction in the center of the circle of dough, turn the dough over the concoction to make a semi-circle, and seal the filling securely by crimping the edges of the dough with the tines of a fork or your fingertips.

Ingredients
Pastry for a double-crust pie or two premade store-bought pie crusts
1 pound ground beef (ground round, ground sirloin)
2 hard-boiled eggs, chopped
1 medium onion, diced
1 tablespoon salt pork or bacon drippings
10 ounces beef broth
¼ teaspoon fresh thyme leaves, diced
2 teaspoons fresh parsley, chopped
4 cloves garlic, sliced thinly, or minced with a garlic press
¾ teaspoon salt

Pinch of pepper

2 tablespoons flour

2 tablespoons dry red wine, or beef broth, if preferred

2 cups vegetable oil, for frying

Directions

Prepare the pastry in advance and refrigerate, or chill premade pie crust dough. Allow the dough to become room temperature (about 20 minutes) before rolling it out. In a 12-inch cast-iron skillet, fry the onion and garlic in the salt pork or bacon drippings until just cooked. Add the ground beef until it's lightly browned. Add herbs, salt, pepper, and wine. Let the mixture simmer for 1 minute, allowing the ingredients to "marry." Sprinkle flour into the mixture. Add the broth and simmer for 10 minutes. Add the chopped eggs, mix them in, and remove the pan from the heat. Allow the mixture to cool. Roll the pie pastry out to about ¼-inch thickness. Cut out circles using a tea cup saucer, or a metal biscuit cutter (5-inch diameter). Put 3 tablespoons of the meat mixture onto one side of the circle. Moisten the edges of the dough with water and fold the pastry over the other half of the meat. Crimp the edges (seal tightly) with your fingertips or the tines of a fork. In a Dutch oven or 12-inch skillet, heat the shortening or canola oil to 360°F. Fry until golden brown—about 3 minutes per side. Drain on a wire rack. (Yields 6 to 8 servings.)

> **Tidbits:**
> After frying and draining each pie, place it on a wire rack in a rimmed baking sheet in a warm oven. As you fry the remaining pies, this will keep the cooked ones warm before serving.

> **Tidbits, Too:**
> This dough recipe can also be used for making fried fruit pies.

WILD BLACKBERRY COBBLER

Cobbler has been around since early American colonial women were unable to find suitable suet and equipment to make their traditional puddings. Instead, the women stewed fruit and covered it with a layer of uncooked biscuit or pastry dough and baked it, either in a Dutch oven with coals on the lid, or as a deep-dish pie with a crust on the bottom and the top. Typically, today's cobbler is a one-crust dessert.

The multi-drupelet blackberry (a drupelet is one of many small bumps that make up the fruit) grows wild along the trails of Tennessee. Sam Houston likely went blackberry picking with strict instructions from his mother: watch out for snakes and watch out for chiggers! While watching out for those chiggers and snakes, Sam picked blackberries for cobbler, pie, fried pie, jam cake, sauces, jelly, and for snacking (enjoying the fruits of his labor, so to speak). Elizabeth Houston likely used a one-crust pastry for cobbler.

Surely Elizabeth Houston would have employed this newer, simpler cobbler recipe had it been available. But baking powder was not invented until 1845. Mrs. Houston likely added pearl ash to her flour as a "raising agent."

Whether baked in a single, or double crust, or as prepared in this recipe, with no "crust," timeless, wild blackberry cobbler is a many "drupelet" thing.

Ingredients
1 stick (8 tablespoons) of butter
1 cup flour
1 cup sugar
2 teaspoons baking powder
½ teaspoon salt
¾ cup whole milk
2 cups fresh blackberries

Directions
Preheat the oven to 350°F. Melt butter in an 8×8-inch baking dish. In a separate bowl, stir ½ cup sugar into the fruit. Set aside. In a medium-sized bowl, sift together the flour, sugar, baking powder, and salt. Make a well in the middle of the flour mixture and pour in the milk. Stir until just combined. Pour the batter into the baking dish of melted butter, but do not mix. Pour the fruit-sugar mixture over the batter, but do not mix. Bake for 35 minutes until the "crust" rises over the fruit mixture and turns golden brown. Serve warm with a dollop of whipped cream or your favorite ice cream.
(Yields 6 servings.)

SOURWOOD HONEY SHORTBREAD

The sourwood stick Sam Houston cut and used as "an emblem of ornament and authority over [his] pupils" in the little log schoolhouse came from a Sourwood Tree (also known as Lilly of the Valley). Sourwood honey, grown mostly in the Appalachian Mountain region, has a unique tanginess unlike that of sweet honey.

Adding sourwood honey to a shortbread recipe would most certainly have pleased Sam Houston.

Ingredients
1 cup butter (two sticks)
2½ cups all-purpose flour
⅓ cup sourwood honey
¾ cup pecans, finely chopped
1 teaspoon vanilla

Directions
Preheat the oven to 300°F. Beat the butter, honey, and vanilla in a large bowl with an electric mixer until light and fluffy. Add flour, 1 cup at a time, beating well after each addition. If the dough becomes too stiff to stir, knead in the remaining flour by hand. Work in the nuts. Pat the dough into a shortbread mold or ungreased 10-inch cast-iron skillet. Score the surface with a knife so that it can be divided into 10 wedges; prick the dough deeply with fork. Bake for 35 to 40 minutes. Cool the shortbread in the pan on a wire rack for 10 minutes. Remove it from the pan. Cut into wedges while warm. Drizzle with sourwood honey, if you like. (Yields 10 servings.)

A Tribute to Sam Houston's Scottish Culinary Heritage

Many of Tennessee's early settlers immigrated to the newly established colonies from Scotland. Sam Houston's lineage can be traced back to his great-great-grandfather Sir John Houston. Sir John built a family estate in Johnstone, Scotland, in the late seventeenth century. His second son, John Houston, immigrated to Ulster, Ireland, during the English plantation era, which lasted from the early eighteenth century until the start of the American Civil War in 1861; hence, the term "Scots-Irish." After several years in Ireland, John Houston immigrated to the American colonies with his family and settled in Pennsylvania in 1735. As the area began to fill with Lutheran German immigrants, Houston decided to move his family along with other Scotch-Irish immigrants who were migrating to the Shenandoah Valley of Virginia.

Surely the beauty of Tennessee's rolling hills and pasturelands reminded these Scots of home. Scottish immigrants in Tennessee farmed oats, barley, corn, carrots, and potatoes, which provided a basis for their agricultural community.

To celebrate Sam Houston's Scottish lineage, I feature food and drink from Johnstone, Scotland, with recipes passed down through generations.

MENU
Blackberry Sweet Tea
Scotch Barley Soup
Scotch Summer Salad

BLACKBERRY SWEET TEA
Blackberries are one of the best fruits for jam, jelly, juice, pie, cobbler, tea, and wine known to man. Blackberries grow in wild patches along the trails of Tennessee as well as among the bramble bushes of Scotland.

Tidbits:
"Muddling" occurs when the back of a spoon or a baseball-shaped object (often made of marble or wood) is used to release the flavor of an ingredient, such as mint or other herbs, spices, and fruit.

Ingredients
3 cups fresh or frozen (thawed) blackberries
1¼ cups sugar
1 tablespoon chopped (or muddled) fresh mint
Pinch of baking soda (to soften any bitter taste)
4 cups boiling water
2 family-size regular tea bags
2½ cups cold water

Directions
Combine the blackberries and sugar in a large container. Crush the blackberries well with a wooden spoon. Muddle the mint and add it and the baking soda (a pinch) to the blackberry

mixture. Set aside. Place the tea bags in a large pitcher. Pour 4 cups of boiling water over the tea bags; cover and let stand for 3 minutes. Drain and discard the tea bags. Pour the tea over the blackberry mixture; let it stand at room temperature for 1 hour. Pour the tea mixture through a wire-mesh strainer into a large pitcher, discarding the solids. Add sugar. Add 2½ cups of cold water, stirring until the sugar dissolves. Cover and chill. Garnish with fresh mint leaves or lemon slices—or both, if desired. (Yields 6–8 servings.)

SCOTCH BARLEY SOUP
The taste of grass-fed lamb or beef, barley, carrots, turnips, leeks, and peas simmered in its own hearty broth is a favorite in Scotland and along the trails of Tennessee.

Ingredients
2 to 3 pounds lamb (or beef) shanks with bones (remove most of the fat)
3 quarts beef stock
1 cup pearl barley
1½ cups carrots (1 large carrot cut into ½-inch pieces
2 cups turnips (one white or yellow turnip cut into ½-inch pieces)
2 cups leeks (1 leek, cleaned and rinsed *very* well, and cut, green leaves
    included, into 1-inch pieces), or use a store-bought frozen brand
1½ cups celery (2 ribs celery cut into 1-inch pieces)
1½ cups white onion (1 large onion peeled and sliced)
2 cups fresh or frozen peas
2 teaspoons salt
½ teaspoon freshly ground black pepper
Worcestershire sauce for garnish (optional)

Directions
Place the shanks and water in a large saucepan or stockpot and bring to a boil over high heat. Using a tight wire-mesh kitchen strainer (sieve), skim off and discard any residue that rises to the surface of the water and continue to do so for the next 5 minutes. Reduce the heat to low, cover, and simmer for 1 hour. Skim again and discard any surface fat and scum. Add the barley and bring to a boil. Cover and cook over low heat for 45

minutes. Using tongs or a slotted spoon, remove the shanks from the pot and set them aside to cool. Add the remaining ingredients to the pot and bring the mixture to a boil. Cover and turn heat down to medium low and simmer the mixture for 30 minutes. When the reserved shanks are cool enough to handle, pick any meat from them and stir it into the pot, allowing the flavor of the meat to mingle with the soup mixture for 10 minutes. Serve the hot soup in large bowls, sprinkling each serving with a shake or two of Worcestershire sauce if desired.
(Yields 10 servings.)

SCOTCH SUMMER SALAD
Cabbage, leeks, tomatoes, and fruit are the basic ingredients in simple salads specific to Scotland and Tennessee.

Ingredients
1 cup shredded white cabbage
2 stalks celery, chopped
2 large carrots, grated
1 bunch green onions (scallions), cleaned and chopped with roots removed
2 whites of leeks, cleaned (*very* well) and chopped
3 medium beefsteak tomatoes, chopped
1 medium apple, peeled, cored, and diced
4 tablespoons olive oil
1 tablespoon freshly chopped basil
Salt and freshly cracked pepper

Directions
Toss all the ingredients with the olive oil in a large salad bowl; season with salt and pepper. Chill for one hour.
(Yields 6 servings.)

Chapter 5

THE CHESTER INN STATE HISTORIC SITE

Built 1797
Jonesborough, Tennessee

Taproots

To all people who have claims to lots in the Town
of Jonesborough are requested to come forth
with their claims, if any, on the first day of
March next, at the house of James Reed, when the
commission will set to adjust said claims . . .

—William Chester,
secretary pro tem of the municipality of Jonesborough

Jonesborough, Tennessee's oldest town, has stories to tell. Tales of conflict with indigenous peoples. Sagas of hard times suffered by settlers struggling to find a market for their surplus goods. In its early days, the well-worn bricks of Main Street—once a Native American trail—spoke to its burgeoning population, and the roar of an approaching steam-engine locomotive announced that a tiny rural community was developing into a major trading center.

The story of North Carolina statesman Willie (pronounced "Wylie") Jones pushing for expansion beyond the Appalachian Mountain range is noteworthy. Jonesborough, his time-honored namesake, was established in 1779. Jonesborough evolved into Washington County (the first county

named after George Washington) while Tennessee was still part of North Carolina.

But as Jonesborough tells its story, the Chester Inn State Historic Site and Museum sets the stage. It showcases the oldest commercial wooden-frame building in a town known for its treasured antiquities and architecture.

Dr. William P. Chester was more than a frontier physician when he moved from his home in York County, Pennsylvania, to Jonesborough in 1794. Having trained extensively in Lancaster, Pennsylvania, Dr. Chester was more inclined to reach for a new herbal potion than a scalpel, and whenever possible, he avoided the traditional prescriptions of bleeding,

The Chester Inn today.

sweating, and purging. Patients flocked to the doctor's office, including one of Tennessee's most distinguished founding fathers, statesman and first governor, John Sevier, whose diary entries indicate that he regularly employed the services of Dr. Chester.

Dr. Chester was a visionary and entrepreneur. Recognizing a shortage of food and lodging for travelers on the Great Stagecoach Road, he designed the Chester Inn to meet a need in his embryonic community while supplementing his income.

In those early days, town lots were purchased on paper by number. Dr. William P. Chester purchased Lot Number 26, on May 15, 1797, for the sum of seventy-four dollars. On this piece of prime real estate, Dr.

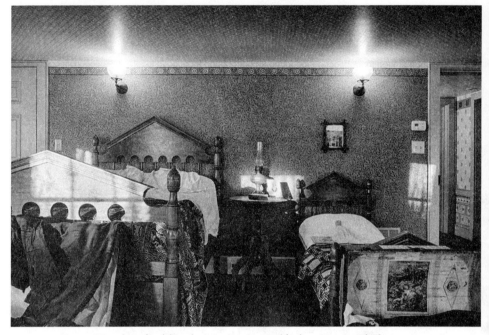

Handcrafted by their great-grandfather James Phelps,
this "three-quarter bed," daybed, candle-stand, and trunk was
donated by Pat McLean and her brother James "Mickey" Scott
in honor of their late brother John Morgan Scott III as an addition
to the upstairs lodging room.

Chester built the town's first stagecoach hotel, the Chester Inn—a three-story, wooden-frame building at 116 Main Street. Here, a traveler was provided a bed for the night, a stable with provisions for his horse, and a decent breakfast and dinner.

Built in the Federal style—an American revival of Roman architecture especially associated with Thomas Jefferson and Benjamin Latrobe—the Chester Inn is the largest structure in Jonesborough and served for more than 175 years as an inn, hotel, and apartment house. Ivan Allen, great-grandson of William P. Chester Jr., described the inn as follows:

> On the North side of Main Street, just west of the public square, he [Dr. William P. Chester] erected what was then the largest building in town

Guests at the Chester Inn could while away the hours
in a lodging room with a view of Main Street.

and one of the largest in the western country. There was a lower story of
brick at the street level, occupied as shops, with two frame stories above.
The entire eastern end of the second floor was the public room around
whose great open fireplace guests and townspeople could mingle. The
remainder of the frame portion was divided into guest rooms. Two halls
ran across the building—from front to back—with a stairway in each
leading to the upper story. On the front were two small roofless porches
projecting over the sidewalk, connected by a narrow catwalk and reached
at either end by a flight of steps from the street level. Upon these porches
the lower halls opened.

Chester Inn became known as "the finest inn on the Western Frontier,"
hosting notable guests, including three United States presidents—Andrew
Jackson, James K. Polk, and Andrew Johnson. Other people important
to Tennessee's early history also stayed at the Chester Inn. Said to have
been among these dignitaries are John Caldwell Calhoun, seventh U.S.
vice president under President Andrew Jackson; Judge David Campbell,

prominent politician; Hugh Lawson White, former governor of Mississippi; and George Bancroft, politician, writer, and secretary of the navy under the eleventh U.S. president, James Knox Polk. The celebrated botanist Andre Michaux, who enthusiastically encouraged the cultivation of cotton as a source of wealth, traveled through Jonesborough and was, perhaps, a guest at the inn.

In early days, the Chester Inn offered beds that lined the walls of two large rooms on the third floor of the east side of the building. A weary traveler could rent a single bed for the night or, for a lesser price, share a double bed with a fellow traveler.

Dr. Chester operated his apothecary shop from the basement level of the inn through the early 1800s. The basement was at street level, facing the pedestrian walkway along Main Street. This frontage of windows and doors has a long history of shops, including barbers, milliners, cobblers, and confectioners, to name a few.

The Chester Inn offered featherbeds—considered a luxury at the time—and fireplaces in every room provided extra warmth and comfort. Andrew Jackson spent many a night at the establishment.

Jackson was a guest at the inn when he was threatened by mob violence. In later years, as president (1829–37), he hosted a large reception at the inn before the Victorian front porch—whose predominant feature was the ornamental "gingerbread work" around the cornices and over the windows—was added. George M. Sprinkle, master craftsman and artisan, produced much of this type of ornamentation at the inn and around Jonesborough, leaving his genius to posterity.

Dr. Chester eventually left Jonesborough, moved west, and opened a string of Chester Inns. His grandson Ivan and several other relatives stayed in town and are buried in the Old Jonesborough Cemetery.

Through the past two centuries, the building has had a number of names, including the Bell Tavern (ca. 1820–60), the Union Hotel (ca. 1860–80), the Planters' House Hotel (ca. 1880–1900), and the Jonesboro Inn (ca. 1900s).

During and after the Civil War, the Chester Inn was known as the Union Hotel (obviously reflecting the new proprietor's sentiments). On September 15, 1880, the building was sold and became the Planter's House Hotel. Approximately ten years later, the inn was sold and reconfigured as apartments.

In 1945, three prominent Jonesborough businessmen, including the city's current mayor J. T. Whitlock, purchased what was now the Jonesboro Inn. They saved it from demolition and the construction of a service station on the site. In the 1950s, the Bennett family changed the inn back into apartments, each with its own efficiency kitchen.

Finally, in 1987, Bennett sold the Chester Inn to the Tennessee State Historical Commission. It was restored in the 1990s to its 1880–90s façade and redesigned to be more like a working office, with the exception of the parlor and dining rooms.

Like Jonesborough, the Chester Inn has a long and storied history. Today, Jonesborough is the "Storytelling Capital of the World" and home to the National Storytelling Festival. The Chester Inn Museum, housed in the Chester Inn, is owned by the State of Tennessee and operated by the Heritage Alliance of Northeast Tennessee and Southwest Virginia.

Address and Contact Information
The Chester Inn
116 West Main
Jonesborough, TN 37659
(423) 753 4580
www.heritageall.org

Timeless Recipes

A two-story brick and frame addition, used as a
kitchen and dining room with guest rooms above,
stood at the rear.

—Ivan Allen, great-grandson of William Chester Jr.

Although menus from the Chester Inn have not come to light, Paul M. Fink's book *Jonesborough: The First Century of Tennessee's First Town, 1776–1876* offers—through period photographs, including images of lading receipts and other items that show the prices of local and imported produce, livestock, crops, and dairy products—a glimpse into foods the Chester Inn would likely have served, particularly on special occasions, such as hosting Andrew Jackson and other dignitaries as dinner guests.

The midday meal and largest meal of the day would be dished up from farm to table. Supper was a light offering such as soup and cornbread.

The kitchen remained a kitchen until the inn was converted into private efficiency apartments in the 1950s. The State of Tennessee restored the structure in the 1990s and converted the former kitchen area into office space.

CHESTER INN BREAKFAST MENU (1799)
Candied Bacon
Stack of Pumpkin Flapjacks (5) with Butter and Maple Syrup
Stewed Apples
Moravian Sugar Cake (Coffee Cake)
Coffee

CANDIED BACON
Pork was a mainstay on the east Tennessee frontier. In the life of young Andrew Jackson, however, "Bacon" had a double meaning.

Having just turned twenty-one and studying in Jonesborough for his law exam, Andrew Jackson was staying about two miles out of town at Mayor Christopher Taylor's home (a two-story log residence built in 1778 and now located next to the Chester Inn State Historic Site and Museum). As one version of the story goes, in an early court case, Jackson was opposed by Waightstill Avery, a Princeton-educated, seasoned attorney with an impressive law practice. Inexperienced in jurisprudence, Jackson continually referred to his favorite authority—Matthew Bacon's *A New Abridgement of the Law*—ending each argument with "Bacon says . . ." During the course of the trial, Avery not only ridiculed Jackson's constant reference to Bacon but his seeming lack of legal knowledge. Jackson's temper flared. Friends tried to intercede. Still, Avery's antagonism continued the next day in court. Jackson is said to have written a note to Avery, challenging him to a duel.

The custom of the day mandated that such a challenge be carried out. Jackson and Avery met at sunset on a hill in the outskirts of Jonesborough. Tempers had cooled but *code duello*—a set of rules for one-on-one combat—had to be enforced. Both gentlemen fired their pistols in the air.

Afterwards, Avery, carrying a small package, handed it to Jackson as they faced each other in the field and reportedly said, "Had I mortally wounded you, I know of nothing that would have so cheered your last moments as your beloved bacon." After unwrapping the package, Jackson discovered, not the law book, as he might have expected, but a piece of well-cured bacon. Fisticuffs might have ensued had not cooler heads prevailed.

Ingredients
1 pound thick-cut bacon (12 to 14 slices)
½ cup brown sugar
⅓ cup maple syrup

Directions
Preheat the oven to 400°F. Place the strips of bacon on a wire rack and onto a foil-lined baking pan. In a small bowl, combine the brown sugar and maple syrup. Mix well. With a small pastry brush, paint the top of the bacon strips with the brown sugar/maple syrup mixture. Bake in the preheated oven for 15 minutes. Remove the bacon from the oven. Turn the bacon over and paint the other side with brown sugar/maple syrup. Bake for another 15 minutes, or until the bacon reaches the desired level of crispness. (Yields 14–18 slices.)

Tidbits:
A teaspoon of ground cinnamon or a grind or two of black pepper adds another dimension of goodness to this treat. A sprinkle of cayenne pepper adds heat.

PUMPKIN SPICE FLAPJACKS

Dr. Chester was becoming a prominent landowner in Jonesborough. In 1799, the crop of potatoes, turnips, and pumpkins promised a bountiful fall harvest in Washington County. Surely the Chester Inn cook could transform a creamy pumpkin-spiced batter into a tasty stack o' jacks—one of Andrew Jackson's favorite foods.

Ingredients
1½ cups milk, plus 2 tablespoons
1 cup pumpkin puree

Tidbits:
Flap jacks, on the Tennessee frontier, were made with pearl ash—first mentioned by Amelia Simmons in her 1796 cookery book, American Cookery. Pearl ash was used in frontier foods as a leavening agent made from wood ashes. Baking powder, a combination of baking soda and cream of tartar, was discovered by a British chemist, Alfred Bird, in 1843. Baking soda, imported from England during the Colonial era, was first manufactured domestically in a New York factory around 1840.

1 egg
2 tablespoons vegetable oil
2 cups all-purpose flour
3 tablespoon brown sugar
2 teaspoons baking powder
1 teaspoon baking soda
1 teaspoon ground allspice
1 teaspoon ground cinnamon
½ teaspoon ground ginger
⅛ teaspoon ground cloves (a pinch)
½ teaspoon salt

Directions

In a large mixing bowl, combine the milk, pumpkin puree, eggs, and oil. In a separate bowl, whisk the flour, brown sugar, baking powder, baking soda, allspice, cinnamon, ginger, and salt. Stir the dry ingredients into the pumpkin mixture until just combined. Over medium heat on a lightly oiled griddle or fry pan, pour ¼ cup of batter for each flapjack. When the batter begins to bubble, flip the 'jack. Brown on both sides. Serve hot off the griddle. Slather with butter, maple syrup, and/or your favorite jam.

(Yields 6 servings.)

STEWED APPLES

Apples were prepared in a number of ways in Washington County. They were eaten raw, dried, baked into pies, cakes, and breads, and turned into cider and brandy. This simple side dish at the Chester Inn breakfast table may have been just what the doctor ordered—dispelling that old "apple a day" adage.

Ingredients
1 to 2 apples per person, peeled, cored, and chopped
Dash of apple juice or cider
1 teaspoon sugar per apple

Directions
Place the chopped apples, cider, and sugar in a heavy sauce pan or Dutch oven. Heat the mixture until it bubbles. Stir and cover it with a lid. Turn the heat down to simmer. Add more cider if needed and continue cooking until the apples are fork-tender. Serve with a sprinkle of cinnamon.

MORAVIAN SUGAR CAKE (COFFEE CAKE)

In 1793, the French botanist and explorer André Michaux made one of his flora-collecting tours through Jonesborough. Six years later, the Moravian missionaries Abraham Sleiner and Frederick Schweinitz, traveling to Cherokee villages along the Great Stagecoach Road, made their way to Jonesborough. In their journals they describe the frontier town as "one long street with nearly 30 houses and is growing, as are all the towns in the back country. The innkeeper, with whom we stopped, looks after an apothecary shop as well as a hotel." The innkeeper hosting these missionaries was Dr. William P. Chester.

Moravians, a pious Germanic people, founded the area of Winston-Salem, North Carolina, in 1766. Sugar cake, an Easter-morning tradition, is still served to members of the Moravian Church.

Ingredients
3 eggs, beaten
1 package dry yeast
1 extra-large russet potato, peeled and quartered
1 cup warm potato water
1 cup sugar
½ cup butter (1 stick), softened
1 cup mashed potatoes
½ teaspoon salt
5 cups all-purpose flour
1½ cups brown sugar

1 teaspoon ground cinnamon
1 stick butter

Directions
In a medium sized saucepan, boil the quartered potato in 2 cups of water until tender. Remove the softened potato quarters from the pan, reserving the water. Pour 1 cup of the hot potato water into a large mixing bowl and allow to cool until just warm. Dissolve the yeast in the warm potato water until it bubbles. Stir in the sugar, softened butter, and mashed potatoes. Add the beaten eggs, flour, and salt until well combined. Turn the dough out onto a floured surface. Knead the dough for 10 minutes or until it is smooth and elastic. Turn the dough into a large, oiled bowl. Cover with plastic wrap. Let the dough double in size—1 to 2 hours. Punch the dough down. Turn the dough out onto a floured surface. Roll out into a rectangle. Place the dough into a greased 12x18x 2-inch sheet cake pan, or two 13x9x2 inch cake pans. Pat out and spread thinly. The dough should touch the sides of the pan. Melt the butter, brown sugar, and cinnamon in a saucepan. With your fingertips, punch closely spaced, deep holes all over the top of the cake. Pour and spread the melted butter, brown sugar, and cinnamon mixture on top of the cake. Let it rise for 1½ hours. Preheat the oven to 350°F. Bake for 30 minutes or until the top is lightly browned.
(Yields 24 servings.)

> **Tidbits:**
> *The time and energy spent in making this cake are well worth the effort.*

CHESTER INN DINNER MENU
Chicken Fried Lamb Chops with Saw Mill Gravy
Buttermilk Biscuits
"Leather Britches"
Scalloped Turnips
Nell Baxter's Cottage Pudding

CHICKEN FRIED LAMB CHOPS WITH SAWMILL GRAVY
Pork, beef, lamb, turkey, chicken, and goose were mainstays in Washington County and likely would have been served at the Chester Inn. Sheep,

however, being a significant farm animal, were used as much for meat as for their fibers. This was especially true of young, tender lambs.

Leg of lamb and lamb chops seasoned with rosemary were favorites of Andrew Jackson. Besides roasting, stewing, and boiling, pan frying was frequently used in frontier food preparation. Chicken-fried lamb chops go especially well with sawmill gravy.

As the story goes, the gravy's name came from loggers who accused their cook of using sawdust as a substitute for cornmeal when the gravy was too thick. Logging camps were common on the Tennessee frontier. In fact, the first Jonesborough courthouse, as described by historian J. G. M. Ramsey in his book *Annals of Tennessee,* "was built of round logs, fresh from the adjacent forest and covered in the fashion of the pioneers, with clap-boards."

In this two-part recipe, the gravy should be made first.

Ingredients
Sawmill Gravy
1 tablespoon bacon drippings
3 heaping tablespoons of stone ground white cornmeal
½ teaspoon salt
2 cups whole milk

Chicken-Fried Lamb Chops
Oil for frying
2 teaspoons kosher salt
1 tablespoon freshly ground black pepper
2 teaspoons fresh, minced rosemary
2 cups all-purpose flour
12 single-rib lamb chops (2 chops per person)
2 cups buttermilk

Directions
For Sawmill Gravy: In a heavy-bottomed, cast-iron saucepan, add the bacon drippings and cornmeal. Cook over medium heat, whisking constantly—about 10 to 12 minutes—until the mixture turns peanut-colored (roux). Whisk in the milk, salt, and pepper. Bring the mixture to a boil, continually

whisking. Reduce the heat and simmer for 15 more minutes, whisking frequently. The sauce should thicken enough to coat the back of a spoon. (Yields 1¾ cups.)

For Lamb Chops: Add 1 inch of oil to a straight-sided, 3-inch-deep cast-iron pan. Preheat the oil in the frying pan to 365°F. In a medium sized mixing bowl, whisk the salt, pepper, and rosemary with the flour. Dredge the lamb chops in buttermilk, then into the seasoned flour mixture. Slowly add the chops to the preheated oil—about 4 per batch. Fry 2 minutes per side for medium doneness. Drain on a wire rack and serve with gravy. (Yields 6 servings.)

BUTTERMILK BISCUITS

This old-fashioned recipe engages a couple of "new-fangled" methods and equipment to achieve the perfect balance of biscuit goodness for your gravy. Use a high-quality, whole-fat buttermilk such as Cruze Farm Buttermilk, available in markets like Whole Foods.

Ingredients
1 stick butter, frozen
2½ cups self-rising flour
1 cup chilled whole-fat buttermilk
Parchment paper
2 tablespoons extra butter, melted

Tidbits:
"Self-raising" (self-rising) flour was invented in 1845 when Henry Jones patented his formula: 1 teaspoon of baking powder and a pinch of salt to 1 cup of flour.

Directions
All ingredients including the bowl, wooden spoon, and rolling pin—should be chilled. Preheat the oven to 475°F. Grate the stick of frozen butter using the large holes on a box grater. Scrape the grated butter into the flour and gently combine with a cold spatula. Make a well in the center of the flour mixture. Pour in the chilled buttermilk. Using a chilled wooden spoon, stir the mixture together about 15 times until fully moistened. Turn the dough out onto a floured

surface. Roll the dough into a rectangle of ½-inch thickness. Fold the dough in half and roll out again. Repeat this procedure 5 times, layering the dough to ½-inch thickness. Cut biscuits out using a 2½-inch biscuit cutter. Place the biscuits together on a jellyroll pan lined with parchment paper. Bake at 475°F for 15 minutes. Remove from the oven and brush the tops with 2 tablespoons melted butter.
(Yields 12 biscuits.)

"LEATHER BRITCHES"
According to the website *The Food Timeline: American Presidents' Food Favorites,* one of Andrew Jackson's favorite dishes was "leather britches."

To be clear, these leather britches are dried greens beans. Long before the invention of pressure cookers and canning, folks dried almost everything edible they couldn't preserve.

Heirloom beans—beans that have not been genetically modified or crossbred with any other variety for at least fifty years—are perfect for drying, as are wax beans and pole beans. Preserve a piece of history—plant heirloom seeds.

Ingredients
2 pounds of beans (string beans, wax beans)
1 large ham hock, scored
1 large yellow onion, sliced
¼ teaspoon lard (optional)
Salt, to taste

Preparing the Beans
Pick (literally) or purchase your string beans or wax beans (about 2 pounds) in the spring, wash them, and set them out to dry in the sun. After the beans dry, string them together using a darning needle threaded with white store string (kite string works, too). In other words, stick the needle through the middle of the bean pod—not through the bean itself but through the center—leaving both ends of the bean loose. String until the string is full of beans. Hang the string of beans in a clean dry place like an attic or sunroom. The beans will become dry and wrinkled. This process generally takes about 2½ weeks.

Tidbits:
Hanging the strings
of beans near a
fireplace or wood-
burning stove
allows a smoky
essence to infuse the
bean pods.

Directions
Rinse the dried beans and remove the stem and the natural string from the center of the bean. Remove the beans from the store-bought strings. In a large pot, soak several strings of the dried beans or "britches" overnight until they become soft. Drain and rinse well. In fresh pot of lightly salted water, add the beans, ham hock, and onion. Bring to a boil and then reduce heat to a simmer. Cover and cook over low heat all day. Season to taste and serve hot.
(Yields 8–10 servings.)

SCALLOPED TURNIPS

The humble turnip is one of early Washington County's most copious crops. Scrub and slice this root vegetable, layer it with butter, onion, flour, and milk, and bake it in a hot oven until fork-tender. This side dish was a well-rounded addition to any square meal served at the Chester Inn.

Ingredients
4 tablespoons butter
½ cup thinly sliced onions
4 cups peeled, sliced turnips
2 tablespoons flour
1 teaspoon salt
Freshly ground pepper
1 cup whole milk
½ cup light cream

Directions
Preheat the oven to 375°F. Melt the butter in a small sauce pan. Whisk in the flour to make a roux (a cooked mixture of butter and flour used to thicken sauces). Into the roux, slowly whisk the milk and cream. Add salt and pepper to taste. Layer an 8×8-inch Pyrex dish with sliced turnips and

onions, drizzling the roux over each layer. Finish with remaining roux. Bake for 45 minutes or until the turnips are tender. (Yields 4–6 servings.)

NELL BAXTER'S COTTAGE PUDDING

This original recipe from Mrs. Eleanor "Nell" Baxter is included in her cookbook *Receipt Book of Tried Receipts: A Homemade Cookbook.* The "receipts" begin in 1895 and continue into the mid-twentieth century when the Chester Inn became the Planter's House Hotel and later the Jonesboro Inn.

Mrs. Baxter's wedding dress is displayed periodically at the Heritage Alliance Museum in Jonesborough. The following text comes from the exhibit label:

> Eleanor Walker Lampson was born in 1864 in Jonesborough and was a life-long resident. She and Mr. Elbridge J. Baxter wed on June 8, 1893 at 8:00 p.m. that evening. They were married at the Second Presbyterian Church, current home of the Central Christian Church on Main Street. This is the dress she wore 123 years ago.
>
> Elbridge and Eleanor "Nell" Baxter lived in the Greek Revival home at 127 East Main Street in the early 1900s. They had a daughter named Martha Baxter. Many of her toys, books and memories are in the collections of the Jonesborough/Washington County History Museum and Archives.

Ingredients
1 cup sugar
2 tablespoons butter
3 eggs
1 cup sweet milk
3 cups flour
2 teaspoons baking powder
½ teaspoon salt

Original Directions
Rub the butter and sugar together. Separate the egg yolks from the egg whites. Add the beaten egg yolks, milk, and flour. Lastly, add the beaten eggs whites. Bake one hour. Eat with sauce.

Tidbits:

The "sauce," as mentioned in the original recipe, was likely a thinner version of the pudding. Chocolate or caramel sauce works well drizzled over this dessert.

Updated Directions

Preheat the oven to 350°F. In a medium sized bowl, sift together the flour, baking powder, and salt. Set aside. Separate the egg yolks and egg whites. With a hand mixer, whip the egg whites until they form soft peaks. In a large mixing bowl, or stand mixer, cream the butter, sugar, and egg yolks together until they're well combined. Stir the milk into the creamed mixture and slowly add the flour until the mixture forms a smooth batter. Fold the egg white gently into the mixture. Pour the mixture into an 8x8-inch baking dish. Bake for one-hour or until the pudding is relatively firm. Allow the pudding to set. Serve warm.

(Yields 6 servings.)

Chapter 6

CRAGFONT STATE HISTORIC SITE

Built 1798–1802
Castalian Springs, Sumner County, Tennessee

Taproots

Cragfont was the scene of many a festival in which
our grandfathers and grandmothers participated.
The General was given to great and generous
hospitality. The magnates of the nations were often
entertained in its halls including Andrew Jackson
and Marquis De Lafayette.

—Nashville newspaper, 1890

The highway leading north from Nashville through Gallatin's charming
sidewalk shops and churches suddenly transforms into a two-lane country
road. Pushed around like a piece of string, Highway 25 gradually heads
east. A sharp left turn onto a dusty, gravel side road winds around blue-
grass pasturelands. And it leads ever upward into the untroubled, lovely,
long-ago world of Cragfont.

Cragfont's design reflects the balanced, well-proportioned architectural style and grandeur of the Georgian era (1714–1830). The historic
mansion's first owner, James Winchester, was a lawyer, Sunday school
teacher, Revolutionary War captain, and brigadier general in the War
of 1812. He enlisted stone masons from his home state of Maryland to
fashion the massive structure for his wife, Susan, and their eight daughters
and six sons.

The grandeur of beautiful Cragfont today.

Constructed of limestone on a craggy hillside with Bledsoe's Creek at its base, Cragfont is said to have been designed in the shape of Christ's cross. The front section—wide across the top and flanked by enormous fireplaces on each end—boasts an elongated rear wing with corresponding side porches or "galleries" as its trunk. A second-story ballroom upon which Andrew Jackson and other dignitaries waltzed and in which his young daughter Susan practiced piano (her sheet music still leans upon her music desk) was added around 1810. Large, almost floor-to-ceiling ballroom windows offer a glimpse down into an elaborate, well-manicured garden. Winchester's granddaughter, Susan Black Winchester Scales, in

The parlor walls' original "diamond-and-pearl, vertical, "sliced egg" border and "snowflake filler" match that of renowned New England stencilers Moses Eaton Jr. and his father.

her book *Long, Long Ago: Reminiscences at Cragfont,* described "the wicket gate with large cabbage roses and syringa. Virgin's Bower clamored over the summerhouse and hung long wisps of bloom which made a bower of beauty . . . jonquils and Sweet William. Over the garden wall was the big shining pond whose clear water kept it evergreen. It was a beautiful place for a little girl and her nurse to spend long summer days. When we were tired of games and 'make believe' we could fish from the garden wall." Today, this magnificent flower garden flourishes and is as beautifully maintained as it was "long, long ago."

The kitchen with its original flagstone floor features a large
limestone cooking fireplace with a solid-wood lintel. To the right
of the fireplace, a built-in oven with a cast-iron door may have
turned out skillets of Aunt Delphy's soda biscuits.

Cragfont's floors and walls—fashioned from poplar, white ash, cherry,
and walnut hewn from the site's surrounding forest—are meticulously
preserved. Original stenciled walls and Winchester family heirlooms grace
the large parlor just off the main entryway and are displayed throughout
the home. Across the hallway from the parlor, General Winchester's private office is replete with memorabilia, including tokens of his election
to the first Tennessee legislature, credentials as speaker of the House, as
well as the original commission—signed by President James Madison—

appointing him a brigadier general in the War of 1812. Epaulettes worn by General Winchester in that war are displayed, along with a three-hundred-acre land grant presented to him by President James Monroe—a reward for his service in the American Revolution. His Revolutionary War rifle hangs on the wall—a silent witness to the bloody battle for God, home, and country.

Interestingly, General Winchester, General Andrew Jackson, and Judge John Overton surveyed, named, and established the city of Memphis in 1819. At that time, Memphis—named after the ancient capital of Egypt—was only about four blocks long with a population of nearly fifty people. The Winchesters' eldest son, Marcus, was appointed the city's first mayor.

More than a footnote in history, however, is the Battle of Raisin River (aka the Battle of Frenchtown) during the War of 1812. General Winchester's unfortunate decision to override the commander of the Northwest Territory, William Henry Harrison (later to become the ninth U.S. president), by employing an unsuccessful strategy to invade Canada, resulted in the highest number of fatalities of any battle during the war. Winchester's men—some five hundred Tennesseans and Kentuckians—were captured and imprisoned in Quebec for over a year. "Remember the Raisin!" became the battle cry for the War of 1812, a cry that echoed through the small town of Monroe, Michigan (formerly Frenchtown). The city of Monroe and the banks of River Raisin were the site of one of the largest military engagements in the war between the United States and Great Britain, Canada, and their Native American allies—a fierce battle for control of the Great Lakes region.

General Winchester returned to his beloved Cragfont after the war. Owning nearly one hundred enslaved workers, he ran his sizeable tobacco farm, engaged in land speculations, and helped develop the state of Tennessee until his death in 1826. Having a strong interest in the Classical Era, he named Castalian Springs, Tennessee, after Castalian Springs on Mount Parnassus in Greece. The names of three of his sons—Marcus, Brutus, and Valerius Publicola—are reminiscent of ancient Rome.

The general's wife, Susan, remained at Cragfont until her death in 1864. General and Mrs. Winchester are buried in the property's family cemetery alongside family members, including his daughter Almira and her husband, Alfred Royal Wynne of Wynnewood State Historic Site in

Castalian Springs. The Winchester family's enslaved workers lived in row houses—which provided a large living area and loft for each family—located some sixty feet north of the family cemetery. The slave quarters eventually succumbed to weather and age.

Several generations of Winchesters lived at Cragfont. After the devastation of the Civil War, the family sold the mansion and moved to Memphis to start anew. Over the years several families occupied Cragfont. During the late 1950s, the Tennessee Historical Commission acquired Cragfont, and the magnificent mansion is listed on the National Register of Historic Places and open to the public.

Address and Contact Information
Cragfont State Historic Site
200 Cragfont Road
Castalian Springs, TN 37031
(615) 452-7070
www.cragfont.net

Timeless Recipes

> . . . and I could as soon forget Aunt Delphy as her
> kitchen, stone-flagged and splendidly equipped; a great
> open fireplace with spit and crane, big skillet with legs
> and a top, wherein those delicious soda biscuits were
> baked. Our old cook, Aunt Delphy, was so famous for
> her "soda biscuit" that a visitor once said her "monu-
> ment" should be built of them.
>
> —Susan Black Winchester (1771–1864)

In her memoir *Long, Long Ago: Reminiscences of Cragfont,* Susan Black Winchester Scales, granddaughter of James and Susan Black Winchester, guides us through her grandmother's recollections of Cragfont's broad hardwood hallways, even venturing down a set of wooden steps to the "stone-flagged and splendidly equipped" kitchen where meals were prepared by Delphy, their African American cook and nursemaid.

An unfinished manuscript titled "My Mother: A Biography," chronicles life at Cragfont before, during, and after the Civil War. The text includes descriptions of domesticated geese, fruits to be dried, of jellies, preserves, pickles, and catsups to be made by the hands of enslaved African American workers.

Within the pages of the manuscript are descriptions of domesticated geese, fruits to be dried, of jellies and preserves and, pickles, and catsups to be made by the hands of slaves. Apples and peaches and other fruits were peeled and set out to dry piece by piece on scaffolds where young African American girls were stationed with fly brushes made from boughs of nearby bushes, which they waved up and down to keep insects away. And there were walnut trees and clusters of wild fox grapes, persimmons, and "the sweetest of mulberries" for gifts of friendships and to be stirred into desserts and jams. There were herbs, bitter and sweet, mint and sage, sweet marjoram and lavender and tansy and rue, and "never, never, never to be forgotten Sweet Betsy."

MENU
Soda Biscuits
Roast Goose with Wild Rice and Wild Fox Grape Stuffing
Mushy Peas with Mint
Savory Carrot Soufflé
Black Currant Pound Cake
Persimmon Pudding
Rose Geranium Cake with Rose Frosting
Blackberry (or Mulberry) Liqueur

SODA BISCUITS
Soda biscuits are timeless. In the Antebellum Era, however, soda biscuits were a mixture of flour, salt, lard, and a leavening agent—most likely pearl ash, a residue of wood ashes. Shaped and patted by the Winchesters' enslaved African American cook, whom the children affectionately nicknamed "Aunt Delphy," these biscuits were fashioned into a dough sturdy enough to bake on top of a chicken casserole or even for use as a piecrust. After shoveling white-hot wood coals from the fireplace onto the lid of

her cast-iron skillet nestled in embers, the old cook knew precisely when to lift that lid, revealing her batch of golden-biscuit perfection.

Today, we barely bat an eyelash when tossing a teaspoon or two of baking soda into our baked goods. We pop them into our convection ovens and listen for a "ding!" from the built-in timer.

The following recipe is adapted from Walter N. Lambert's *Kinfolks and Custard Pie: Recollections and Recipes from an East Tennessean.*

Tidbits:
Pearl ash was only in use for a short time period, about 1780–1840, until saleratus, which is chemically similar to baking soda, was introduced and used more frequently.

Ingredients
2 cups all-purpose flour
⅓ cup shortening
¾ cup buttermilk
½ teaspoon salt
1½ teaspoon baking soda

Directions
Preheat the oven to 400°F. Whisk together the flour, salt, and baking soda in a large bowl. Work in the shortening and blend until the mixture resembles coarse cornmeal. Add the buttermilk and stir to make a reasonably soft dough. Turn the dough out onto a floured surface and knead lightly 5 or 6 times or until the surface of the dough is just smooth. Roll or pat out the dough until it is about ½ inch thick. Cut the dough with a 2½-inch biscuit cutter. Rework and reroll until all the scraps have been used. Place the biscuits on a lightly greased cookie sheet with the sides touching. Bake until golden brown on top (about 15 to 20 minutes). Serve hot with butter.
(Yields 12 biscuits.)

ROAST GOOSE WITH WILD RICE AND WILD FOX GRAPE STUFFING

Only a plump, domestic goose roasted and stuffed with wild rice and fox grapes, served with an assortment of peach, apple, mulberry, currant, and persimmon filled puddings, pies, and cakes, was fit for a Winchester. Purplish-black fox grapes—parent of such cultivars as Catawba and Concord—add a musky, "foxy" sweetness to rice stuffing. Although there is no written record of rice as part of Cragfont's agricultural yield, the grain could easily have been imported from rice-producing plantations in the South Carolina lowcountry. Additionally, an assortment of garden-fresh vegetables mingled with herbs and spices from the kitchen garden was likely prepared by Aunt Delphy.

Ingredients

1 eight-pound fresh or frozen goose
2 cups cooked wild rice
⅔ cup chopped, toasted pecans
1 cup fox grapes, cut in half and seeded
½ cup yellow onion
1 celery stalk, thinly sliced
1 teaspoon ground sage
1 teaspoon ground thyme
Salt and pepper to taste

Directions

Preheat the oven to 350°F. In a large bowl, mix together the pecans, cooked wild rice, grape halves, onion, and herbs. Season to taste with salt and pepper. Remove the bird's innards—neck, gizzard, and heart and reserve for the broth. Wash the bird inside and out. Pat dry. Trim any excess fat from the bird. With the point of a sharp knife, prick the entire surface of the goose, being careful not to cut into the flesh. Rub the goose inside and out with a mixture of kosher salt and pepper. Fill the cavity of the bird with the stuffing mixture. Cover the bird loosely with aluminum foil. Roast in the preheated oven for 2½ to 3 hours. Juices should run clear when the bird is pricked where the thigh is attached to the

Tidbits:
A shallow roasting pan fitted with a V-rack and convenient handles is perfect for goose. Reserve the considerable amount of goose fat for frying potatoes or cooking winter greens, such as kale or chard.

Tidbits, Too:
Goose breast is best eaten medium-rare or medium. After about an hour of cooking, remove the goose and carve the breast out with a sharp boning knife. Place the goose back in the oven to finish cooking. When ready to serve, cut the goose breast in half and sear in a sauté pan with the goose fat.

body. Remove the goose from the roaster. Allow the bird to rest for 15 minutes before carving.

(Yields 4–6 servings.)

Variant Recipe Using Broiler Chickens
Substitute two 4-pound broiler chickens for the 8-pound goose and prepare as follows: Preheat the oven to 350°F. Rinse the chickens inside and out. Pat dry with a paper towel. Salt and pepper both birds inside and out to taste. Follow the above directions for preparing the stuffing. Stuff the chickens with the wild rice mixture. Place the chickens side by side on a flat wire rack in a heavy-duty 12x18 inch roaster pan (2 to 2½ inches deep). Roast for one-hour and thirty minutes. Prick the chicken between the leg and breast. When the juices run clear, the chickens are likely done. A meat thermometer inserted into the thickest part of the thigh (not touching the bone) should read between 160 and 165°F. Remove the roaster from the oven. Let the birds rest for 15 minutes to allow the juices to settle before carving.

(Yields 4 servings per bird.)

MUSHY PEAS WITH MINT

Snap peas are typically planted in Tennessee gardens in March or April—while the ground is slightly cool—and picked at the height of harvest about sixty days later, according to David W. Sams, Professor Emeritus, Plant and Soil Scinece, at the University of Tennessee Agricultural Extension Service.

Legumes—beans, peas, and the like—were cooked and served fresh or dried for use in Cragfont wintertime meals. Mint was muddled fresh or hung up to dry in bunches in the kitchen with other herbs.

Ingredients
4 tablespoons olive oil
2 bunches scallions, chopped (green and white parts)
2 handfuls fresh mint leaves, finely chopped
2 pounds fresh or canned green peas
2 tablespoons butter
Salt and pepper to taste

Directions

Heat the olive oil in a pan and sauté the chopped scallions. Add the peas and chopped mint. Cover and allow the mixture to steam until the peas soften. With a fork, mash the peas until you achieve a mushy consistency; or, puree the peas in a food processor or with an immersion blender for a smoother consistency. Stir in the butter and season with salt and pepper. (Yields eight ¼-cup servings.)

CARROT SOUFFLÉ

A soufflé is served during the holidays or as a special gesture of hospitality. This simple yet elegant side dish could be presented on Winchester china for the family and the plethora of prominent guests seated in the well-appointed dining room of magnificent Cragfont.

Ingredients

1 tablespoon unsalted butter, softened, plus more for the baking dish

2 pounds carrots, peeled and cut into ¼-inch thick rounds

1 tablespoon kosher (coarse) salt

1 cup whole milk

1 cup saltine cracker crumbs

¾ cup grated sharp white cheddar cheese

⅓ cup very finely chopped yellow onion

¼ teaspoon freshly ground black pepper

3 eggs, whisked with a mixer until foamy

Directions

Preheat the oven to 350°F. Butter a 2-quart shallow casserole dish. Set aside. Place the carrots in a large pot and add water to cover them by one inch. Add the salt and bring the water to a boil. Reduce the heat and simmer until the carrots are tender and can be pierced with the tip of a sharp knife—about 10 minutes. Strain the carrots and transfer to a large bowl. With an immersion blender, puree the carrots. Stir in the milk, cracker crumbs, cheese, onion, butter,

Tidbits:
A drizzle of sorghum syrup, with a sprinkle of ground cinnamon or nutmeg, works well with this recipe adapted from Sam Beall's Blackberry Farm Cook Book.

salt, and black pepper. Fold in the foamy, beaten eggs gently. Transfer the mixture to the prepared buttered casserole dish. Bake for 40-45 minutes until the soufflé is puffed and lightly golden on top. Serve warm. (Yields 8–10 generous servings.)

BLACK CURRANT POUND CAKE

Black and red currants flourish from June through August in Tennessee's humid summers and limestone-laden soil, the perfect mixture of climate and clay. One can imagine these sweet-tart-bejeweled shrubs picked clean by the deep-purple-and-rubicund-stained fingers of the Winchester children—all in anticipation of a sugary treat. The leaves of the Sweet Betsy plant—also known as Carolina allspice—are aromatic when bruised, leaving a tang in the air with their spicy breath. The fragrant blossom, described as a delicate blend of pineapple, strawberry, and banana, was sometimes used in place of cinnamon. In addition to using the coveted clove and nutmeg, perhaps Aunt Delphy swirled a generous sprinkling of "never, never, never to be forgotten Sweet Betsy" into her toothsome cake batter.

Ingredients
1 cup dried currants
½ cup black walnuts
¼ cup brandy
2 cups butter, softened
8 eggs, room temperature
2½ cups sugar
¼ teaspoon salt
4 cups all-purpose flour
½ teaspoon ground nutmeg
¼ teaspoon cinnamon

Tidbits:
A gentle sifting of powdered sugar on top of these cakes makes a pretty presentation and an even sweeter taste.

Directions
Preheat the oven to 325°F. In a jar, combine the currants and brandy. Cover tightly and soak at room temperature for several hours or overnight. Drain. Cream the butter and sugar until the mixture is light and fluffy. Add eggs, one at a

time, beating well after each one. Add in the flour, nutmeg and cinnamon. Blend well. Fold in the currants and black walnuts. Grease the *bottom only* of two 9×5×3-inch loaf pans. Turn the batter into the pans evenly. Bake for about 60 minutes. Turn the loaves out onto a wire rack to cool. (Yields 9 slices per loaf.)

PERSIMMON PUDDING

The American persimmon *(Diospyros virginiana)*—sometimes called "possumwood" or "sugar plum"—buds, blossoms, and bears fruit from Connecticut to Florida, continuing west of the Appalachians into Tennessee and farther to Texas. A persimmon tastes like a cross between a peach and an apricot. Early frontier settlers learned from Native Americans how to transform the sweet and spicy pulp—high in vitamin C—into delicious repasts.

Cragfont persimmons grew wild. Winchester's enslaved workers knew better than to pluck astringent, unripened persimmons—round with fruit the size of a quarter. After the fruit turns orange and rosy cheeked in the fall, a persimmon tree—lightly shaken—delivers a shower of sweet, succulent, seed-bearing drupes for treats or to be fermented into brandy.

This persimmon pudding would be a grand finale for family and guests spending Thanksgiving or Christmas with the Winchesters at festive Cragfont. (The recipe is adapted from "The United States of Thanksgiving," *New York Times,* November 18, 2018, www.nytimes.com.)

Ingredients
4 tablespoons butter, melted, plus more for the dish
Pulp from 5 American persimmons (2 cups) trimmed and chopped
2 eggs, beaten
2 cups sugar
1 teaspoon baking soda
1½ cup buttermilk
1½ cups all-purpose flour
1 teaspoon baking powder
¼ cup heavy cream
¼ teaspoon salt
½ teaspoon vanilla extract
Dash of cinnamon

Tidbits:

Using a sharp knife, cut off the leaf-like flower and stem. Slice the persimmon into thin wedges or into slices as you would a tomato.

Tidbits, Too:

During the Civil War, persimmon seeds were used as buttons. They were also roasted and ground as a substitute for the limited supply of coffee beans.

Directions

Preheat the oven to 350°F. Generously butter a 9×13-inch baking dish. Puree the prepared persimmon pulp in a food processor or with an immersion blender until smooth. Strain the pulp through a fine mesh strainer into a bowl, using the back of a spoon or spatula to push the puree through. Measure out two cups of pulp. Combine the eggs, sugar, and persimmon pulp in a large bowl. Beat with an electric mixer on medium speed until the ingredients are well mixed. Stir the baking soda into the buttermilk, then add to the persimmon mixture and beat to combine. In a separate bowl, sift together the flour and baking powder. Beat the flour mixture into the persimmon mixture in 3 batches, alternating with the cream and ending with the flour mixture. Stir in the melted butter, salt, vanilla, and cinnamon. Transfer the batter to the prepared baking dish. Bake until the pudding is set, 1 hour to 1 hour and 15 minutes.

(Yields 10–12 servings.)

ROSE GERANIUM CAKE WITH ROSE FROSTING

The rose geranium flowering plant, known as *Pelargonium graveolens,* may have been cultivated in the Winchester garden, although the plant is not native to Tennessee. Perhaps these leaves were one answer to unavailable flavorings in the South during times of war. Brushing against its leaves or a whispering breeze releases a fragrance akin to dabbing one's wrist with rose water. Heavenly!

This cake is my personal favorite. I infuse the sugar with the rose-scented florae. And after swaddling sticks of butter in the fragrant leaves overnight, I'm ready to bake a luscious layercake, sheet cake, cupcakes, or mini-cupcakes. This geranium variety is available in seed or plant form from local or mail-order greenhouses in the spring.

Scented rose geranium cake and flavorings—including syrup and pot-pourri—have been a culinary favorite since Colonial times. This pretty-in-pink fragrant frosting gives new meaning to "the icing on the cake."

Ingredients
Rose Geranium Cake
12 rose geranium leaves
1 cup butter (2 sticks)
1¾ cups sugar
6 *fresh* egg whites (not from a carton)
3 cups sifted cake flour
1 tablespoon baking powder
½ teaspoon salt
¾ cups milk
½ cup water

Rose Frosting
1½ cups rose scented geranium white granulated sugar
2 *fresh* egg whites (not from a carton)
⅓ cup cold water
¼ teaspoon cream of tartar
⅛ teaspoon salt
5 drops red food coloring

Directions
For the Cake: Preheat the oven to 350°F. Gently rinse the rose geranium leaves and allow them to dry. Wrap 6 leaves around each stick of butter then wrap in foil or plastic wrap and chill overnight. When ready to begin the cake mixture, remove the leaves and set aside and allow the butter to soften slightly. In a large bowl, cream the softened butter and sugar until light and fluffy. Add the egg whites two at a time, beating well after each addition. In a separate bowl, sift together the flour, baking powder, and salt. Combine the milk and water into a 2-cup or larger measuring cup. Alternately add the flour mixture and liquid to the creamed butter, sugar, and egg mixture; begin and end with the flour mixture. Beat smooth after

each addition. Butter and flour two 9×1½-inch round cake pans. Bake in the preheated oven for 30 to 35 minutes. Cool in the pans for 10 minutes. Turn out onto a wire rack and allow the cakes to cool further.

For the rose geranium scented white granulated sugar: Pour 1½ cups of sugar into a glass jar or container. Press 3 or 4 large scented rose geranium leaves into the sugar. Mix the sugar and leaves together until they are well-combined. (Remove the leaves from the sugar before preparing the frosting.)

For the Frosting: In the upper pan of a double-boiler, stir together the scented sugar, egg whites, water, cream of tarter, and salt. Beat for 1 minute with an electric hand mixer. Place the upper pan over boiling water. The upper pan should not touch the boiling water in the lower pan. Cook while beating the mixture to stiff peaks—about 7 minutes (do not overbeat). Remove from the heat. Add 5 drops of red food coloring. Beat until the frosting mixture is well combined and has reached spreading consistency—about 2 minutes. Layer the two cakes together by frosting thinly in between the layers and generously covering the cake. (Yields 12 slices.)

BLACKBERRY (OR MULBERRY) LIQUEUR

After settling on his acreage near Bledsoe's Creek in 1785, James Winchester built a mill, cotton gin, and distillery—most likely refining alcohol from his various crops of grain such as wheat, rye, and corn. Blackberries grew wild in bushes across the Winchester acreage. Sipping this prized liqueur after a sumptuous meal with his guests was the height of refinement. Yet, even as they reclined in the "galleries," libations in hand, mulberry leaves stirred in the breeze while winds from the north blew colder. As with all things timeless, this liqueur ages well.

Ingredients
One 6-cup glass container with screw-top lid
1 cup water
3 cups sugar
3 cups vodka
3 cups fresh blackberries, or mulberries, slightly mashed

Directions

Mix the water, sugar, and vodka in a large pot on the stove. Over medium-high heat, stir the mixture until the sugar is completely dissolved. Let cool before continuing. Pour the cooled sugar mixture into a 6-cup container (a tall mason jar works well). Add the berries to the container. Screw the lid on tightly. Allow the mixture to infuse for at least 10 days. Turn the container upside-down once a day to keep it mixed well. Strain the liqueur through a tiny-mesh wire sieve into a clean glass container and discard the berries; or, pour the berries over ice-cream or use in dessert such as pie filling. Strain again, if needed, through a kitchen cheese cloth. Store in the tightly capped mason jar or in gift bottles. Keep in a cool, dark place. (Yields 1 quart.)

Tidbits:
Substitute the vodka with white grape juice or apple cider with a dash of lime juice, if desired.

Chapter 7

MARBLE SPRINGS STATE HISTORIC SITE

◆━━━━━━━━━━━━━━━━━━━━━━━━━━━━━━━━◆

Established 1801–1815
Knoxville, Tennessee

Taproots

Dear Sir: Your affectionate and much esteemed
letter of the 12th has come to hand and am happy to
hear your family is well, but very sorry to learn you
are so much afflicted with the Rheumatism. I wish you
could spend a summer at Marble Springs. Probably the
Water would relieve you as it has done me.
I am very confident it was that water alone
that gave me any relief.

—John Sevier to his son George Washington Sevier, June 1812

Marble Springs State Historic Site is the final home of one of Tennessee's most important founding fathers and its first governor, John Sevier. Born in Rockingham County, Virginia, on September 23, 1745, Sevier was the eldest of Valentine and Joanna Goad Sevier's seven children. Sevier migrated east to Tennessee, married, and remained in the forefront of frontier life as a pioneer, soldier, Indian fighter, and statesman.

Recognized as a natural-born leader, John Sevier was elected to head up the newly formed Watauga Association, the government of the first American frontier settlement west of the Appalachians in East Tennessee. Here, he began to play a key role both militarily and politically in Tennessee's early development.

The replica of a rustic "log and chinking" period tavern
at Marble Springs State Historic Site.

In July 1776, the Cherokees began a series of well-orchestrated attacks on the East Tennessee Watauga settlements. Led by John Sevier,
the Wataugans drove away the onslaught and swiftly counterattacked.
With the help of militia from North Carolina and Virginia, John Sevier
and his band of soldiers invaded the heartland of the Cherokees, torching
their towns. According to the *Tennessee Blue Book* (2009–2010), "Sid-
ing with the British during the American Revolution proved disastrous
for the Cherokee, as it gave the Americans a reason to reduce the tribe's
military power and therefore encroach further on their land."

In 1780, Colonel Sevier fought at the Battle of King's Mountain, considered a turning point in the Revolutionary War, thanks to the brav-

A chalkboard menu rendering the cost of a meal, beverage, and bed on the Tennessee frontier.

ery of the Overmountain Boys. He defended pre-Tennessee statehood in Washington County (still part of North Carolina) during battles with the Cherokees in the 1780s and 1790s. Sevier served for three years as the only governor of the short-lived State of Franklin and was brigadier general of the Southwest Territory during the 1790s.

As recompense for his service as a Revolutionary War soldier, the State of North Carolina presented Brigadier General John Sevier with 375 acres of prime Tennessee pastureland. Sevier dubbed his military reward "Marble Springs" after discovering substantial deposits of Tennessee Rose Marble and six continuously bubbling springs on his acreage.

Today, Marble Springs is situated on 35 acres of Sevier's initial plot. The cabin—reconstructed with historical accuracy—still stands on its original site, with additional log structures giving visitors a glimpse into frontier life during the eighteenth and nineteenth centuries.

John Sevier served as Tennessee's governor from 1796 until 1801 and from 1803 to 1809—with term limits preventing another consecutive term. After his final term as governor, Sevier, ever popular with the people, was

elected to three terms in the United States House of Representatives. He served there until his death in 1815.

As the nation celebrated General Andrew Jackson's victories in the Creek War and the Battle of New Orleans, President James Madison signed the Treaty of Ghent, ending the War of 1812. After the war's con-

The Tavern House at Marble Springs.

clusion, President Madison appointed Sevier a commissioner of a congressional delegation that was tasked with determining the boundary between Georgia and the Creek territory near Decatur, Alabama.

After satisfactorily surveying the landscapes, Sevier, approaching his seventieth year and weary of travel, longed for his beloved Marble Springs.

Upon returning, he contracted a fever, yet still mustered enough strength to attend an Indian festival known as the "Green Corn Dance" and was apparently rejuvenated by the activities.

Upon returning to Fort Decatur, Alabama, however, Sevier's health suddenly took a turn for the worse. Realizing he might be nearing death, Sevier asked his men to carry him across the Tallapoosa River. He sought a spring located about a mile away so that he could taste the cool, clean water. Ever the believer in natural remedies, Sevier likely hoped this elixir would help restore his health. Unfortunately, he never reached that spring.

John Sevier served his country until his death on September 24, 1815. He was buried along the Tallapoosa River near Fort Decatur, Alabama and later reinterred in Knoxville, Tennessee. According to Robert E. Corlew's entry on Sevier in the *Tennessee Encyclopedia of History and Culture*:

> Sevier was a product of the frontier and a hero to Tennesseans who understood and appreciated his diverse career. When, in 1887, his body was reinterred on the courthouse lawn in Knoxville, a monument was erected whose inscription well describes his life of public service: "John Sevier, pioneer, soldier, statesman, and one of the founders of the Republic; Governor of the State of Franklin; six times Governor of Tennessee; four times elected to Congress; a typical pioneer, who conquered the wilderness and fashioned the State; a protector and hero of Kings Mountain; fought thirty-five battles, won thirty-five victories; his Indian war cry, 'Here they are! Come on, boys!'"

SARAH HAWKINS SEVIER, JOHN SEVIER'S FIRST WIFE AND "TENNESSEE'S FIRST FIVE STAR MOTHER," 1761–1780

She was the love of his youth; the inspiration of his manhood; a gallant, courageous, Colonial and Revolutionary patriot; her descendants number many notable leaders of men.

—Inscription on Sarah Hawkins Sevier's tombstone
Old Knoxville Courthouse

Sarah Hawkins was just fifteen years old when she married the handsome, daring, sixteen-year-old Indian fighter and frontiersman, John Sevier.

The year was 1761. Sarah likely met John Sevier at the large trading post established by her father inside the local stockade in Frederick County on Virginia's frontier. Sarah Hawkins Sevier was, indeed, the love of John Sevier's youth. She is Tennessee aristocracy.

Sarah embodied the biblical definition of "helpmeet" through her timeless recipe for a successful marriage: dedication to serving her husband, family, and country. When the ever-present Cherokees led a surprise attack on Sevier and his neighbors, the small band of settlers mustered and drove them away—using almost all of their bullets. Borrowing a page from the ideals of another brave patriot, Abigail Adams, courageous Sarah built a bonfire and, kneeling before it, melted lead and molded bullets, supplying enough to ensure her family's safekeeping until nightfall.

During the next nineteen years of marriage, the Seviers produced ten children—Joseph, James, John, Elizabeth, Sarah, Mary Ann, Valentine, Rebecca, Richard, and Nancy—their lineage propagating notable political leaders.

In the spring of 1780, while building a new grist mill on the shore of the Nolichucky River, "Nolichucky Jack"— Sevier's nickname—was warned of an impending Indian attack. Gathering his family, Sevier, Sarah, and their children made it safely inside the stockade. Sadly, Sarah, having recently given birth to their tenth child, died early the next morning. That evening, Sevier and his men laid Sarah to rest in the heart of the forest. As a sign of love and respect, all of their children were present—including their newborn.

The John Sevier–Sarah Hawkins Chapter of the Daughters of the American Revolution in Johnson City, Tennessee, honored her memory, erecting a monument next to her husband's tombstone on the lawn of the Old Knox County Courthouse in Knoxville.

CATHERINE "BONNY KATE" SEVIER,
JOHN SEVIER'S SECOND WIFE, 1780–1815
Brightest star among pioneer women of this state.

—Inscription on Bonny Kate Sevier's tombstone
Old Knox County Courthouse, Knoxville, Tennessee

John Sevier established his farm residence at Marble Springs in 1792. He and his second wife, Catherine "Bonny Kate" Sherrill Sevier, spent time in the three-room log dwelling with several of their youngest children, as well as at their fine residence in Knoxville, until his death in 1815.

The Sevier's courtship is said to have begun during a surprise Indian attack as Catherine was milking a cow outside the walls of Fort Watauga (Fort Caswell) in northeast Tennessee. Settlers inside the fort quickly closed the gates, unintentionally locking her out. Bonny Kate outran the attackers and scurried up the walls of the stockade into the waiting arms of Sevier, who pulled her to safety while shouting, "Jump, my Bonny Kate! Jump!" Twenty-six-year-old Catherine married John Sevier in 1780, shortly after the death of John's first wife, Sarah Hawkins Sevier.

Catherine "Bonny Kate" Sherrill Sevier became the first "first lady" of the newly formed state of Tennessee. Bonnie Kate held the title "first lady" six times (totaling twelve years): from 1785 to 1788, when her husband was governor of the short-lived State of Franklin, and during his terms as the first and third governor of Tennessee, 1796–1801 and 1803–9.

Bonny Kate Sevier not only cared for their eight children—Catherine, Ruth, George Washington, Samuel, Polly, Eliza, Joanna, and Robert—but she also spun flax into wool for the uniforms her husband and two sons wore in the Battle of Kings Mountain.

Originally buried in Russellville, Alabama, with the help of Daughters of the American Revolution, Catherine "Bonny Kate" Sherrill Sevier was reinterred in 1922 next to her husband on the lawn of the old Knox County Courthouse in Knoxville.

Address and Contact Information
Marble Springs State Historic Site
1220 W. Governor John Sevier Highway
Knoxville, TN 37920
(865) 573-5508
(865) 712-9076
www.marblesprings.net

Timeless Recipes

Sevier once captured thirty Indians. Not knowing
what to do with them he brought them to Marble
Springs. The Indians liked their "prison"
(and no doubt Bonny Kate's fine cooking)
so well they refused to leave.

—*Country Cookin' Cookbook,*
Governor John Sevier Farm Home

Early pioneer methods of planting were not original. Everything from cooking techniques to growing corn and building log homes was taught to settlers by Native Americans or brought to America from England.

Sevier learned to cultivate sorghum, white sweet potatoes, and sugar beets, as well as pole beans, root vegetables such as white potatoes and turnips, and members of the gourd family such as pumpkins and a variety of squash on his acreage. Still, corn was the primary crop on John Sevier's Marble Springs farmstead, as it was in Tennessee country before and after statehood.

Livestock, including beef, lamb, hogs, geese, and chickens, were cared for by the ten to twenty African American enslaved workers at Marble Springs. Surely the Seviers grew herbs in their kitchen garden, not just for seasoning food but for medicinal purposes.

MENU
Indian Pudding
Three Sisters' Stew with Pork and Corn Dumplings
Sorghum Caramel Corn

INDIAN PUDDING
Mrs. Sarah Hawkins Sevier did not live to see Marble Springs, yet it's fitting to share a recipe she would have served John and their children on the East Tennessee frontier. A close relative of England's "Hasty Pudding"—sweetened porridge made by boiling water or milk with wheat flour—Indian pudding is made with freshly ground cornmeal.

Adapted from Amelia Simmons's 1796 classic, *American Cookery*, this recipe for Indian pudding is baked in a 9-inch buttered pie pan, or an 8×8-inch buttered casserole dish, with cornmeal from Old-Mill.com.

Tidbits:
Serve Indian pudding with a scoop of ice cream, whipped cream, or maple syrup. A coveted sweetener on the east Tennessee frontier, maple syrup grew to be an industry before the turn of the century.

Tidbits, Too:
"White flint cornmeal fresh from the mill works best," according to Martha McCulloch-Williams's Dishes and Beverages of the Old South (1913).

Ingredients
2 cups half-and-half
1¼ cups cornmeal
6 tablespoons raisins
6 tablespoons sugar
1½ teaspoons each: ground cinnamon, nutmeg, cloves
3 tablespoons butter
3 eggs, lightly beaten

Directions
Preheat the oven to 350°F. In a medium saucepan, heat the half and half over medium heat. Slowly add the cornmeal, whisking gently until fully incorporated and the mixture begins to thicken. Remove from the heat. Slowly whisk in the raisins, sugar, spices, and butter. Once well-blended, return the pan to the burner. Continue whisking until the mixture is fairly thick. Remove from the heat. In a mixing bowl, whisk the eggs. Add the egg to the cornmeal mixture, blending thoroughly with a wooden spoon. Pour the mixture into a greased, 9-inch pie plate or 8×8-inch, greased casserole dish.

Bake for 30 minutes or more. Insert a knife blade into the center of the pudding; if it comes out clean, it's done.
(Yields 8–9 servings.)

THREE SISTERS' STEW WITH PORK AND CORN DUMPLINGS

According to Cherokee legend, corn, beans, and squash are three inseparable sisters who only grow well and thrive when they're planted side by side. Corn, the straight and tall oldest sister, watches over her two siblings. Squash, the middle sister, flourishes low to the ground, her large leaves warming the feet of her older sister. Bean (or pea), the baby sister, is the weakest and grows up "hugging" her big sister, Corn, who provides support and protection.

Corn, beans, and squash complement each other nutritionally as well. Corn provides carbohydrates. Beans are rich in protein–offsetting the lack of amino acids in corn. Squash produces vitamins and delicious oil from its seeds.

The planting season of "three sisters" is marked by a festive ceremony commemorating the first harvest of green corn on the cob, called the Green Corn Dance, much like to the one attended by John Sevier after surveying the boundary lines in Alabama during his final days.

Incorporating the abundance of agriculture at Marble Springs, perhaps Bonny Kate served her husband, John, a nutritious bowl of three sisters stew. The following recipe includes pork and some delicious corn dumplings.

Ingredients
Stew
2 tablespoons vegetable oil
1-pound trimmed pork loin, cut into 1-inch cubes
1 teaspoon garlic, minced
1-pound butternut squash, peeled and cubed
2 medium red bell peppers, diced
2 cups corn, fresh or frozen
2 cups beef stock
2 cups tomatoes, diced
2 tablespoons tomato paste
2 cans pinto beans, drained
1 teaspoon chili powder
1 teaspoon cumin
1 teaspoon oregano
Salt and pepper to taste

Dumplings
½ cup yellow cornmeal
½ cup all-purpose flour

2 teaspoons baking powder
½ teaspoon salt
½ teaspoon sugar
1 egg
⅓ cup milk
1 tablespoon unsalted butter, melted
½ cup cooked fresh, thawed frozen, or drained canned corn kernels

Directions

For the Stew: In a cast-iron Dutch oven or stock pot, over medium heat on your stovetop, brown the pork cubes in the oil of your choice (I use vegetable oil) with salt, pepper, and garlic—being careful not to burn the garlic. Add the squash, onion, red pepper, and corn. Sauté until each vegetable is slightly tender. Add the beef stock. Bring the mixture to a simmer. Add the remaining ingredients. Simmer over low heat for 30 minutes. (Yields 12 servings.)

For Dumplings: In a large bowl, whisk together the cornmeal, flour, baking powder, salt, and sugar. In a small bowl or glass measuring cup, whisk together the egg, milk, and butter. Add the liquid to the dry mixture, stirring until just combined. Fold in the corn kernels until just combined. After the stew has simmered for 30 minutes, drop the batter by heaping tablespoons on top of the simmering stew. Cover and cook for another 15 minutes or until a wooden toothpick inserted into the center of dumplings comes out clean. With a serving ladle, allow one or two dumplings per bowl of stew.
(Yields 16 dumplings.)

SORGHUM CARAMEL CORN

Long before the invention of microwave popcorn, "Bonny Kate" Sevier may have had the perfect recipe for "campfire family fun" at Marble Springs: freshly popped Indian corn bathed in bacon bits from their hefty hogs, slathered in sorghum fresh from the field and tossed to popcorn perfection in a salty-sweet snack.

Ingredients
Two 3.2-ounce bags microwave popcorn, popped and ready
    (24 cups popped)
1½ cups crisply fried bacon, chopped into bits (1 pound bacon)
1 cup unsalted roasted peanuts (optional)
1 cup (2 sticks) butter, melted
2 cups firmly packed, light brown sugar
½ cup sorghum syrup
1½ teaspoon salt
1 teaspoon baking soda
1 teaspoon pure vanilla extract

Directions
Preheat the oven to 250°F. Place the popcorn, bacon bits, and peanuts in a large, lightly oiled bowl. Melt the butter in a large cast-iron skillet. Stir in the brown sugar, sorghum syrup, salt, baking soda, and vanilla extract. Bring the mixture to a boil, stirring constantly with a wooden spatula. Boil without stirring for 3 minutes—or until a candy thermometer registers 240°F. Pour the sorghum mixture over the popcorn mixture and stir until thoroughly coated. Divide the mixture between 2 lightly greased, 15×10-inch jellyroll pans and spread into a thin layer. Bake at 250°F for 1 hour, stirring every 15 minutes. Cool completely (about 45 minutes) on wire racks sprayed with cooking spray. Break into pieces and serve.
(Yields 4–6 servings.)

> ***Tidbits:***
> *For a less clumpy mixture, stir the popcorn in the jelly roll pan constantly for 5 minutes after removing from the oven.*

John Sevier's Timeless Recipe: A Cure for Rheumatism

John Sevier believed in a holistic approach to treating illness. He kept recipes on hand to cure everything from an "Abscess to Whooping Cough," as shown in his *Journal of John Sevier (1745–1815)*. Perhaps this is one of the reasons why Sevier employed the services of Dr. William P. Chester, founder of the Chester Inn in Jonesborough: both men preferred natural remedies for "what ails you."

In a letter to his son George, John Sevier prescribed his cure for rheumatism (the opening quotation of this chapter), suggesting a dip in the burbling, pure water of Marble Springs, along with the following instructions:

Take a handful of the inside bark of prickly ash 6 inches long, the same quantity of red earthworms, and about the same quantity of both those articles of the oil of hog's feet, & stew all slowly together until the worms are dissolved: strain out the sediment and anoint with the oil.

Chapter 8

HAWTHORN HILL STATE HISTORIC SITE

◆——◆

Built ca. 1805
Castalian Springs, Tennessee

Taproots

It afforded me very great pleasure indeed to know that
you were all so comfortably situated around our old
family hearthstone . . . where so many desolate have
been comforted, where so many have been fed and
where so many weary travelers have found rest.

—Humphrey Bate Sr. to his mother, 1866

Standing in stately repose, amid red cedar trees and scrub bushes, Hawthorn Hill was home to five generations of the Humphrey Howell Bate family. Colonel Humphrey Howell Bate, a veteran of the War of 1812, served in Troop No. 3 of the Tennessee Volunteer Calvary. Troop No. 3 was led by Colonel John Coffee in the Natchez Expedition of 1813. Bate's decendants include a Civil War veteran; an internationally known countess; the man whose band, the Possum Hunters, was an original member of the Grand Ole Opry; and a Confederate general, United States senator, and Tennessee governor.

Hawthorn Hill was so named for the Hawthorn shrubs *(Crataegus monogyna)* growing prolifically across its arable acreage. The two-story brick structure is an expression of early-nineteenth-century craftsmanship, and its design is representative of the antebellum rural farmhouse

Hawthorn Hill State Historic Site.

(*antebellum* is a Latin phrase meaning "before the war"—in particular, the Civil War). Elegant, Federal-style architecture enhances its decorative Flemish bond brickwork—popular during Tennessee's early settlement era. The doorsteps, now over two centuries old, are made of white ash. Its walls are joined by original pegs, roughly hewn from pine. Stepping into the two-story structure, the room's wood mantle and brick hearth are original to the circa 1805 house, and decorative stenciling on the upper wall of the front room likely dates back to the 1820s. Upstairs, original graffiti of a Confederate flag and ladies in hoop skirts from the Civil War era adorn the walls untouched; this is amazing for a home having numerous owners and at times sitting abandoned. In fact, few major changes

This classic six-string guitar, circa 1899, was owned and played by Sewell Chenault in Dr. Humphrey Bate's first band, the Castalian Springs Band.

have been made to the house since being owned by the Bate family. The outbuildings—a kitchen, at least three slave cabins, a smokehouse, a carriage house, a stone fence, and later additions—did not survive.

Hawthorn Hill is situated on a 10.45-acre plot and retains 4.38 acres of original agricultural pasture west of the house. The initial 400-acre plot was received by Charles Carter of Sumner County in 1795. This was a land grant from North Carolina for his service in the Revolutionary War. Carter moved to Smith County (named for Daniel Smith, surveyor, senator, and builder of his magnificent home, Rock Castle, now a state historic site in Sumner County) and began selling portions of his land. Carter deeded 208 acres to John Bearden, who likely began construction on the brick house. In 1817, Colonel Humphrey Howell Bate purchased the property and moved to the home with his first wife, Elizabeth Pollock Brimage, and two of their surviving five children; James H. and Thomas West Bate. Three years after moving to Hawthorn Hill, Elizabeth died.

Colonel Bate later married Anne Franklin Weathered, the daughter of William Weathered (owner of nearby Locust Grove Plantation), on her seventeenth birthday. Their union produced nine children—eight of whom reached adulthood: Mary Eliza Spivey (1823–1883), Eugenia Patience (1826–1906, later Countess Eugenia Patience Bass Bertinatti), Willa Anne (1828–1859), William George Weathered (1831–1912), Agnes Elizabeth (1834–1920), Amanda Malvina (1836–1872), Henry Clay (1839–1917), Humphrey Howell Jr. (1844–1911), and Aaron Spivey (1846–1863).

Several Bate family members became distinguished Tennesseans. James H. Bate, elder son of Elizabeth and Colonel Bate Sr., settled in the Castalian Springs community and built a beautiful brick home in 1839–40 on Rock Springs Road.

Born at Hawthorn Springs, James's son, William Brimage Bate (1826–1905), enlisted in the Confederate Army. He was promoted to brigadier general in 1862 and was eventually elected twenty-sixth governor of Tennessee in 1882 and 1884. William also served as a United States senator, dying in office.

Eugenia, one of Colonel Bate's daughters, married Council Bass, a wealthy Mississippi plantation owner in 1842. Widowed in 1855, Eugenia married Chevalier Guiseppi Bertinatti, Italy's 1865 ambassador to the United States. They lived at his family estate near Turin and at The Hague in Holland.

Dr. Humphrey Howell Bate Jr. carried on his father's medical practice at Hawthorn Hill. He eventually built a new home and moved the practice a half mile east of Hawthorn Hill. Dr. Bate Jr. was an original member of the Grand Ole Opry.

Address and Contact Information
Hawthorn Hill State Historic Site
495 Old Highway 25
Castalian Springs, TN 37031
Call Wynnewood State Historic Site for further information,
(615) 452-5463

Timeless Recipes

For nearly eleven years, Dr. Bate and his "Possum
Hunters" opened our radio program in WSM's first
studio. It is now housed in a tabernacle which seats
four thousand people. . . .

—George D. Hay, American radio personality and founder of the
original Grand Ole Opry radio program on WSM-AM in Nashville,
Our Shield Magazine, June 22, 1936

Dr. Humphrey Howell Bate Jr. discovered a timeless recipe for a life well
lived: love people, share your passion, and place service above self.

When Humphrey Bate Jr. was a boy growing up at Hawthorn Hill,
a former enslaved worker piqued his interest in music when he showed
him how to play a few simple tunes on the harmonica. From that moment
on, young Bate continued to hone his skills—performing on steamboats
running up and down the Cumberland River. During those years, he developed his musical repertoire, from classical to folk music, as he honed
his own trademark sound. Dr. Humphrey Howell Bate Jr. became one of
the foremost contributors to the early development and growth of country
music.

Following in his father's footsteps, the younger Dr. Bate served in the
Medical Corps during the 1898 Spanish American War, having gradu-
ated from the University of Nashville Medical School (later Vanderbilt
University Medical School) in 1897.

After serving in the war, Dr. Bate—despite offers to move to "the
city"— returned to Castalian Springs to take over his father's medical
practice at Hawthorn Hill. Even as his musical interests increased, he
didn't pay serious attention to music as a career until around 1925, when
he finally put his band together.

As the lead harmonica player, Bate added Stanley Walton and Burt
Hutcherson on guitar; Oscar Albright on bowed string bass; Albright's
son, Buster, on guitar, harmonica, Jew's harp, and tipple (a small chor-
dophone guitar); Oscar Stone on fiddle; and Walter Ligget on banjo. Bate
invited his daughter, Alcyone, to join the band as a vocalist who played

ukulele and piano. Alcyone Bate (Beasley) is recognized as the first female artist to perform on the Grand Ole Opry.

Dr. Bate and his string band performed on one of the newly established country radio stations, WDAD in Nashville, until October 1925, when he and his band, along with Uncle Dave Macon, played a benefit show at the Ryman Auditorium. Originally named the Union Gospel Tabernacle by saloon owner and wealthy riverboat captain Thomas Ryman, the building was constructed in 1892 by Captain Ryman as a tabernacle for the Reverend Samuel Jones to preach the gospel. Captain Thomas Ryman, after hearing Reverend Jones's fiery rhetoric on the death, burial, and resurrection of Jesus Christ one Sunday morning, was a changed man.

After several years and a litany of prestigious guests and events, the tabernacle was renamed the Ryman Auditorium in 1904 to honor Captain Ryman. The benefit show was broadcast over WSM radio one week before the arrival of George Dewey Hay, known on the Opry as "The Solemn Ol' Judge." WSM, a company radio station founded in 1925 by Nashville-based National Life and Accident Insurance Company, used the first letters of their three-word advertising motto, "We Shield Millions," as call letters.

By 1926, Dr. Bate became a regular on the WSM "barn dance" program, which later became the Grand Ole Opry. While the Bate band is not considered one of the founders of the Grand Ole Opry, the string-band music they produced was a key factor in developing the show, which influenced several other artists, such as the Crook Brothers and Uncle Dave Macon. "The Ol' Solemn Judge," George D. Hay, later named Bate's band the "Possum Hunters."

George D. Hay considered Dr. Bate "Dean of the Opry" because of his keen ear for good music, his genuine interest in people, and his ability to recruit new artists, which helped expand the Opry's musical repertoire. Dr. Bate utilized large orchestras featuring popular individual soloists—a first on the Opry.

With his appreciation for different genres of music, Humphrey Bate Jr. began recruiting "up-and-coming" artists, giving them exposure—a tradition that remains to this day. Among those recruited was DeFord Bailey, the first African American harmonica player on stage, later nicknamed the "Harmonica Wizard." The experiences Dr. Bate gained growing up in the rural setting of Hawthorn Hill helped him develop his musical interests and enabled him to be a guiding light and friend to gifted musicians.

Known for his love of fried pies and country ham with biscuits and red-eye gravy, Dr. Humphrey Howell Bate Jr. would appreciate this timeless menu featuring his favorite foods.

MENU
Cathead Biscuits
Country Fried Ham with Red Eye Gravy
Hominy Grits
Sorghum Butter
Hawthorn Jelly
Quince Preserve Fried Pie

CATHEAD BISCUITS
Named for the way they bake up as "big as a cat's head," this dough can be pinched off in handfuls and rounded out, cut out with a biscuit cutter, or shaped the old-fashioned way using a sizeable tin can. A 3- or 4-inch coffee can works well here.

No one knows exactly when this baked good grew (so to speak) into today's giant-sized phenomenon. But as sure as there were fried pies at the Opry, Dr. Bate partook of the crispy crust and fluffy crumb of this biscuit—sopping up some red-eye gravy goodness.

Ingredients
2¼ cups soft winter wheat, low-protein flour
½ teaspoon baking soda
1 teaspoon salt
2 teaspoons Rumford Baking Powder (contains no aluminum)
5 tablespoons unsalted butter, chilled
1 tablespoon bacon grease
1 cup cold buttermilk

Directions
Preheat the oven to 375°F. In a large bowl, sift together the dry ingredients. Work the butter and bacon grease into the flour until the mixture

resembles coarse meal. Make a small well in the center of the flour mixture and pour in the buttermilk. Blend together with a rubber spatula until a soft dough forms. Turn the dough out onto a generously floured board and knead 4 or 5 times. Pinch off a portion of the dough about the size of an extra-large egg and pat out with your hands. Or roll the dough out to ½-inch thickness and cut out biscuits with a 4 to 6-inch cutter. Place the biscuits with the sides touching on a lightly greased cookie sheet. Bake for 12–15 minutes or until those "heads" are golden brown. (Yields 6 "catheads.")

COUNTRY HAM AND RED EYE GRAVY

Before Dr. Bate Sr. and his enslaved workers went about the business of working his 208 acres of wheat, rye, corn, and sorghum cane—as well as tending a varying number of sheep, hogs, and cattle—Lucinda "Aunt Cindy" Stanfield, their faithful cook and housekeeper, prepared fine hearty breakfasts, one of which became young Humphrey's forever favorite meal.

Aunt Cindy continued to live at Hawthorn Hill as a freed person long after the din of Civil War cannon fire subsided.

Ingredients
1 tablespoon bacon grease
⅔ cup fatty ham scraps
1 teaspoon all-purpose flour
1 cup strong black coffee
Four ¼-inch-thick slices of hickory-smoked country ham with fat rind
Pepper to taste

Directions
Heat the bacon grease in a medium skillet over medium heat. Fry the ham scraps until browned (about 5 minutes). Remove to a plate, reserving grease in the pan. Fry the ham slices in the reserved grease, turning both sides until just browned, about 5 minutes per side. Reduce the heat and simmer until the ham slices are slightly crusty on both sides. Remove the ham from the skillet. Set aside. Cover to keep warm. Reduce the

heat to medium-low and sprinkle the flour over the pan drippings. Cook and whisk for 2 minutes. Increase the heat to medium-high and pour the strong black coffee into the pan using a wooden spatula to scrape up bits of ham stuck to the bottom of the skillet. Turn the heat back to medium-low and simmer, whisking until the flour and fat are combined and thickened. Return the ham to the pan to warm through. Sprinkle with pepper. Serve immediately.
(Yields 4 servings.)

HOMINY GRITS

Hominy grits, or "grits," as they're called in the South, are dried kernels of white or yellow corn—hull and germ removed—ground into tiny grains and boiled in water until they reach the consistency of smooth, creamy porridge. A more finely ground hominy produces cornmeal, corn flour being the most finely ground.

"Grits" can be nestled near scrambled eggs or under eggs cooked "sunny-side up." They're delicious topped with a lump of country butter or with your favorite cooked greens, cheese, and shellfish. Or, as Dr. Bate might have preferred, plated under some country fried ham saturated with red-eye gravy.

Ingredients
1 cup water
¼ cup white or yellow stone-ground corn grits
Generous pinch of salt

Directions
Bring 1 cup of water to a boil. Stir in the grits and salt. Simmer on low heat, covered, for about 30 minutes, stirring occasionally. Add water if the mixture is too thick. Stir. Serve immediately with a pat of butter, sprinkled generously with black pepper.
(Yields 4 servings.)

Tidbits:
Pour the cooked grits into a loaf pan and refrigerate until firm. Remove the "grit loaf" from the pan and cut into slices. Coat with melted butter and sear on both sides in a skillet until browned and warmed through. Serve "grit cakes" as a side dish with meals. A drizzle of sorghum syrup works well here.

SORGHUM BUTTER

Sweet sorghum cane is a subtropical grass, first imported to America from Africa in 1853. The production of sorghum syrup became a major Tennessee byproduct by the late nineteenth century.

To this day, sorghum syrup makers abide by traditional procedures —utilizing refitted nineteenth-century sugar-cane processing machinery and feeding raw cane through the machinery by hand.

Hawthorn Hill is noted for having raised "cane" on its acreage. To reap a fall harvest, Colonel Bate would have planted sorghum seed the first week in May, when the ground was dry enough and the weather was warm.

Perhaps he produced the sweet syrup, deemed ready when its thick boiling juice coats the back of the ladle.

Ingredients
1 cup butter (2 sticks), softened
½ cup sorghum syrup

Directions
Stir together the butter and syrup until well combined. Serve immediately or keep chilled in a glass container for up to one month.

HAWTHORN JELLY

Hawthorn Hill was named for the abundance of Hawthorn shrubs bearing small, red, oblong fruit, growing prolifically across the hillsides and swales of the Bate homestead.

"Haws"—the fruit produced by hawthorn shrubs—although edible, are mostly used in cakes, pies, jams, and jellies. When picked in early spring, their delicate white-and-fuchsia blossoms and young leaves can be added to salads. Hidden within its branches, however, are long, sharp, thorns guarding red, bedecked fruit. These thorns are thought to be of a variety used in the "crown of thorns" placed on Christ's head at his crucifixion. The Hawthorn shrub is ideal as a hedge. Dr. Bate may have used "haws" for medicinal purposes such as treating high blood pressure.

Today the Hawthorn shrub has all but disappeared, making haws difficult to find. The flowering quince, however, produces fruit prolifically throughout Sumner County.

We will never know whether Aunt Cindy filled her fried pies with hawthorn jelly. But Dr. Humphrey Howell Bate Jr. would surely appreciate both fruit fillings from his homestead.

Ingredients
2 pounds (1 quart) of hawthorn berries (haws),
    stalk, twigs, and leaves removed
2 cups hawthorn berry juice
2 cups granulated sugar
Juice of one large lemon (I prefer Meyer lemons)

Directions
Wash and drain the haws. Place the haws into a heavy saucepan and cover with 2 cups of water. Bring the water and the berries to a boil. Turn the heat down and simmer the berries for 1 hour, mashing the berries with a potato masher every 20 minutes. Using cheese cloth, muslin, or a jelly bag, strain the berry pulp overnight, allowing the hawthorn berry juice to drip into a glass container. In a heavy saucepan, combine the sugar and lemon juice. Add the strained hawthorn juice. Stir to combine. Boil the sugar/berry juice/lemon mixture at a rapid boil for 10 minutes, stirring constantly, until the jelly has thickened. Skim off any foam from the jelly mixture. Pour into sterilized jars and screw on the lids. (Yields 1 pint jar of clear jelly or two ½-pint jars.)

Tidbits:
Pie dough for quince preserves can be used for hawthorn jelly fried pies.

QUINCE FRIED PIE
Flowering quince grows more prolifically today in Castalian Springs than the once ubiquitous hawthorn shrub. In his 1987 classic book, *Southern Food: At Home, on the Road, and in History,* award-winning writer, journalist, and southern food historian John Egerton describes the flowering quince, or *Chaenomeles,* as "rock hard, fairly dry, and sour as can be at 2 inches in diameter. They're still good as a source of pectin and acid for preserves and hardier and less disease prone than *Cydonia oblonga* (or, common quince.)" If quince cannot be found, Tennessee pears such as the Ayres (named for Dr. Brown Ayres, president of the University of Tennessee from 1904 to 1919) are a worthy substitute.

Ingredients
Quince Fried Pie Filling
4 large quince, washed, peeled, cored, quartered, and diced
1 tablespoon freshly squeezed lemon juice
¾ cup light brown sugar
2 tablespoons butter
¼ cup heavy cream
¼ teaspoon each: ground cinnamon, ground ginger, and ground nutmeg
¼ teaspoon salt
1 teaspoon vanilla extract

Dough
2 cups all-purpose flour
3 tablespoons sugar
1 teaspoon salt
1 cup (2 sticks) unsalted butter, cubed, ice cold
¼ to ½ cup ice water

Directions
For Preserves: Toss the quince in lemon juice to prevent browning. Drain. In a medium bowl, whisk together the brown sugar, flour, cinnamon, ginger, nutmeg, and salt. In a large saucepan combine the quince with the sugar, butter, cream, spices, and vanilla. Cook over medium heat, stirring frequently until the quince is tender and the mixture is caramelized (about 1 hour). Set aside to cool before assembling the pies.

For Dough Preparation: In a medium bowl, whisk together the flour, sugar and salt. Cut in the butter until the mixture resembles coarse crumbs. Dribble in just enough ice water so that when mixed, the dough just comes together. Turn the dough out onto a lightly floured surface and gather it into a mound. Knead the dough gently 2 or 3 times and divide it into 2 equal portions. Shape the portions into disks and wrap each one in plastic wrap. Refrigerate the disks for about 30 minutes while preparing the filling.

Rolling Out the Dough: On a large floured countertop, roll out each pie crust disk (separately) to about ⅛-inch thickness. Using a round 3-inch cookie cutter (or glass or small bowl), cut the dough into circles and place them on a parchment-lined baking sheet to chill for at least 30 minutes. Place 2 teaspoons of cooled quince filling into the center of each chilled dough circle. With your fingertips, wet the edges of each circle with water. Fold the dough over the filling, wet the outside edges, and use the tines of a fork to seal the edges. Place the pies on a platter by the stove. Place a wire rack over a paper-towel-lined baking sheet for the pies after they are fried. Place a medium-sized bowl of sugar or confectioner's sugar next to the pies.

Frying the Pies: You'll need 2 cups of clarified butter or peanut oil for frying. In a 12-inch cast-iron skillet, heat the oil over medium-high heat to 350°F. Carefully slide 2 or 3 pies into the hot oil. They should sizzle. Fry for 1 to 2 minutes. With a slotted spatula, carefully flip the pies and fry for another 1 or 2 minutes until they are golden brown. Carefully transfer the pies to the prepared baking sheet. Repeat with the remaining pies. Roll the hot pies in sugar to coat them thoroughly or sprinkle them with a dusting of confectioner's sugar. Set them on a wire rack to cool.
(Yields 16–20 pies.)

Tidbits:
Clarified butter lacks the water and milk proteins found in normal butter, which makes it less likely to splatter or burn.

Chapter 9

PRESIDENT JAMES K. POLK HOME AND MUSEUM STATE HISTORIC SITE

◆———————————————————————◆

Built 1816
Columbia, Tennessee

Taproots

Under the benignant Providence of Almighty God, the
representatives of the States and the people are again
brought together to deliberate for the public good.

—President James Knox Polk

Known throughout his life as a man of high moral integrity, clear vision, and purpose, James Knox Polk is highly regarded as a United States president. Today's historians consider him to be among the top twelve presidents. At age forty-nine, he became the youngest president to enter the White House at the time.

Although recognized as governor of Tennessee (1839–41), chairman of the Ways and Means Committee, and Speaker of the House in 1835, James K. Polk became nationally known as the Democratic "Dark Horse" candidate with his unexpected selection by political colleagues to run for the presidency. Polk captured 50 percent of the popular vote and 170 electoral ballots, defeating the expected victor, Henry Clay, who opposed the annexation of Texas, a political "hot potato."

Considered the last strong pre–Civil War president, Polk established four basic goals for his administration: reduce the tariff (government-imposed taxes on imports or, less often, exported goods), build an

The James K. Polk Ancestral Home.

independent federal treasury, settle the boundaries of the Oregon Territory with the British, and acquire the territories of Texas and California. During his four-year presidency, Polk accomplished his goals and oversaw the founding of the United States Naval Academy and the Smithsonian Institute.

Historian and political advisor Arthur M. Schlesinger Jr. once said, "A coldly practical man, Polk set for himself certain precise objectives to be achieved while he was president. And achieve them he did during his single term of office from 1845–1849. To get Oregon and Washington for the country, he risked the threat of war with Great Britain. He did go to war with Mexico to acquire California and most of the territory of the present states of our Southwest including Texas and the state of Wisconsin."

By the end of his presidency, James K. Polk had acquired over 800,000 square miles of western land, doubling the size of United States territory, including Arizona, Nevada, California, and Utah, as well as sections of New Mexico and Colorado.

Polk also approved a compromise with Great Britain for the land that is now Idaho, Oregon, Washington, and parts of Wyoming and Montana. With the expansion of U.S. borders from the Atlantic to the Pacific came the fulfillment of "Manifest Destiny"—a term coined by political writer and Democratic Party advocate John Louis O'Sullivan. The term describes the nineteenth-century belief in the United States that settlers were destined to extend the country's national territories from the Atlantic to the Pacific to enhance its social, political, and economic influence.

In the course of Polk's political career, he served as chief clerk of the Tennessee Senate, captain (and later colonel) of the Tennessee militia, a state representative, U.S. congressman, Speaker of the House, governor of Tennessee, and president of the United States. Polk chose George Mifflin Dallas (son of Alexander Dallas, U.S. treasury secretary under James Madison), mayor of Philadelphia, U.S. senator from Pennsylvania, and the man for whom the city of Dallas, Texas, is named, as his vice-presidential running mate.

Having promised to serve as a one-term president, Polk retired on March 5, 1849. While on his goodwill retirement tour, he contracted cholera in New Orleans and died in Columbia, Tennessee, on June 15, 1849, three short months after leaving office. He was just fifty-three years old.

Sarah Polk, his wife of twenty-five years, remained a widow for the next forty-three years of her life—and always dressed in black. She was awarded a five-thousand-dollar annual pension, a first for any First Lady.

THE POLK ANCESTRAL HOME

James Knox Polk's father, Samuel Polk, was a land surveyor, farmer, and military man. Samuel served in the War of 1812. Because money was hard to come by on the frontier, surveyors were usually paid in land grants. Ambitious and entrepreneurial, Sam Polk began amassing large

The dining room featuring original items
from the White House and Polk Place.

tracts of land in Maury County, Tennessee. His enormous success as a
surveyor and farmer— raising livestock and growing tobacco, cotton,
and corn—would enable him to send his son, James, to the best schools
in the area and to the University of North Carolina at Chapel Hill, where
he graduated with honors in 1818.

Samuel Polk, now a wealthy, respected member of his community, grew
weary of the twelve-mile round-trip buckboard ride from his farm to the
public square of Columbia. This prompted him to purchase additional
land in town, including a piece of prime real estate near the public square.
In 1816, what is now the James K. Polk Ancestral Home was constructed
on the edge of Columbia. At that time, the town's population was just
three hundred.

Many homes around the square were pieced together, mostly from
logs cut from surrounding timberland. But wood, even when covered with
clapboard, proved an unreliable source of security. Bricks provided a perfect (albeit expensive) substitute. For his two-story home, Samuel utilized
an eighteenth-century pattern of brick laying known as Flemish bond.

The detached period kitchen has been beautifully reconstructed
across the brick courtyard of the home.

The Polk home was considered the finest building in Columbia. Imagine
James's surprise when, after two years away at college, he returned home
to Columbia and found his family home was no longer a small log cabin
in the surrounding prairie where he had grown up but the most beautiful
building in town!

Polk's perception of his father and grandfather—who traded moderate
success in North Carolina for greater success in Tennessee—may have
provided seed for his idea of westward opportunity and expansion. For
James Knox Polk, the West signified opportunity based on the premise
that if you keep pushing westward, you can make a better life for yourself.
This became a driving force throughout his presidency.

POLK'S BURGEONING POLITICAL CAREER

During two years in the finest local schools in Murfreesboro—Tennessee's state capitol from 1819 to 1825—Polk's strict work ethic enabled
him to excel in his studies. After enrolling in the University of North
Carolina at Chapel Hill as a sophomore in 1816, he more than lived up

to the reputation he had earned as a scholar and man of honor in Tennessee. His active membership on the college debate team helped earn him the nickname "Napoleon of the Stump" during his political career and piqued his interest in the study and practice of law. Perhaps Polk and his college roommate, William Dunn Mosely, Florida's first governor, encouraged each other in the study of jurisprudence. John Y. Mason, a fellow classmate and friend at UNC, later served as attorney general in Polk's presidential cabinet.

When he returned to Columbia at twenty-three years of age, and after living for several years at his parent's home, Polk began serving as law clerk for the renowned trial attorney Felix Grundy in Nashville. Grundy was a man of considerable importance (Grundy County, Tennessee, is named for him). Through Grundy's powerful political connections, Polk became acquainted with and remained a staunch supporter and friend of Andrew Jackson. Polk even earned the nickname "Young Hickory." Felix Grundy continued to mentor Polk throughout his political career.

While clerking for Grundy, Polk was chosen clerk of the state senate and spent time in Murfreesboro. Admitted to the bar in 1820, he opened his first law office in a log structure two blocks from his home in downtown Columbia, paid for and built by his father. Samuel Polk also purchased James's first set of law books. A rough-hewn log replica of Polk's law office stands on its original site today and is open to the public.

In 1823, while Polk was in Murfreesboro during his first year in the Tennessee General Assembly, Andrew Jackson introduced him to Sarah Childress. A courtship ensued. On January 1, 1824, Sarah Childress, aged twenty, married James Knox Polk, aged twenty-eight, in a well-attended outdoor ceremony on the lawn of her parents' plantation in Rutherford County.

Polk's political career rose rapidly after he married Sarah, who was considered the most politically dominant wife since Abigail Smith Adams. In an age when a woman's life was confined to childbearing and homemaking, Sarah and James remained childless—perhaps because of Polk's ill-advised childhood gallbladder operation, which he survived with no anesthetic. Yet, having no children allowed them to focus time and energy on Polk's burgeoning political career.

Mr. and Mrs. James K. Polk purchased Felix Grundy's beautiful mansion in Nashville, renaming it "Polk Place." Mrs. Polk continued living at Polk Place for the remainder of her life—forty-two years beyond her husband's death. James K. and Sarah Childress Polk are buried on the grounds of the state capitol building in Nashville.

After his father's death in 1827, James executed the will to ensure his mother would remain in their beautiful Columbia home until her death in 1852. Samuel and Jane Knox Polk are buried in Greenwood Cemetery, Maury County, Tennessee. Samuel Polk's home remained in the family for many years. After being purchased by the State and Memorial Association in 1929, it was opened to visitors in 1930. Seven years later, the purchase of an additional portion of the original Polk lot permitted reconstruction of the dining room and kitchen on their original foundations. The detached period kitchen has been beautifully reconstructed across the brick courtyard from the home.

The James K. Polk Ancestral Home and Museum displays original furnishings, some of James and Sarah Polk's personal belongings, and over thirteen-hundred artifacts and documents, including Polk's books. Collectibles from his political campaign, the official notification of his election to the presidency, the Bible upon which Polk placed his hand as he was sworn into the presidency, the Polk White House china, and oil portraits of President and Mrs. Polk, rendered by George Peter Alexander Healy, are also featured at the museum. Healey, the most prolific and popular portrait artist of his era, is the earliest known photographer of the White House interior.

The state historic site also features the adjacent "Sister's House," which was home to two of Polk's sisters: Jane Maria Walker, whose husband James Walker was Columbia's first newspaperman and whose son, Joseph Knox Walker, served as President Polk's private secretary, and Ophelia Hays, wife of Dr. John Hays. Built in 1818, the charming brick dwelling serves as a visitor's center, museum, and gift shop.

In accordance with its purpose, the Polk Memorial Association and the State of Tennessee continue to perpetuate the memory of James Knox Polk, the eleventh president of the United States.

SARAH CHILDRESS POLK

Elizabeth Whitsett Childress and her husband Joel Childress, a prosperous plantation owner and surveyor, surrounded their daughters, Sarah and her older sister, Susanna, with wealth and refinement befitting upper-class women of the era. Believing in equal education for their children, the Childresses sent both daughters to Bradley Academy, the local private boy's academy's. The girls were tutored after the boys left for the day. Later, the sisters attended a fashionable school in Nashville, where they learned to play the piano and were introduced to the finest and most polished of Middle Tennessee society.

Wanting yet more for their daughters, the Childresses sent Susanna and Sarah—who had just turned fourteen—to the best girls' school in the South: the female academy conducted by the Moravians in Salem, North Carolina. Sarah and Susanna, accompanied by their eldest brother Andrew, traveled over five hundred miles on horseback to reach the Moravian Female Academy in Salem, North Carolina.

The strict moral code of the school and its unusually strong curriculum, which included English, grammar, Bible study, history, music, drawing, and sewing, were forever ingrained in Sarah and surely became an attractive part of her personality and nature.

While living in the White House, one of Mrs. Polk's most notable changes in protocol—still practiced today—was instructing the Marine Band to begin playing "Hail to the Chief" when President Polk entered the room at official functions. The First Lady wanted to ensure that guests notice her husband when he made his entrance, and while a strict traditionalist, Mrs. Polk oversaw the installation of the first gaslights at the White House.

As a warm, vivacious hostess, First Lady Sarah Childress Polk earned the admiration and esteem of leading figures of the day while maintaining an active social life—entertaining less lavishly than their predecessors, President John Tyler and his second wife, Julia Gardiner Tyler.

Address and Contact Information
President James K. Polk Home and Museum State Historic Site
301 W. 7th Street
Columbia, TN 38401
(931) 388-2354
www.jameskpolk.com

Timeless Recipes

If I should be so fortunate as to reach the White
House, I expect to live on twenty-five thousand dollars
a year and I will neither keep house nor make butter.

—First Lady Sarah Childress Polk
From *James K. Polk: A Biographical Companion*, 2001

After two-term president Thomas Jefferson left office March 4, 1809, Honoré Julien, Jefferson's French chef de cuisine, stayed in Washington to start a catering business. Chef Julien became the official White House chef in 1801, passing his culinary knowledge on to his son Auguste, who later had the opportunity to cater White House banquets during the Polk presidency.

Mrs. J. E. Dixon, the wife of a senator and a guest at one of the Polk's dinners, described the evening fare as offering more than 150 different items, "all in the French style." According to Mrs. Dixon, the menu included soup, fish, green peas, spinach, duck breast, turkeys, birds, oyster pies, potatoes like snowballs, croquettes poulet (chicken croquettes), pate de foie gras (duck and chicken liver), jellies, oranges and lemons, Charlotte Russe, ices and pink mud, sweet meats, and everything one can imagine, all served in silver dishes and tureens with the famous gold-plated knives, forks, and special spoons for dessert. President Polk ate little at these political affairs, preferring plainer fare such as corn pone and ham.

Family meals were another matter entirely. President and Mrs. Polk had brought their enslaved African American cook, Coakley (no other name mentioned), from Tennessee to the White House. Coakley, who kept the kitchen fireplaces stoked to assure a hot breakfast, lunch, and dinner for President and Mrs. Polk, slept in a room near the White House kitchen.

SELECTIONS FROM PRESIDENT POLK'S WHITE HOUSE DINNER MENU

Potage Crème d'Asperge (Cream of Asparagus Soup)
Chicken Croquettes with Béchamel Sauce

Duck Breast in Cherry-Port Wine Reduction
Snowball Potatoes
Charlotte Russe

POTAGE CRÈME D'ASPERGE
(CREAM OF ASPARAGUS SOUP)

When the White House's French chef prepared a menu for the steady stream of Polk's political dignitaries—friend and foe—the fare was often considered lavish, diverse, and, at times, exotic. While producing a daily "soup to nuts" menu, however, the chef bore in mind this president's preference for plain food, while still pleasing the palates of his guests—without the use of today's modern conveniences.

Asparagus, a springtime vegetable, could easily be replaced with corn in late summer, mushrooms in fall, and root vegetables, such as pumpkin or squash, in winter. Each could be well employed in this potage—a French word meaning "thick soup."

Ingredients
2 tablespoons butter
1 medium yellow onion, minced
8 ounces asparagus (30 or 40 spears; 2 cups, roughly chopped)
1 cup half and half
1 cup chicken stock
⅓ cup cooked short-grain white rice
Salt and pepper to taste

Directions
Melt the butter in a medium-sized saucepan over medium-low heat. Add the onions and sauté until they are translucent and begin to brown around the edges. Add the asparagus, milk, chicken stock, and cooked rice. Simmer over medium-low heat for 10 minutes or until the asparagus is soft. Set aside to cool or chill in the refrigerator for 15 minutes. Pour the soup into a blender and blend on low speed, slowly increasing to high speed. Once the soup has reached a creamy consistency, return it to the pot and reheat over medium-low heat. Add salt and pepper to taste.
(Yields 4 cups.)

CROQUETTES POULET (CHICKEN CROQUETTES) WITH BÉCHAMEL SAUCE

Croquettes (from the French *croquer*, "to crunch") are small, oval-shaped meat rolls, dipped in egg batter, rolled in breadcrumbs, and fried to crisp deliciousness. In this recipe, the chicken (*poulet*, in French) croquettes are drizzled with delicious béchamel sauce in the manner White House caterer Auguste Julien prepared them for President and Mrs. Polk over a century ago. Perhaps these croquettes were served on the elegant Polk White House china displayed today on the dining room table in the James K. Polk Ancestral Home.

Béchamel sauce, known in culinary circles as basic "white sauce," is seasoned with onion and nutmeg. The cream sauce is named after its originator, Louis Marquis de Béchamel, steward of Louis XIV of France.

Ingredients
Croquettes Poulet
2 tablespoons butter
3 tablespoons all-purpose flour
2 teaspoons ground mustard
¼ teaspoon salt
⅛ teaspoon pepper
1 cup milk
2 cups cooked, finely shredded chicken
¼ cup chopped green pepper
1 tablespoon minced parsley
1 tablespoon finely minced yellow onion
1 teaspoon lemon juice
¼ teaspoon paprika
Pinch of cayenne pepper (optional)
1½ cups dry bread crumbs
1 egg
2 tablespoons water
Oil for frying

Béchamel Sauce
5 tablespoons butter
5 tablespoons all-purpose flour
4 cups milk
½ teaspoons salt
½ teaspoon freshly grated nutmeg
Cracked pepper to taste

Directions
For the Croquettes: Melt the butter in a large saucepan over medium heat. Whisk in the flour, mustard, salt, and pepper until smooth. Gradually add milk, stirring constantly; bring to a boil. Continue stirring for 2 minutes until the mixture thickens. Remove from the heat. Add shredded chicken, green pepper, parsley, onion, lemon juice, paprika, and cayenne pepper. Refrigerate for 2 hours or more. Shape the chilled chicken mixture into six 4×1-inch logs. Pour the breadcrumbs into a shallow dish. In another dish, whisk together the egg and water. Roll the moist logs in bread crumbs (pressing the crumbs into the logs), then in the egg mixture, then again in breadcrumbs. Heat about 3 inches of peanut oil in a Dutch oven or deep fat fryer to 350°F. Lower the logs into the hot oil a few at a time. Fry for 1 to 2 minutes, turning until golden brown. Drain on paper towels. Serve immediately, drizzled with béchamel sauce.
(Yields 6 croquettes.)

For the Sauce: Heat the butter in a medium saucepan over medium-low heat. Slowly whisk in the flour. Continue whisking until the mixture (a "roux") turns a light-golden color (about 6 to 7 minutes). Heat the milk in a separate pan until almost boiling. Add the hot milk to the roux 1 cup at a time, whisking continuously until the mixture is very smooth. Bring the mixture to a boil. Lower the temperature to simmer. Simmer for 10 minutes, whisking constantly until the mixture thickens. Remove from the heat. Season with salt, pepper, and nutmeg. Stir. Set aside until ready to use. Pour over the chicken croquettes.
(Yields 4 cups.)

DUCK BREAST IN A CHERRY-PORT
WINE REDUCTION SAUCE

Duck breast, when served by Auguste Julien to White House dignitaries, was considered an exotic treat. Indeed, French cooking was perceived as beyond the skills of the American homemaker until, in the 1950s, Julia Child turned the spotlight on the simplicity of using wine and herbs to enhance the flavor of everything from roasted chicken to whipped cream desserts. And there's no need to brandish one's shotgun. Today's home cook has the obvious advantage of purchasing duck ready to *cuis* (French for "cook") along the trails of Tennessee . . . to the White House and back. The following recipe is adapted from my June 2009 edition of *Bon Appétit* magazine.

Ingredients

Two 4- to 6-ounce duck breasts (skin-on)

2 tablespoons cold butter, divided

¼ cup shallots, minced

1 large garlic clove, smashed and diced

½ teaspoon lemon thyme, finely minced

12 pitted sweet, red cherries, halved—fresh or frozen, thawed

½ cup chicken broth

3 heaping tablespoons tawny port wine
   (or substitute with apple juice, or cider)

1 tablespoon orange blossom honey

1 teaspoon cornstarch dissolved in two
   teaspoons water

Lawry's seasoned salt and ground pepper

> **Tidbits:**
> If you prefer duck breast "well done," finish the meat in a preheated, 425°F oven for 10 minutes. Spoon the sauce over the sliced meat when serving.

Directions

Using a sharp knife, score (slash) the skin in one-inch increments. Do not cut into the meat. Season the duck breast with seasoned salt and ground pepper. Melt 1 tablespoon butter, the garlic clove, and thyme in a large, cast-iron skillet over medium-high heat. Add the duck breast, skin side down, to the bubbling butter and cook until the skin is browned and crispy—about 5 minutes. Turn the breasts over, reduce the heat to

medium and cook until browned to desired doneness—about 5 minutes. Transfer to a platter to rest. "Tent" (prop up aluminum foil in an inverted "V" to cover and keep warm) the duck with foil for about 10 minutes. Pour off all but two heaping tablespoons of drippings from the skillet. Add the shallots and stir over medium heat for about 30 seconds. Add the broth, cherries, port wine, and honey. Increase the heat to medium-high. Continue to stir until the liquid reduces slightly. Add 1 tablespoon of butter. Allow it to melt. Whisk in the cornstarch mixture. Season with salt and pepper to taste. Thinly slice the duck. Spoon the sauce over the meat and serve immediately.
(Yields 2 servings.)

SNOWBALL POTATOES
White House Snowball Potatoes, served with pomp and circumstance, were stuffed with the finest French cheese.

Ingredients
4 large russet potatoes, peeled and quartered
1 tablespoon salt
4 ounces French brie or soft, white melting cheese, cubed
1 cup bread crumbs
Salt and pepper to taste

Directions
Preheat the oven to 375°F. Put the potatoes in a large pot filled with water until the potatoes are just covered. Add a tablespoon of salt. Bring the water to a rolling boil and cook until the potatoes are very soft (about 40 minutes). Drain the potatoes and mash them until smooth and creamy. Add salt and pepper to taste. Cut the white cheese into ½-inch cubes. Prepare a baking sheet with foil and coat with vegetable spray or rub with oil. Pour the bread crumbs into a small bowl. While the potatoes are still warm, form them into 2-inch balls and insert 1 cheese cube into each center. Roll the potato balls in the breadcrumb mixture until fully coated and place them on the greased cookie sheet. After every third ball, wash and dry your hands so that the potatoes will form evenly with no breadcrumbs sticking to your hands. Bake for 20 to 25 minutes.
(Yields 8 servings.)

CHARLOTTE RUSSE

Russian Charlotte, or Charlotte Russe (pronounced CHAR-lot rooce) is a cold dessert of Bavarian cream set in a baking dish lined with ladyfingers—an egg-based, sweet sponge cake shaped like a finger.

Some historians say the confection was invented by the famous nineteenth-century French chef Marie-Antonin Carême to honor Sofia Charlotte (1744–1818) of Mecklenburg-Strelitz, Germany, wife of King George III of Great Britain, and Carême's Russian employer at the time, Czar Alexander I (*Russe* being the French word for "Russian").

Serving Charlotte Russe at a White House soirée surely pleased President Polk, whose Mecklenburg County, North Carolina, birthplace—Charlotte, North Carolina—was so named to honor Queen Sofia.

Ingredients
1 envelope unflavored gelatin
3 tablespoons cold water
¼ cup dry sherry
1 tablespoon vanilla
1 cup whipping cream, stiffly whipped
2 large egg whites (room temperature)
¼ cup sugar
10 store-bought ladyfingers, split lengthwise
Fresh fruit slices or berries (optional)

> **Tidbits:**
> The success of this dessert lies in not overly whipping the egg whites.

Directions
In the top of a double-boiler over boiling water, dissolve the gelatin and cold water, stirring until the gelatin dissolves. Add the sherry and vanilla, stirring until combined. Let the mixture cool to room temperature. Gently fold the gelatin mixture into stiffly beaten whipped cream. Set it aside. Beat the egg whites in a medium mixing bowl until soft peaks form. While continuing to beat the egg whites, gradually add sugar, 1 tablespoon at a time, until they are stiff and glossy. Fold the beaten egg whites into the whipped cream mixture. Line the sides of a 1½-quart serving bowl with

ladyfingers (split the sides open facing the inside of the bowl.) Pour in the filling; chill until set. Garnish with fresh fruit slices, blueberries, raspberries, or the like. Spoon into individual serving bowls.
(Yields 6–8 servings.)

James K. Polk's Favorite Home-Cooked Food

Cornpone is said to have been one of James K. Polk's favorite foods. Introduced to frontier settlers by the Indians, cornpone, a rudimentary form of cornbread, is made from a thick, soft dough of ground corn and water. It's shaped by hand into a small cake and fried in a skillet over an open fire. 'Pone was a staple on Samuel Polk's breakfast, lunch, and dinner table and gobbled by his young son, James, when he was a barefoot boy living on his father's farm on the outskirts of Columbia. The delicious cake was likely a part of meals in the "finest home in Columbia."

This modern-day cornpone recipe employs baking powder and milk instead of water. Coakley, the Polk's enslaved cook, likely made 'pone for the president during his years at the White House—a welcome taste of home.

CORNPONE
Ingredients
1 cup yellow cornmeal
½ teaspoon salt
2 tablespoons bacon drippings
1 teaspoon baking powder
½ cup milk

Directions
In a medium bowl, whisk together the cornmeal, salt, and baking powder. Make a well in the center of the dry ingredients. Add the milk and bacon drippings. Stir well. Make 4 'pones (flattened circles) and drop them in a hot, greased, cast-iron skillet. Cook until golden brown, flipping each 'pone once. Serve immediately with butter, jelly, or honey.
(Yields 4 'pones.)

Chapter 10

SABINE HILL STATE HISTORIC SITE

◆————————————————————————————————————◆

Built 1818
Elizabethton, Tennessee

Taproots

Returning from the war in the South, General Taylor
soon turned his attention to the construction of a new
home in Happy Valley. There he had acquired a large
holding of lands. A part of this came from his father;
and the larger portions were purchased by him until
he owned there above 3,000 acres of land, covering
the major part of Happy Valley, so widely known in
Tennessee and the South for its natural charms and
historic background. . . . The house yet stands on an
eminence overlooking the Watauga.

—Samuel Cole Williams, "Brigadier-General Nathaniel Taylor"
East Tennessee Historical Society's Publications 12 (1940)

Sabine Hill is located in Carter County on a hill overlooking the western
entrance to Elizabethton (pronounced Eliza*beth*ton.) This site is the first
established democratic association of free American-born men and women
west of the Appalachians. The site is known as the Watauga Association
and Sycamore Shoals in the area known as Happy Valley.

Constructed by the War of 1812 veteran Brigadier General Nathaniel Taylor and his wife, Mary Patton Taylor, Sabine Hill was built circa

1818. The home was originally constructed on a foundation of sturdy logs—with the bark still attached—"with more attention to interior detail than that of its exterior," according to former Tennessee Supreme Court justice Samuel Cole Williams in his 1940 biographical article on Taylor. Williams further noted that Taylor's land had been the site of a 1775 treaty with the Cherokees; it was also the location of Fort Caswell (aka Watauga Fort), which was "attacked and besieged by the Indians" the following

This sweeping view of Sabine Hill State Historic Site includes the detached kitchen with its original chimney and fireplace behind the main residence.

year. In 1780, during the American Revolution, the Kings Mountain men rendezvoused at the site.

Taylor's Federal-style two-story frame dwelling was originally constructed to replicate the nearby Carter Mansion (ca. 1780). Constructed by John Carter and his son Landon Carter—early settlers along the Watauga River for whom Carter County is named—the Carter Mansion is the oldest frame house in Tennessee, and it was the first with glass windows.

The west parlor features original flooring and wainscoting.
The original ceiling, and trim around the doorframe (not pictured)
is of Prussian Blue. Two shades of red ochre, and a colonial blue
make up the wallpaper "medallions."

Typical of a Federal-style home, Sabine Hill has a symmetrical five-bay "nine-over-nine" front-window façade. It also boasts traditional mixed-width pine boards over hand-hewn timber hand-laid by Taylor's enslaved workers to support the flooring. Elaborate, delicately carved fireplace mantels feature hand-wrought wood trim. A charming fanlight transom was added over the front entrance several years later, and the original stairwell borders are tastefully engraved with ornate scroll-work. Flooring throughout the house is original. Today, reproduction glass fills the original "nine-over-nine" window frames.

Taylor family patriotism is reflected in their choice of interior paint colors, a tribute to the American flag—red molding, white walls, and Prussian-blue wainscoting (paneling on the lower part of a wall). The blue ceiling is original. Brick chimneys—fashioned in common bond style—grace each side of its weatherboard-siding exterior, which was replaced in the 1950s. As a result of a Historic American Building Survey (HABS) in 1936, Sabine Hill's split-shingle roof was replaced with galvanized iron.

General Nathaniel Taylor's father, Andrew Taylor Sr., came to the Watauga Settlements from Rockbridge County, Virginia, in 1776–77. Born in Armagh, Antrim, Ireland, around 1728–32, Andrew Sr. married Elizabeth Wilson—one of twin daughters of John Wilson, his first cousin—who bore ten children. When Elizabeth died, Andrew Sr. married her twin sister, Ann, who bore two children: Nathaniel and a daughter, Elizabeth.

Andrew Sr. received a land grant of 627 acres from Charles Robertson, Esq., and through several other land grants, he received another 481 acres on Buffalo Creek. He fought in the Battle of Kings Mountain with his son, Andrew Jr., taking part in the decisive victory over Major Patrick Ferguson and the British in the Revolutionary War.

Andrew Sr. wrote his will on May 22, 1787, and died sometime between May and November 30, 1787. He is buried in the old Taylor Cemetery in Carter County. He was the great-grandfather of Tennessee congressman Nathaniel Green Taylor as well as two Tennessee governors: Robert Love Taylor, 1887–91, 1897–99; and Alfred Alexander Taylor, 1921–23. Both were born in the Happy Valley area of Elizabethton. Their "brother-against-brother" race for governor—named for a similar familial military campaign in medieval England, the "War of the Roses"—is a colorful episode in Tennessee history.

General Nathaniel Taylor was born on February 4, 1771, at Mill Creek in Rockbridge County, Virginia. He began his military career by being elected sheriff and as one of the officers in Tennessee's state militia. At age twenty-two, as a militia captain, he fought the Cherokees around the Nolichucky River (Unicoi County) in 1793.

Among his many battles, Taylor and his mounted troops chased the Cherokees to the French Broad River. They later joined forces with General John Sevier—future first governor of Tennessee—and his men, who were on their way to Georgia for another bloody conflict with the Indians.

When Carter County was formed from a pocket of Washington County on April 9, 1796, Nathaniel Taylor owned nearly fifteen hundred acres of prime real estate. He inherited some of the land from his father and purchased some from his neighbor John Tipton. Elizabethton, originally named Tiptonville, was renamed to honor Landon Carter's grandmother, Elizabeth McLin Carter.

When General Taylor died in 1816, two years before Sabine Hill was finished, his wife, Mary "Polly" Patton Taylor, finished the home around 1818. Sabine Hill served as home and headquarters of the Taylor family estate, with their more than twenty enslaved workers, for decades. Mary Taylor outlived her husband by thirty-seven years, presiding over Sabine Hill until her death in 1853.

Today, Sabine Hill is situated on four acres of rolling hills. The structure's evolution from endangered relic to restored living history has been a lengthy process. Although the Taylor family remained the technical property owners, family members vacated the home at some point during the late nineteenth century, relinquishing their property rights around 1947.

In 2007, having passed through various owners and a plethora of repairs and alterations, Sabine Hill was nearly sold to a developer who planned to demolish the historic structure to build condominiums. The fine citizens of Elizabethton, unwilling to let go of their treasured antiquity, purchased the dilapidated historic home.

In 2008, the Tennessee Historical Commission acquired Sabine Hill. Residents of Elizabethton, endeavoring to raise money toward the restoration of the home and property, began holding fundraisers. Their goal was fully realized in 2012 when the Tennessee General Assembly awarded the Tennessee Historical Commission $1.1 million for research and restoration of Sabine Hill. Meticulous research ensued in an effort to restore Sabine Hill to its original grandeur.

Mathew J. Mosca, a nationally recognized consultant in the field of historic paint research and restoration, sampled paint from all the mantels. Using the samples, he created paint recipes to match the mansion's original colors. According to Mosca, a mere thirty-eight years before the construction of Sabine Hill—as the Overmountain Men mustered for the Battle of King's Mountain—the world of "color" consisted of drab, basic browns and pale yellows made from walnut-dye and plant pigments.

Two years after the War of 1812 ended, however, Scottish scientist Sir David Brewster invented the kaleidoscope—a tube containing loose pieces of colored glass which, when reflected by mirrors or glass lenses set at an angle, creates delightful color patterns. Brewster named his kaleidoscope after the Greek words *kalos* (beautiful), *eidos* (form), and *scopos* (watcher). His "beautiful form watcher" invited folks into a world they might never have imagined. This new technology forever changed the way people interacted with their surroundings. Mesmerized by unique colors and excited about the freedom and possibilities they might experience, people began designing fabrics and accoutrements in bright colors and patterns like the colors and patterns adorning the interior of Sabine Hill.

Upon discovering that the walls in Sabine Hill were made of wood and that three different wallpapers had been papered over old plaster, the Tennessee Historical Commission enlisted the help of Adelphi Paper Hangings of Sharon Springs, New York. The company specializes in reproducing wallpaper from original documents, which are, in turn, hand-printed by skilled artisans using the same methods and materials employed in the eighteenth and nineteenth centuries. Wallpaper was re-created based on what was known about the frontier in Washington County and North Carolina—actually, Tennessee by then—and what papers were being used at that time. Red ochre and a version of Prussian blue grace the walls of Sabine Hill today—with Mathew J. Mosca providing original color design recipes.

Beautiful, historic Sabine Hill, once a faded photograph in Tennessee history, flung open its elegantly fashioned front doors in the fall of 2017.

Address and Contact Information
Sycamore Shoals State Historic Area, Sabine Hill State Historic Site
2328 West G Street
Elizabethton, TN 37643
(423) 543-5808

Timeless Recipes

I give my large Bible containing the family record to
my son, A. W. Taylor and the balance of my Bibles to
Mary Dulany, my daughter. . . . If after the payment of
all the above bequests there shall remain a fund in the
hands of my Executors, I require them to pay thereof

to the American Bible Society or to such agent as they
shall appoint to receive it two hundred dollars or such
other less sum as may be in their hands after (?) payment—if nothing, then this bequest is to be void.

—Mary "Polly" Patton Taylor, Last Will and Testament, 1853

Mary "Polly" Patton Taylor dedicated her life to her home and family, providing food for their bodies as well as their souls and managing meals with
the help of the Taylors' enslaved workers. Sabine Hill's original kitchen
was most likely detached from the home—as it appears today—and may
once have been a small log house. John Tipton and his family lived in a
log structure that burned down on what was then Tipton property.

This section of property, purchased from Tipton by Nathaniel Taylor,
raises speculation that the Taylor kitchen is attached to the old Tipton
chimney and fireplace. Elements of the original indoor kitchen are restored
based on data as to when the kitchen was first built. Original wood plank
wallboards concealed beneath layers of wall paper are restored. The mantel on the south side of the space appears to be original.

The artfully crafted fireplace, with its segmental arch, is composed of
rough-cut limestone blocks from Crab Orchard, Tennessee. The crown
and baseboard molding have been replaced. The floor covering consists
of modern three-inch pine plank flooring.

Nathaniel Taylor, having purchased acreage from his neighbor John
Tipton, became a large landowner in Elizabethton's interdependent farming community. Sheep, horses, hogs, mules, and cattle peppered the Taylor
landscape and barnyards. Corn was the primary crop.

MENU
Irish Soda Bread
Savory Tomato and Cheese Cobbler
Buttermilk Lamb
Buttermilk Fried Quail
Blueberry Upside-Down Skillet Cake
Sylvia's Sausage Dressing

IRISH SODA BREAD

Andrew Taylor Sr. made his way from Ireland through Virginia to the Watauga Valley in 1776–77 to put down roots. Branches of the Taylor family tree are recognized and admired not only for what they accomplished but for their willingness to serve their country.

Traditional Irish Soda Bread is made with basic ingredients: flour, baking soda (instead of yeast), buttermilk (to activate the baking soda), and salt. As per Irish tradition, the sign of the cross is slashed across the top of the dough "to ward off evil spirits" before placing the loaf in the oven.

Ingredients
3½ cups all-purpose flour
1 teaspoon baking soda
2¼ teaspoons salt
1½ cups buttermilk

Directions
Preheat the oven to 425°F. Brush a baking sheet with melted butter or coat with nonstick cooking oil spray. In a large bowl, combine the flour, baking soda, and salt. Make a well in the center of the flour mixture and gradually stir in the buttermilk, continually stirring until the dough can be gathered into a ball. Place the dough ball on a lightly floured surface and pat into an 8-inch round loaf. Place the loaf on the oiled baking sheet and score (slash) a ½-inch X into the top of the dough with a baker's lame (pronounced "lahm," meaning "blade" in French) or a small, very sharp knife. Bake at 375°F for 45 minutes, or until the top is golden brown. (Yields 1 loaf.)

> *Tidbits:*
> This loaf may need more than 1½ cups buttermilk, as directed. Add up to ½ cup more buttermilk, 1 tablespoon at a time, until the dough holds together.

SAVORY TOMATO AND CHEESE COBBLER

Yellow corn—grown, dried, and ground into meal on the Taylor acreage— paired well with home-grown tomatoes, especially when combined with garden-fresh herbs and a mild, buttery cheese. It is fitting that shortly after Tennessee was granted statehood on June 1, 1796, the words "Agriculture and Commerce" were emblazoned on the Great Seal of Tennessee in 1801. These words were officially adopted as Tennessee's state motto in 1987.

In 2003, the tomato was designated the official state fruit by Tennessee's 103rd General Assembly. The luscious red fruit, enriched by Tennessee's nutritious soil continues to enhance the flavor of salads, sandwiches, stews and sauces. There is speculation that the Cherokees were growing tomatoes over 100 years before the white man set foot in "the new world."

Ingredients
Cobbler Filling
1 tablespoon vegetable oil
1 medium yellow onion, diced
1 large, red, ripe tomato, chopped
2 large garlic cloves, finely minced
3 pounds assorted small tomatoes, halved
1 tablespoon white wine vinegar
1 tablespoon cornstarch
Salt and cracked black pepper to taste
1 teaspoon fresh thyme leaves, chopped

Cornbread Topping
1½ cups self-rising flour
½ cup stone-ground yellow cornmeal
½ teaspoon baking powder
8 tablespoons cold butter, cut into ¼-inch pieces
¾ cup shredded cheddar cheese
1 cup cold buttermilk

Directions
For the Filling: Preheat the oven to 375°F. In a 12-inch cast-iron skillet, sauté the onion in the heated vegetable oil until it is soft and tender. Add the large chopped tomato, garlic, and 1½ cups small, halved tomatoes and sauté until they are soft and tender. Remove from the heat and add the vinegar, cornstarch, salt and pepper, and thyme. Place the remaining

small halved tomatoes in a 13×9-inch baking dish and spoon the sautéed onion and tomato mixture from the skillet over them. Toss to coat.

For the Cornbread Dough: Combine the flour, cornmeal, and baking powder. Gradually add the butter pieces until the mixture resembles small peas. Chill the mixture for 15 minutes. Stir the shredded cheese into the chilled flour mixture. Make a well in the center of the flour mixture and pour in the cold buttermilk. Mix until just combined. In ½-cup increments, drop the cornbread mixture on top of the tomato mixture. Do not spread. Bake for 30 to 35 minutes. Allow the cobbler to cool for 15 minutes before serving.
(Yields 6–8 servings.)

BUTTERMILK LAMB

Sheep, a general term for the animal, grazed in the rolling pasturelands of Sabine Hill long before "grass-fed" became a fashionable, healthy alternative to today's supermarket meat.

The meat of lamb, a young sheep, is more tender than mutton—the meat of an older sheep. The acid content of buttermilk breaks down connective tissue, transforming the meat into a delectable main dish enhanced by the bite of red onion and fresh dill from the kitchen garden.

Ingredients
2- to 3-pound leg of lamb
1 qt. buttermilk
3 teaspoons fresh dill weed, finely chopped (or 1 teaspoon, dried)
2 teaspoons garlic powder (or 4 large cloves, minced)
⅓ cup red wine
⅓ cup beef broth
1 large red (purple) onion, sliced into rings
Salt and pepper to taste

Directions
"Butterfly" the leg of lamb (or ask your butcher to do so). Place the lamb in a large container. In a separate bowl, combine the buttermilk with the dill, garlic, wine, and beef broth and pour over the lamb. Place it in the refrigerator to marinate for two days. Preheat the oven to 500°F. Cut the

purple onion into rings and distribute them evenly across the bottom of a roaster pan. When the oven is preheated, place the lamb (the butterfly side should be open) in the bottom of the roaster on top of the onion rings. Pour the buttermilk marinade mixture from the refrigerated container over the lamb. Cover and place in the preheated oven. Allow the lamb to cook for 20 minutes. Turn off the oven and leave the lamb inside to bake for 2 hours; be sure the oven door is closed tightly and *do not open the oven door for the remainder of the cooking time.* After baking, remove the lamb from the oven. Allow the meat to rest for 10 to 15 minutes. Slice. Use the marinade in the roaster for juice.
(Yields 4–6 servings.)

BUTTERMILK FRIED QUAIL

Long before the bobwhite quail—also known as a partridge—was designated the official state game bird of Tennessee in 1988, the small meaty fowl made a mighty tasty meal for early East Tennessee settlers.

It's doubtful the Taylor boys brined their wild-caught covey before soaking them in fresh buttermilk. Today's birds, however, should sit in a brine of ¼ cup kosher salt to 4 cups of water for at least 4 hours to remove the gamey taste. Store-bought, farm-raised quail can simply be battered and fried.

Tidbits:
The bobwhite hen lays 10 to 20 white eggs at a time. Quail eggs are considered a delicacy in today's upscale restaurant kitchens. The nutritional value of quail eggs far exceeds that of chicken eggs with less than half the calories, fat, cholesterol, and sodium.

Ingredients
8 to 16 quail, split in half
2 cups buttermilk
2 tablespoons each fresh herbs
     (chopped rosemary, thyme, parsley)
2 cups flour
1 tablespoon garlic salt
Pinch cayenne pepper
3 cups vegetable oil

Directions
In a medium container, combine the buttermilk with the herbs and spices (except for the garlic salt). Submerge the quail in the buttermilk mix-

ture for as little as an hour or as long as overnight. Cover the container. In a large cast-iron Dutch oven, heat the oil to 325°F. While the oil is heating, prepare the flour mixture—adding the garlic salt—in a brown paper bag. Shake to combine. Remove the quail from the buttermilk mixture. Place a few quail at a time in the brown paper bag and shake. Place the battered quail on a wire rack. Fry the quail in batches of 4 for about 3 to 4 minutes per side. Remove the fried quail from the oil with a long handle wide mesh strainer, or kitchen tongs, and drain on a paper towel. Serve hot and crisp.

(Yields 4 quail per person.)

BLUEBERRY UPSIDE-DOWN SKILLET CAKE

Elizabethton was founded near the site of the old Cherokee village "Wata'gi," meaning "broken waters"—like those found at the convergence of the Doe and Watauga Rivers. The Cherokees contributed greatly to the settlers' knowledge and use of natural plants and herbs. Wild strawberries, blueberries, huckleberries, blackberries and raspberries—providing sustenance as well as medicine to the Cherokees—were shared with settlers in their initial and somewhat symbiotic relationship.

The roots, leaves, and fruit of a blueberry bush, for example, were prepared as tea and used as a muscle relaxant for women during childbirth. Blueberries were boiled down into a thick syrup to treat a sore throat caused by tuberculosis, or "consumption," so named back then because the malady seemed to "consume" the individual.

These round, light-silvery-blue blushing berries with a calyx on top can be homegrown, picked wild, and found at farmers' markets in Elizabethton from June through July.

Ingredients
Blueberry Mixture
4 tablespoons salted butter, melted
½ cup brown sugar
3 cups blueberries, washed and patted dry
½ tablespoon fresh lemon juice

Cake

½ cup butter
¾ cup white sugar
1 egg, lightly beaten
1 teaspoon vanilla
1⅓ cups all-purpose flour
¼ teaspoon salt
2 teaspoons baking powder
¾ cup whole milk
Coarse white sugar for sprinkling on top of finished cake

Directions

For the blueberry mixture: In a 10½-inch cast-iron skillet on the stovetop over medium heat, melt the butter and brown sugar. Stir the lemon juice into the sugar mixture. Add the berries and mix until the berries are coated with the sugar mixture. Set aside.

For the cake: Preheat the oven to 350°F. In a medium sized bowl, combine the butter and sugar and beat with a hand mixer until light and fluffy. Stir in the lightly beaten egg and vanilla. Sift together the flour, baking soda, salt. Add the dry ingredients, alternating with the milk, to the beaten butter and sugar mixture. Stir until just combined. Spoon the batter over the top of the berry mixture in the skillet using the back of a spoon to smooth out the batter. Place the skillet in the preheated oven and bake for 45 to 50 minutes until the top crust is golden brown. Allow to cool in the pan, slightly (about 10 minutes). To invert the cake onto a platter, lay a flat, oven-proof plate on top of the skillet. Carefully but quickly, flip the cake from the skillet to the platter. Tap the skillet several times to make sure all the congealed berry mixture is released from the skillet. Sprinkle sparkling white baker's sugar on top of the cake, if desired. Serve warm. (Yields 8 servings.)

SYLVIA'S SAUSAGE DRESSING

I am delighted to include the recipe for Sylvia's Sausage Dressing which belonged to Mrs. Sylvia Maye Darton Bauer Born in 1916 in Tottenham, Herefordshire, England. Mrs. Bauer arrived in America as a World War

II bride in 1946. She lived much of her life in Maryland and later in Tennessee. Mrs. Bauer's recipe is shared by her daughter, Ms. Jennifer Bauer, park ranger for Tennessee State Parks—Sycamore Shoals State Historic Area, Sabine Hill State Historic Site.

Ingredients
2 cups celery, thinly sliced
1 cup yellow onion, diced
3 tablespoons butter, melted
4 cups day-old bread (a combination of cornbread,
    sourdough, or any day-old bread)
½ teaspoon dried thyme
½ teaspoon dried sage
¼ teaspoon paprika
¼ teaspoon parsley
1-pound pork sausage, broken into small pieces
1 medium red-skinned apple, diced
2 eggs, lightly beaten
2 cups chicken broth, warmed

Directions
Preheat the oven to 350°F. Sauté the celery and onions in butter until they are tender and translucent. Set aside. Over medium heat in a cast-iron skillet, cook the sausage until it's done. Pour off the grease. In a large bowl, combine the day-old bread with the dried thyme and sage, paprika, and parsley. Mix well. To the seasoned bread crumb mixture, add the cooked sausage, celery, onion, and diced apple. Stir in the beaten eggs until they are well combined. Gradually add the warm chicken broth to the dressing mixture until it is moist. Transfer the dressing to a 1½-quart shallow casserole dish. Cover and bake the casserole for 45 minutes or until it's heated through and lightly browned.
(Yields 6–8 side-dish servings.)

Chapter 11

CARTER HOUSE STATE HISTORIC SITE

◆━━━━━━━━━━━━━━━━━━━━━━━━━━━━━━━━━━━━◆

Completed 1830
Franklin, Tennessee

Taproots

Although the [Carter] house withstood the shock
of former conflicts, they seemed as child's play
to the approaching storm. The cellar afforded the se-
curest retreat, and hardly reached before the din
of battle grew appalling . . . the children cowering
at the feet of their parents while bullets rained and
cannon balls went crashing through.

—Fountain Branch Carter,
describing the Battle of Franklin, November 30, 1864

The Carter House was built of brick and mortar fashioned on-site by the hands of Fountain Branch Carter and his enslaved workers. General Jacob Dolson Cox of the Union Army took over and used the Carter House as his headquarters in the Battle of Franklin. Fought on November 30, 1864, as part of the Franklin-Nashville Campaign, the Battle of Franklin was a turning point in the defeat of the Confederate States of America. It was one of the bloodiest conflicts of the Civil War.

The first of the Carter lineage, Giles Carter, came to Virginia in 1676. Fountain "Fount" Branch Carter was a sixth generation Carter, born on April 6, 1797, in Fairfax, Virginia, to Francis Watkins and Sarah Holcomb

Carter. Around 1806, the erudite Carter family, seeking prosperity, and new horizons, pulled up their ancestral stakes in Halifax County, Virginia. They journeyed west into the virgin fields of Middle Tennessee, settling near Abram Maury's tiny community of Franklin, named for founding father Benjamin Franklin.

The Carter House
as it stands today.

One can imagine a young Fount Carter riding on horseback from his
farm in Waddell's Hollow, reining his mount to a halt on the crest of a
hill overlooking the fledgling town. Gazing down into the small collection of buildings sprinkled along the dusty, wagon-wheel-rutted main
street of Franklin, he might have envisioned the tiny village expanding

The kitchen, one of the original outbuildings, was added by
Fountain Branch Carter after he built the house in 1830.

into a bustling, thriving community—the place he would call home. But
he could not have foreseen future generations who would stand on this
same crest overlooking the site of a bloody battlefield or that the life he
had yet to live would be changed forever.

While building his life, Fount Carter met Mary "Polly" Atkinson, a
Franklin native. Their marriage certificate, dated June 28, 1823, is on file
at the Williamson County Courthouse. Mary, born in 1806, gave birth
to the first of their twelve children in 1824. Their sons included Nisan
Red Carter (1824), Moscow Branch Carter (1825), Orlando Hortensius
Carter (1827), William Augustus Carter (1829), James Fountain Carter
(1831), Samuel Atkinson Carter (1833), Theodrick Carter IV, called "Tod"

Heavy artillery fire was not enough to hold back the onslaught
of Union forces during the Second Battle of Franklin.

(1840), and Francis Watkins Carter (1842). Moscow Carter was the only
surviving son from the first seven years of their marriage.

Their daughters—Mary Alice Carter (1835), Sarah Holcomb Carter
(1837), Annie Vick Carter (1838), and Frances Hodge Carter (1844)—
grew to adulthood without their mother, who died of influenza in 1852
at the age of forty-six. Fountain Carter never remarried and reared their
youngest child to adulthood as a widower.

For several years the family lived in town, where Fount worked as a
merchant in his storefront on Franklin's public square. There, he fashioned
and sold handmade boots. Eventually, he turned the boot shop into a
general store and passed the business operation over to two of his sons,
Moscow and James.

In 1829, F. B. Carter purchased nineteen acres of level acreage and
built the Carter house—a one-and-a-half-story brick home for his small
family. He built it on a stone foundation, and his handmade cedar shingles
are said to have lasted nearly fifty years.

F. B. Carter built the main house in the Federal style, popular between 1780 and 1830. The layout of the six-building compound—smokehouse, slave house, kitchen, farm office, and garden—were built within a short distance of each other. Although no longer standing, he also built a cotton gin to process his cotton as well as that of his neighbors. The rash of Civil War bullet holes riddling the main house, farm office, and detached kitchen are visible reminders of the devastating effects of the horrific war.

The interior of the Carter home is aesthetically pleasing in form and functionality; it exhibits fine taste without excess. The first-floor family room, which also served as a bedroom, features a frame-and-panel door to the main hall fashioned in the popular Cross and Bible style of the era. The well-appointed parlor was likely used for family gatherings and celebrations. The thick stone walls and floors of the finished basement, with its large fireplace, served as the family dining room, comfortable in any season.

On November 30, 1864, the Carters, with their neighbors, the Albert Lotz family, and several slaves, took refuge in the adjoining storage cellar as the Battle of Franklin raged around them. In those five desperate hours, savage, bloody, hand-to-hand combat raged in their front yard, extending for hundreds of yards east and west. The sounds of Union soldiers running into the house and up and down the staircase reverberated overhead while the terrified families cowered in the basement below. When the battle was over, dead, dying, and wounded soldiers lay scattered and piled on top of one another on the grounds around the Carter House. The Battle of Franklin left nearly 10,000 casualties—2,000 dead, 6,500 wounded, and nearly 1,000 missing.

Fount Carter's three sons enlisted in the Confederate Army in May 1861. Tod continued to serve after his two older brothers left the field. Moscow retired in August 1862, and Francis, having been wounded at the Battle of Shiloh, was captured and remained a prisoner of war until the Civil War ended on May 9, 1865.

Young Tod Carter, on a much-needed furlough, was visiting his family at the Carter farm as the Battle of Franklin began. Refusing to sit out a battle on his own property, Carter led a desperate charge and was mortally wounded southwest of the main house. He took nine bullets that day—one lodging in his skull. He died two days later, on December 2,

1862, in the family sitting room, surrounded by family and friends. Tod Carter was just twenty-four years old.

Carter House was purchased by the State of Tennessee in 1951 and opened to the public in 1953. The Carter House State Historic Site, managed by the Battle of Franklin Trust, is dedicated to the Carter family and all Americans who fought in the Civil War.

Address and Contact Information
Carter House State Historic Site
1140 Columbia Avenue
Franklin, TN 37065
(615) 791-1861

Timeless Recipes

Order of my orchard transferred from the book of
1869, at which time most of the trees were planted. Beginning at the Southeast corner of the orchard near the
Columbia Turnpike, running thence west;
finishing at the North end.

—Agricultural diary of Moscow Branch Carter, January 1, 1870

Fountain Branch Carter's initial nineteen-acre farm grew exponentially to 288 acres by 1860; his cotton gin produced a cash crop of nearly twelve thousand pounds of cotton. The production of wheat, oats, corn, and Irish potatoes flourished in Tennessee's high heat, which was perfect for growing some of today's crops: corn, melons, tobacco, and cotton.

F. B. Carter died on August 22, 1871, at the age of seventy-four. In his last will, he divided his land holdings among his surviving children, grandchildren, and in-laws, leaving Moscow the house and the most productive pieces of farmland. He also left land rights to several enslaved workers, including a substantial amount to the former family slave Eliza and her son. Descendants of the Carter family slaves are said to live in and around the Franklin community.

The Carter house kitchen remained functional from its initial construction through the Civil War and beyond. Journal records indicate that many of the Carter children moved back home to the family farmhouse before Fount's death. Records indicate that Moscow Carter wanted to hire a cook, but there is only speculation as to who did the cooking for the family after the Civil War.

The years following the Civil War were difficult. The Carter family put forth considerable effort rebuilding their farm and restoring their livelihood. Moscow Carter was moderately successful, but the farm was never as profitable as it was before the war. Moscow sold the house and farm in 1896.

MENU
Millet Drop Biscuits
Mint Julep
Cider Braised Pork Rib Roast with Cabbage and Potatoes
Smoked Brisket
Smoked Green Beans
Raspberry-Peach Jam
Orange Pudding (Pie)
Corn Flour Cakes

MILLET DROP BISCUITS

October 12—General Robert Edward Lee died of paralysis.
October 15—Cut my millet in the young orchard.
October 16—America [his wife, nicknamed "Mec"]
returned from Nashville.

—An entry from Moscow Carter's 1870 journal

Tidbits:
Lightly toasting the millet adds a nuttier flavor to this tasty grain.

Ingredients
2 cups millet flour
1 tablespoon baking powder
1 teaspoon salt
6 tablespoons cold butter, cut into tablespoons
¾ cup cold buttermilk
2 medium eggs, lightly beaten

Directions

Preheat the oven to 450°F. Grease one cookie sheet. Whisk together millet flour, baking powder, and salt until well combined. Cut in the butter until the mixture resembles small peas. Stir in the buttermilk and beaten eggs until just combined. Drop the mixture in rounded tablespoons onto the greased cookie sheet. Bake for 10 to 12 minutes or until the edges are slightly browned. Remove the biscuits from the cookie sheet immediately and place on a wire rack to cool. Serve immediately with butter and raspberry-peach jam.

(Yields 10–15 biscuits.)

Tidbits, Too:
If you can't find millet flour in stores, make your own by purchasing raw millet seed and grinding it into flour using a small grain mill or coffee grinder; 2 cups raw millet seed equals 2 cups millet flour.

MINT JULEP

In the fall of 1862, Tod Carter, having received his second promotion to assistant quartermaster in the Confederate Army, became a correspondent for the *Chattanooga Daily Rebel*. He wrote his column under the pen name "Mint Julep." Perhaps the Carter men occasionally sipped this quintessential southern libation.

The mint julep, a cocktail mixed with bourbon or Tennessee whiskey, sugar, and mint, originated in eighteenth-century Virginia and was gulped by farmers at dawn as their "eye-opening" equivalent to today's coffee. According to the *Old Farmer's Almanac* (founded in 1792), mint is a symbol of virtue. A member of the herb family, mint grows prolifically throughout Tennessee and likely grew in the Carter's kitchen garden.

"Julep" is derived from the word *julab*, meaning "rose water," and consequently, the name of an Arabic drink made with rose water and syrups. Drinking julab is thought to enhance one's quality of life.

Traditionally, a mint julep served in a silver or pewter cup indicates a person of means.

Ingredients

1 silver cup or old-fashioned glass (6 to 8 ounces)
10 mint leaves, muddled to a paste

1½ teaspoons super-fine sugar
Splash of seltzer water
Crushed ice
2½ ounces good Tennessee whiskey

Directions
Tear the mint leaves into small pieces and place them in the bottom of the glass. Sprinkle sugar on top of the leaves. Muddle these together until small mint pieces break down into a paste. Adding a splash of Seltzer water helps dissolve the sugar. Fill the glass with crushed ice and add the whiskey, or lemonade. Stir gently. Garnish with a mint leaf. Serve immediately.
(Yields 1 cocktail.)

APPLE CIDER BRAISED PORK RIB ROAST WITH POTATOES AND CABBAGE

Moscow Branch Carter kept copious notes in his 1870 agricultural diary. His massive apple and peach orchards—"Beginning at the Southeast corner of the orchard near Columbia Turnpike, running thence west"— produced prolifically.

Moscow planted six different varieties of apple trees, a total of ninety-six trees. One diary entry notes, "All the trees are Yellow Harvest, north to the old orchard and garden are Wine Saps." Regarding his rural holdings, he recorded, "My stock consists of two mules, Nelly and Sam, and Nelly's colt, 2 milk cows and calves, and 5 dry cattle, and 24 head of hogs."

In his March 25 diary entry, Moscow indicated planting twelve rows of Shaker russet potatoes. And on November 12, he noted, "In looking over my stock of winter cabbage, I am able to congratulate myself with having fallen on the right plan, at least, for once. . . . The season has been one of unusual dryness and, yet, my cabbages have shown no signs of having suffered by it. They are fine now. Some of the largest heads are to be found in my patch, I ever say. The ground was rich and thoroughly cultivated."

As Moscow Carter set forth to maintain and add to what his father planted, a warm, nutritious meal incorporating the fruit of his labor surely was a satisfying reward.

Ingredients

1 pork rib roast (pork loin, bone-in), about 4 to 5 pounds
5 tablespoons butter
1 cup yellow onion, chopped
3 large garlic cloves, diced
1 medium-sized cabbage
¾ cup apple cider or farm-fresh organic apple juice
1 tablespoon brown sugar or honey
1 tablespoon apple cider vinegar
3 large russet potatoes, peeled and quartered

Directions

Preheat the oven to 325°F. In a large Dutch oven, melt the butter over medium heat. Sauté the onions in the melted butter and brown the roast on all sides. Add the chopped garlic. Remove the core from the bottom of the cabbage. Remove the large outer leaves from the cabbage and slice the whole cabbage into 6 to 8 wedges. In a measuring cup, stir together the apple juice, brown sugar or honey, vinegar, and dried thyme leaves. Pour the mixture over the pork roast and cabbage. Cover and transfer to the oven. Cook for 2 hours. Add the potatoes; cover and bake for an additional 45 minutes to an hour. Pork should register 160°F on an instant-read thermometer.
(Yields 6 servings.)

SMOKED BRISKET

Before and after the war, the Carter smokehouse was filled with meat. Beef and pork were likely rubbed with a mixture of salt, pepper, and sugar and placed in a large, hollow log to dry-cure for six weeks. The "cured" meat was hung from the rafters on hooks above a smoldering fire—perhaps using a mixture of apple and peach wood from their orchard. After several days of smoking, the meat was removed and stored. Smoked meat could be stored for months without risk of spoilage. Today, meat smoked at home can be enjoyed in hours, not days, using a cast-iron or carbon-steel smoker.

The Carter smokehouse still bears the scars of actual bullet holes from the battle. Perhaps some of these "scars" are from "Williams cleaner" bullets, used by the Union army for cleaning muzzle-loading guns. Invented by Elijah D. Williams of Philadelphia, the bullet was designed to expand against the walls of a musket when fired, thus "cleaning" the black powder residue from the interior of the 'rifled' (grooved, for improved accuracy) musket barrel. This type of bullet mortally wounded Tod Carter on December 2, 1864. The actual bullet is displayed under glass in the Carter House Visitor's Center.

Ingredients
1 large (7- to 12-pound) all-natural beef brisket (with fat cap)
Your preferred barbeque spice rub—or kosher salt and pepper

Directions

Tidbits:
Expect to lose about 20 percent of the brisket's weight during cooking.

Rub the brisket liberally on all sides with the spice rub or salt and pepper. Preheat your smoker to 225°F. Place the brisket in the smoker and cook from 3 hours to a maximum of 12 hours, depending on the size of your brisket. If cooking for 12 hours, wrap the brisket tightly in foil after 3 to 6 hours with the fat cap side up. Place the foil-wrapped brisket (fat-cap side up) in a roasting pan and place it back into the smoker. Roast for an additional 3 to 6 hours or until the brisket reaches an internal temperature of 170°F. Remove the brisket from the smoker and allow the meat to rest for 30 minutes. Slice the brisket across the grain. Serve with the smoky juice ladled over the brisket. (Yields about 12 servings, depending on the size of the brisket.)

SMOKED GREEN BEANS

Planted four and a half rows of extra early bunch beans on the south side of the garden.

—Moscow Carter, April 5, 1870

Bunch beans—called "brown bunch beans"—are rare in today's Tennessee gardens. But in the Carter heyday, these beans did not send out "runners," but sat squat on the ground according to Bill Best, heirloom seed aficionado.

The term "green beans" refers to pole beans and snap beans, which are classified based on growth characteristics. Pole beans, for example, are categorized as "climbers" and need a trellis. Snap beans grow closer to the ground without a trellis and are so named for the sound they make when broken into pieces.

Ingredients
6 cups freshly picked green beans, trimmed and snapped
2 cups water, boiling
2 teaspoons apple cider
½ medium white onion, thinly sliced
¼ pound bacon (4 slices)
1 teaspoons pepper
1 teaspoons salt, divided

Directions
Blanch the green beans in salted boiling water (using 1 teaspoon salt) until bright green and crisp (about 5 minutes). In a two-quart, heat-proof casserole dish or aluminum pan, add the green beans, water, and apple cider. Add the onion, bacon slices, and the teaspoons of salt and pepper. Place in a 250°F smoker uncovered for 3 hours. Serve with your brisket and as a side dish.
(Yields 6 cups.)

RASPBERRY-PEACH JAM
The Carter family enjoyed a variety of garden truck from their two-acre tract just behind the main house. Prior to the Battle of Franklin, their fertile Tennessee soil gave birth to potatoes, okra, raspberries, apples, and peaches, according to Moscow Carter's diary. Spreading sweet, tangy, ruby-red, golden-toned fruit between nutty flavored halves of piping-hot millet biscuits is a bite of heaven on earth.

The bountiful garden was destroyed, however, when Federal troops swarmed the Carter property and dug a section of their defensive line through the Carter backyard, resulting in grisly hand-to-hand combat that cost thousands of Confederate and Union soldiers their lives.

Ingredients

1 pound of raspberries, washed and patted dry

3 pounds ripe yellow peaches, peeled, chopped, pits removed

3 cups sugar

6 tablespoons fresh lemon juice

Tidbits:
A hot water bath, or "water bath canner," is used in sterilizing the jars prior to filling and for boiling the jars once they're filled.

Directions

Prepare a boiling hot-water bath and sterilize six ½-pint glass jars and the lids. Combine the chopped peaches, raspberries, sugar, and lemon juice in a large Dutch oven. Over medium-high heat, begin cooking the fruit, stirring frequently as the sugar dissolves and the fruit releases its juices and breaks down. Once the jam is reduced and thickened (reaching a temperature of 220°F on a candy thermometer), remove it from the heat. Ladle the jam into clean, dry, sterilized jars. Wipe the rims with a damp, clean kitchen towel and screw on the lids. Process the jars in the water bath for 10 minutes. Remove the jars from the water bath. Set the jars on the countertop to cool. Leave the jars on the countertop for 12 hours. Store in a dark place.

(Yields six ½-pint jars.)

ORANGE PUDDING (PIE)

Finding an original handwritten family recipe associated with a historic site is exciting and rare. Rarer still are orange trees in Middle Tennessee, where summers are hot and winters freezing. For this reason, citrus trees, olive trees, and the like do not mature. The Carters, however, must have found a way to import and incorporate the fragrant fruit into this velvety dessert.

This recipe is exactly as it appeared on a beautifully handwritten original note card shared with me by the Battle of Franklin Trust. I added the zest of one large orange to the pudding mixture for flavor, and I substitute apple cider for the brandy

Ingredients
½ pound butter (2 sticks)
½ pound sugar (1 cup)
5 eggs
2 tablespoons of brandy or apple cider
Rind of an orange (large)

Directions
Soak the rind of an orange overnight (in water).
The next day boil it in fresh water and mash it
fine (to a paste). Beat the butter and sugar for
the cake (until light and fluffy). Whisk the eggs
(lightly, until combined). Add beaten eggs to
the butter sugar mixture (until just combined).
Stir in the brandy and the mashed orange rind.
Cover your pie plate with a rich paste use a
store-bought pie crust, or employ your favorite pie crust recipe). Bake in a moderate oven
(375°F) for 40 to 45 minutes or until crust is golden brown and the pie
filling is not "wobbly" when shaken.
(Yields 8 slices.)

> **Tidbits:**
> Wash the orange rind
> extremely well using
> an organic liquid fruit
> and vegetable cleaner,
> rinsing the rind after
> peeling.

> **Tidbits, Too:**
> Place the filled pie pan
> on a rimmed baking
> sheet while baking.
> Refrigerate the pie
> before slicing.

Benjamin Franklin: The Art of Eating

Benjamin Franklin, for whom the city of Franklin is named, is known
as one of America's founding fathers. But did you know he was also a
forefather of gastronomy? In one of his letters regarding the Stamp Act,
Dr. Franklin describes corn as cuisine.

In his pamphlet *The Art of Eating,* Franklin responds to a letter by
a European who wrote: "Americans, should they resolve to drink no
more tea, cannot keep that Resolution, their Indian corn not affording
an agreeable or easily digestible breakfast."

Franklin's annoyance waxed almost poetic: "Pray, let me an American,
inform the gentleman, who seems ignorant of the matter, that Indian
corn, take it for all in all, is one of the most agreeable and wholesome

grains in the world; that its green leaves roasted are a delicacy beyond expression; that samp, hominy, succotash and nokehock made of it, are so many pleasing varieties and that jonny or hoe cake, hot from the fire, is better than a Yorkshire muffin" (January 2, 1766).

Fountain Branch Carter planted acre upon acre of Indian corn on his property. Ben Franklin, lover and defender of Indian corn would surely appreciate my recipe for corn flour cakes using fresh corn kernels and finely ground corn flour.

CORN FLOUR CAKES

Ingredients
1½ cups corn flour
¼ teaspoon salt
1½ teaspoon baking powder
4 tablespoons salted butter, softened, cubed
1 cup whole-fat buttermilk
1 tablespoon honey
2 cups fresh corn kernels
4 small scallions, whole, thinly sliced
2 large eggs, separated
1 large egg white

Directions
In a large bowl, stir together the corn flour, baking powder, and salt. In a small saucepan, heat the butter. Stir in the buttermilk and honey until just combined. Set aside, allowing it to cool slightly. Make a well in the center of the dry ingredients. Stir in the buttermilk mixture, two egg yolks, corn kernels, and chopped scallions—scraping the dry ingredients from the bottom of the bowl—until just combined. In a clean, dry, medium sized bowl, beat the 3 egg whites until stiff and they hold their shape. Fold the beaten egg whites into the corn batter mixture. Over medium heat, place the extra butter (about 2 tablespoons; more as needed) in a medium sized skillet. Melt the butter until it just bubbles. Using a ¼-cup measure, scoop out the batter and pour it into the hot skillet. Let the batter fry for about 2 minutes. As the corn cakes begin to sizzle and bubble around the edges,

flip the cakes with a spatula and fry on the other side for about 2 minutes. To serve the cakes warm, place a baking sheet in the oven and lay the cakes on the sheet as you remove them from the pan. Serve immediately with pats of butter and raspberry-peach jam.

(Yields 10–12 small cakes.)

Chapter 12

WYNNEWOOD STATE HISTORIC SITE

◆————————————————————————————————◆

Built ca. 1830
Castalian Springs, Tennessee

Taproots

Castalian Springs Hotel Now Open
For anyone desiring quiet rest, comfortable, cool
nights, fine black Sulphur water and a good table
board at a moderate price. This is an ideal resort.

—George W. Wynne, Mgr.

In 1940, George Winchester Wynne, the fourth-generation family owner
of the Castalian Springs Inn and farm and grandson of Alfred Royal
Wynne, gave the property a new name: Wynnewood. The name would dis-
tinguish the rambling Sumner County structure—the largest nineteenth-
century log edifice in Tennessee—from the surrounding community of
Castalian Springs and give recognition to the Wynne family, longtime
residents of the area.

The property on which Wynnewood stands was discovered in 1772
by Isaac Bledsoe and his older brother Anthony. Hailing originally from
Virginia, both were "long hunters"—that is, eastern frontiersmen ac-
customed to spending lengthy, continuous periods of time hunting in
Tennessee and Kentucky. Following an old buffalo trail, the Bledsoes
discovered a mineral spring flowing through the area of what was then
North Carolina. "Salt licks," as these mineral-rich locations are called,

Wynnewood State Historic Site.

attracted a large variety of wild game and buffalo. The animals derived
nutrition from this salty ground. The Bledsoe brothers staked a claim
here and named the area Bledsoe's Lick.

The beauty of Bledsoe's Lick likely attracted its first known group of
human inhabitants: the North American Mound Builders of the Wood-
land Period. Although distorted by erosion and the ravages of time, a
remnant of their mounds—the fortified pre-Columbian village known
as Chaskepi—can still be seen along Highway 25 at Castalian Springs.

The Bledsoes eventually obtained legal rights to their "claim," built
a fort, and occupied the area with their families around 1784. Anthony
constructed a homestead (Fort Greenfield) and moved into it with his fam-

ily. Unfortunately, Anthony was killed in an Indian attack in 1788. The next year, during the winter months, other settler families, including the James Winchesters and the John Halls, arrived from "over the mountain" into the natural beauty of the land surrounding Bledsoe's Lick under an agreement called the Cumberland Compact. Signed on May 13, 1780, by 256 Tennessee settlers, this document ensured them governance and communal protection. It was the forerunner of the state constitution.

A few years later, Isaac Bledsoe was killed by Native Americans while out tending his field. Just a few months after his death, his son, also named Anthony, was killed in a raid near his property.

After Isaac Bledsoe's death, his 320-acre tract of land—including the mineral springs—was purchased from his heirs by James Winchester. Winchester held on to the property until his death in 1826. It was then divided into two parcels but was eventually deeded solely to Mrs. Almira Winchester Wynne, wife of Alfred Royal "A. R." Wynne, daughter of General James Winchester and his wife, Susan Black Winchester, of Cragfont (see chapter 6). A. R. and Almira Winchester Wynne's marriage produced fourteen children.

A. R. Wynne and his business partners, Stephen Roberts and Humphrey Bate of Hawthorn Hill (see chapter 8), built an inn on his property as a way station for travelers along the Avery Trace, a road spanning nearly two hundred miles of surrounding wilderness. But when the stagecoach route was relocated farther south, the flow of traffic past the inn decreased dramatically. Wynne bought his partners' investment and turned the inn into a family residence. At some point between 1829 and 1837 townspeople changed the name Bledsoe's Lick's to Castalian Springs.

Construction on the Castalian Springs Inn and farm began in July 1829 and was completed in the summer of 1830—the year it opened to the public. The Wynnes moved onto the site in 1834 from their cabins nearby. A. R. Wynne commenced cultivating the mineral springs as a summer spa destination. The main building was designed as a large space containing ten rooms—five upstairs and five downstairs. Fireplaces in eight of the ten rooms added warmth and ambiance to the attractively furnished, rustic, log guestrooms. Rooms on the first floor open to a dogtrot, or breezeway. Rooms on the second floor could be accessed by one of two staircases. The main staircase ascends from the dogtrot.

The Wynnewood parlor. Note the original, period mahogany table from Cragfont. The cranberry glass chandelier is original to Wynnewood.

By the summer of 1839, business at the Castalian Springs Inn was booming. A. R. Wynne had wisely chosen a beautiful, sloping hillside close to a grove of magnificent cedar and hardwood trees near the salt lick for the site of his inn. Guests and boarders drank the sulphur water and bathed in mineral baths. By 1850, Castalian Springs Inn offered the services of a resident physician. The doctor's office still stands today.

People came from across the country to enjoy the inn with its additional recreational facilities built for tennis and bowling. The inn hosted such notable guests as Andrew Jackson, Sam Houston, and even Jesse James.

The original smokehouse remains about fifty feet southwest of the inn. Wynne planted flora along the drive and often received requests in the mail for plants and seeds. Exchanging seeds was customary in those days. Today, seed libraries, such as the one at Thomas Jefferson's Monticello, are operating all over the country. A catalogue of bean seeds from the

The spacious, detached kitchen was designed
to serve guests and family members.

southern Appalachia region can be traced back to Nashville, Tennessee,
in the early eighteenth century and from Nashville to France.

In 1845, Wynne planted a shellbark hickory tree to commemorate the
death of his hero, Andrew "Old Hickory" Jackson. The tree was admired
by friends and patrons of the inn until it was felled by an electrical storm
in 1910.

Castalian Springs, as an inn, mineral springs, and health spa resort, experienced two main periods of operation. The first was from 1830 through
1861; the second, from 1899 until 1915. When the much-anticipated plans
for an electric trolley car connecting Castalian Springs with Nashville
failed to materialize, the grounds became a lovely spot for church picnics
and outings for the next quarter century.

Wynnewood's out-of-the-way location is one reason it remains so well
preserved. Today, this landmark is a unique specimen of the beginnings of
the settling of the Southwest Territory, a distinct destination for travelers,

and a superb example of architecture and landscape from Tennessee's frontier settlement period.

Despite sustaining heavy damage from a 2008 tornado, which destroyed almost half of the two-story structure and many of the old trees, Wynnewood has been restored to its original grandeur. The state historic site reopened on July 4, 2012.

A. R. Wynne died in 1893 and is interred with the Wynne and Winchester family members in a small family cemetery at nearby Cragfont State Historic Site. Several generations of Wynnes lived at Wynnewood until 1971, when George Winchester Wynne and his wife, Eula, in an effort to protect the integrity and history of Wynnewood, deeded the house and property to the Tennessee Historical Commission for interpretation as an historic site. Wynnewood was placed on the National Register of Historic Places in 1971.

Address and Contact Information
Wynnewood State Historic Site
210 Old Highway 25
Castalian Springs, TN 37031
(615) 452-5463
www.historicwynnewood.org

Timeless Recipes

In a very short time a good substantial breakfast
was prepared which the weary soldiers ate
with a good relish. In the meantime,
a courier was dispatched to Gallatin to find
out the strength of the Lincolnites there.

—from the diary of Susan Wynne, daughter of Alfred R. and
Almira W. Wynne, March 16, 1862

A. R. Wynne was a Unionist and a follower of Andrew Jackson's way of thinking. He openly opposed secession. The Wynne family struggled with this juxtaposition throughout the Civil War. Although he seemed to have established good relationships with both sides, A. R. Wynne, like many Middle Tennesseans, eventually became a Confederate when Tennessee seceded from the Union on June 8, 1861, after the Civil War began with the Battle of Fort Sumter on April 12 of that year.

Several days after Union soldiers occupied Gallatin and Hartsville, Wynne's daughter, Susan, wrote in her March 16, 1862, diary entry that forty-three soldiers on horseback, under the command of the notorious Confederate cavalryman General John Hunt Morgan, thundered into the yard of the Castalian Springs Inn. These Confederate soldiers had confiscated—and were dressed in—Union garb. This frightened the Wynnes into believing Union soldiers had come to take over their property.

From the colonial period until the Civil War ended, enslaved workers did the majority of cooking and housework for wealthy slave owners on plantations across Middle and West Tennessee. On the day the Confederates invaded, and despite the war and skyrocketing prices due to food shortages, the Wynne family and their enslaved workers managed to serve Morgan and all forty-three hungry Confederate soldiers a "substantial breakfast" of southern favorites.

There is no written record of what filled the hungry bellies of Morgan and his men that March morning. According to southern tradition, however, their appetites would have been satisfied by sumptuous fare served hot and fresh from the massive twenty-foot kitchen with its enormous stone hearth and fireplace.

THE CASTALIAN SPRINGS INN BREAKFAST MENU
Dandelion Root Coffee
Butternut Squash Fritters
Southern Fried Fowl
Buckwheat Pancakes
Roasted Strawberry Jam
Shellbark Hickory Nut Shortbread Cookies
Skillet Gingerbread
Skillet Gingerbread, Too
Tennessee Sycamore Maple Sugar Cookies

DANDELION ROOT COFFEE

Shortly after the start of the Civil War, hunger and thirst defined the life of a Confederate soldier. Eventually, that lack invaded every aspect of their daily lives, save for the prayers of family and friends.

As Union blockades reduced imports such as coffee to a trickle, southerners began to wish they were not "living in the land of cotton." Realizing that cotton—King of the South—could not be fried, boiled, canned, or stewed, foraging for food and drink became a soldier's daily preoccupation. Dandelion root, as well as other readily available plant sources including sweet potatoes, could be roasted, ground, and "brewed" into a warm coffee-like substitute.

The *Farmer's Almanac* offers this rudimentary "receipt" for dandelion root coffee served during the Civil War. Surely this warm drink helped lift the spirits of Confederate and Union soldiers alike.

Directions

In clean water, scrub 3 thin dandelion roots, drain, pat dry, and place on a baking sheet. Roast at 150°F until the roots are dark and dry (about 4 hours). Cool and grind the roots with a coffee bean grinder or food blender. Add 1 heaping teaspoon of roasted roots to 1 cup of boiling water. Steep for 3 minutes. Strain and serve. Store in a covered jar until used. (Yields 1 cup coffee.)

BUTTERNUT SQUASH FRITTERS

Wynnewood's rich soil produced vining gourd-like vegetables such as yellow crookneck and butternut squash. These nutritious nuggets could be transformed into a tasty accompaniment to breakfast or a midday meal. Butternut squash, a fall vegetable, could be stored in the root cellar.

Interestingly, Confederate uniforms were often the color of "butternut," a yellowish-brown dye made of copperas and crushed hulls from the butternut tree (or white walnut tree—one of two species native to Tennessee). Hence, the term "butternut" became synonymous with the soldier.

Ingredients

1 medium butternut squash (5 cups), peeled, seeded,
    and grated, lightly packed
⅔ cup all-purpose flour
2 large eggs, lightly beaten
1⅔ tablespoons minced sage
⅓ cup vegetable oil
¼ teaspoon salt
Pinch of pepper

> **Tidbits:**
> *Butternut squash can be grated on the large holes of a box grater or in a food processor.*

Directions

Place a wire rack on a rimmed cookie sheet with a paper towel underneath to absorb oil. In a large bowl, combine the grated butternut squash, flour, eggs, minced sage, salt, and pepper. Stir until the mixture is combined. In a large cast-iron pan, heat the oil over medium-high heat. Once the oil is hot, scoop 3 one-tablespoon mounds of the mixture into the pan, pressing them lightly into rounds, spacing them at least 2 inches apart. Fry the fritters for 2 to 3 minutes. Flip them once, and fry for an additional 2 minutes until they are golden brown and cooked throughout. Transfer the fritters to the wire rack and sprinkle with salt. Repeat the scooping and frying process with the remaining mixture.
(Yields 12 fritters.)

SOUTHERN FRIED FOWL

The Castalian Springs Inn was a working farm with a barnyard full of chickens and hogs. Rolling pastureland provided fresh fodder for cattle and sheep as well as deer, bear, and small game. The smokehouse, and salt helped preserve meat.

During the Civil War, every part of an animal was used for food and functionality. Only the chicken breast is used in my recipe. And it's breaded and fried in butter, not oil.

Southern fried fowl is my fancy name for fried chicken. In 1861, the term "chicken bosom" was used in polite southern society or mixed company.

Ingredients
4 boneless "chicken bosoms"
2 cups bread crumbs (seasoned, if you prefer)
1 egg, lightly beaten
1 stick butter
4 lemon slices
2 tablespoons capers
⅓ cup dry sherry
Salt and pepper to taste

Directions
Place the chicken bosoms between two sheets of waxed paper (or in a Ziploc bag.) Pound until flattened. In a large cast-iron skillet, melt the butter until it bubbles. Beat the egg lightly and dredge the flattened chicken until it's coated. Quickly dredge the chicken in bread crumbs until fully coated. Over medium heat, place the chicken in bubbling butter. Turn when it's crispy. Pour in the sherry and capers and cook the liquid down. Place a lemon slice on top of each chicken bosom. Turn the burner down to medium-low heat. Simmer until cooked through. Remove the chicken from the pan and drain on a wire rack. Serve hot.
(Yields 4 servings.)

BUCKWHEAT PANCAKES

Buckwheat was first cultivated in China around the year 1000 and brought, circuitously, to New York's Hudson Valley by Dutch settlers. Eventually, buckwheat made its way south into frontier kitchens and cookery books. Today, it's healthy cuisine for the home cook.

Buckwheat contains considerable amounts of vitamins B1 and B2, is a great source of protein, and offers a plethora of minerals, including copper, zinc, manganese, and calcium. Nutrition aside, these pancakes satisfied the soldier. They were "stick to the ribs" good.

Immortalized in verses from the song "Dixie's Land" written by song bard Daniel Decatur Emmett in 1859, today buckwheat cakes are as popular as ever.

Dar's buckwheat cakes an Injun batter,
Makes your fat a little fatter;

Look away! Look away! Look away! Dixie Land.
Then hoe it down and scratch your gravel,
To Dixie's Land I'm bound to travel.
Look away! Look away! Look away! Dixie Land . . .

Serving buckwheat cakes, however, was not something the cook took lightly. To "hoe it down and scratch your gravel"—or, in modern vernacular, plant, harvest, winnow, and grind the buckwheat into usable flour—was tedious and time consuming. Today we have the option of purchasing this flour pre-ground and packaged. So, go gather some buckwheat flour and get your griddle on!

Ingredients
1 cup buckwheat flour
1 teaspoon baking powder
½ teaspoon baking soda
2 tablespoons sugar
Pinch of salt
1 egg, lightly beaten
1 cup buttermilk (or milk)
2 tablespoons butter, melted
1 tablespoon cooking oil, or bacon
    drippings for greasing the skillet

Tidbits: *This historic recipe was made before the invention of baking powder. For the sake of convenience, however, today's Rumsford Baking Powder works well and contains no aluminum.*

Directions
In a large, cast-iron skillet, or 375°F, preheated, electric skillet, melt 1 tablespoon of butter or bacon grease. Whisk together the dry ingredients. Add lightly beaten egg, buttermilk, and 2 tablespoons of melted butter to the dry mix, stirring after each addition. Drop the batter in ¼-cup measures onto the hot greased skillet or griddle. Fry until bubbles break on the pancake's surface. Flip and fry an additional 1½ minutes until the pancakes are cooked through. Top with butter, fruit, nuts, and maple syrup. (Yields 4 servings.)

Tidbits, Too: *The Old Mill in Pigeon Forge has the best whole grain flours and cornmeal.*

ROASTED STRAWBERRY JAM

Wild strawberries decorate Sumner County's fruitful landscape in mid-May, and, like their colorful cousin, the wild violet, wither into the soil from whence they came by mid-June. Wild strawberries require a goodly amount of sunlight—the likes of which shines on the old Wynne homestead.

For inn patrons, strawberry jam was coveted and held in high esteem at the dining room table for the bite of biscuit or for stashing between stacks of buckwheat 'cakes.

Sugar was "gold" during the Civil War and just as scarce. Instead of wasting the precious staple, Castalian Springs Inn cooks may have roasted this fruit, allowing it to release its own sugar—adding just enough to sweeten the deal.

Ingredients
12 cups fresh strawberries (3 quarts, roughly chopped)
1 cup granulated sugar, divided
1 tablespoon lemon zest
3 tablespoon fresh lemon juice
Generous pinch kosher salt

To Prepare Fruit: Select large, firm, tart strawberries. Wash and drain the berries; remove the caps with a teaspoon.

Directions
Preheat the oven to 425°F. In a large, shallow baking dish (preferably glass, which help berries caramelize), gently toss together the strawberries, ½ cup sugar, lemon zest, lemon juice, and salt. Roast the strawberries for 10 to 15 minutes before stirring. Taste-test to determine the amount of natural sweetness released. Add the rest of the sugar in ¼-cup increments. Roast longer. Taste-test again. Continue roasting for 30 to 40 minutes until the fruit "jam" thickens slightly (jam will thicken as it cools). Refrigerate before using.
(Yields about 2½ cups.)

To "Put Up" and Store: Immediately pour hot jam into hot, sterile jars, leaving ¼ inch of headspace. Wipe the rims of the jars with a dampened clean paper towel; seal with two-piece, metal canning lids. Process the jars in a boiling hot water bath for 15 to 20 minutes. Remove from the bath and cool at room temperature. The lids seal when you hear them "click."

SHELLBARK HICKORY NUT SHORTBREAD COOKIES

This recipe honors Alfred Royal Wynne and the shellbark hickory tree he planted out of respect and admiration for "tough as an old hickory nut" Andrew Jackson, seventh president of the United States. As the story goes, in 1840, A. R. Wynne built a row of guesthouses on his property just east of the inn and a racetrack at nearby Lick Creek. Most guests vacationed at the resort to bathe in the rich, therapeutic mineral waters of the area. Andrew Jackson, an avid horseman, however, became a frequent guest at the racetrack, occasionally bringing one of his favorite thoroughbreds to race against one of Wynne's horses.

A. R. Wynne's enslaved workers may have "tapped" a sycamore maple tree for syrup like the one in which Thomas Sharp Spencer spent the winter. Shellbark and shagbark hickory nuts are similar in taste and appearance.

Ingredients
1 cup (2 sticks) unsalted butter, softened
½ teaspoon salt
1⅔ cup (about 10 ounces) all-purpose flour
¼ cup confectioner's sugar
½ teaspoon vanilla extract (optional)
½ cup finely chopped wild hickory nuts

Directions
With a handheld mixer, cream the softened butter at medium-low speed. When creamy, beat the butter with a wooden spoon until it is light and fluffy. Add the salt, sugar, and flour, stirring until just combined. Fold in the nuts. The dough will hold together but will be slightly dry. Form the cookie dough into a 2×12–inch log and wrap in parchment paper or

plastic wrap. Chill until firm—at least two hours or overnight. When ready to bake, preheat the oven to 325°F. Line two cookie sheets with parchment paper. Slice the cookie dough into ¼-inch slices and arrange 1 inch apart on the cookie sheet. Bake 10 to 12 minutes or until the edges are light golden brown. Let the cookies cool on a wire rack. Serve while slightly warm. Fully cooled cookies may be refrigerated or stored in an airtight container for up to one week.

(Yields about 48 cookies.)

SKILLET GINGERBREAD

I discovered this handwritten recipe for skillet gingerbread on a scrap of paper in a file marked "Recipes" from the Wynne Family Papers at the Tennessee State Library and Archives in Nashville.

Presumably served at the Castalian Springs Inn, the recipe is as follows: "6 eggs, 6 cups of flour, 2 cups of butter, 1 cup sugar, 1 cup molasses, 1 cup buttermilk, 1 teaspoonful of soda, spices to the taste. I sometimes bake in a large skillet."

Directions for preparing the gingerbread, and the dimensions of that "large" skillet were not included on the scrap of paper. The ratio of spices added to the wet and dry ingredients, however, fills my mother's antique, well-seasoned, 14-inch, round, cast-iron skillet.

Surely this recipe was employed when serving a large number of guests or when Confederate soldiers like General Morgan and his men found their way to the inn.

Cooking time varies when using smaller skillets. See "Skillet Gingerbread, Too."

Ingredients
6 eggs
6 cups flour
2 cups butter
1 cup sugar
1 cup molasses
1 cup buttermilk
1 teaspoon baking soda
2½ teaspoons ground ginger

1½ teaspoons cinnamon
1 teaspoon nutmeg
½ teaspoon cloves
½ teaspoon allspice

Directions
Preheat oven to 350°F. Grease and flour a 14-inch cast-iron skillet. In a large mixing bowl, whisk together the flour, sugar, baking soda, salt, ginger, cinnamon, cloves, nutmeg, and allspice. Melt the butter and combine with the molasses. Pour the molasses mixture into the dry mixture and stir until just combined. Whisk together the eggs and buttermilk. Stir into the batter until evenly combined. Pour the batter into the prepared skillet. Bake for 35 minutes and check for doneness. Bake for another 10 minutes or until the cake begins to pull away from the edge of skillet and the center is set when a toothpick comes out clean. Remove from the oven and cool on a wire rack. Gingerbread is best served warm with a dollop of whipped cream or ice cream.
(Yields sixty 1½×2×4-inch servings.)

SKILLET GINGERBREAD, TOO
My recipe is easy to manage, contains similar ingredients and—baked in a 10-inch skillet—yields 8 moist, delicious wedges.

Ingredients
2 cups all-purpose flour
¼ cup granulated sugar
1 teaspoon baking soda
¼ teaspoon salt
1½ teaspoons ground ginger
1 teaspoon cinnamon
¼ teaspoon each cloves and nutmeg
½ cup (1 stick) butter, melted
¾ cup molasses
¼ cup orange juice (or water)
1 large egg
1 cup buttermilk

Tidbits:
If you prefer a spicier gingerbread, add up to ½ teaspoon of finely ground black pepper.

Directions

Preheat oven to 350°F. Grease and flour a 10 -inch cast-iron skillet. In a large mixing bowl, whisk together the flour, sugar, baking soda, salt, ginger, cinnamon, cloves, and nutmeg. Melt the butter and combine with the molasses. Pour the molasses mixture into the dry mixture and stir until just combined. Add juice or water, stirring until the mixture is moistened. Whisk together the egg and buttermilk. Stir them into the batter until evenly combined. Pour the batter into the prepared skillet. Bake for 30 to 35 minutes until the cake begins to pull away from the edge of the skillet. Remove from the oven and cool on a wire rack. Gingerbread is best served warm with a dollop of whipped cream or ice cream.
(Yields 8 servings.)

Thomas Sharp Spencer

In the words of Tennessee historian Walter Durham, "Some stopped to see the stump of the hollow sycamore tree in which Thomas Sharp Spencer spent the winter alone while on a long hunt from southwest Virginia." Thomas Sharp Spencer's reputation obviously preceded him in the admiring eyes of Confederate *and* Union soldiers. Known for his enormous physical strength, Spencer was often characterized as having the strength of "two common men" and that of a lion.

Spencer is generally recognized as the first white settler in Middle Tennessee. Arriving from Virginia in the spring of 1779, he staked his claim on plots of land, built cabins on them, grew food, and spent the winter of 1779 living alone in the hollow of a giant sycamore maple tree at Bledsoe's Creek near what is now Wynnewood, protecting his "staked claim."

Tennessee's native sycamore holds the record for the broadest trunk of any native tree—over ten feet in diameter at four feet above the ground. This form of lodging must have attracted Thomas Sharp Spencer as he sought shelter for the long, cold, lonely winter.

Surely Spencer did not munch maple sugar cookies while living in the hollow trunk of that sycamore. And he may not have known that its sap could be tapped and boiled down into maple syrup. Yet, he would certainly be delighted to chomp these crisp, tasty "cakes," as you will be, too.

TENNESSEE SYCAMORE MAPLE SUGAR COOKIES

Ingredients
½ cup butter
½ shortening
1¼ cup sugar
2 large eggs
½ cup pure maple syrup
2 teaspoons maple flavor extract
3 cups all-purpose flour
¾ teaspoon baking powder
½ teaspoon baking soda
½ teaspoon salt

> **Tidbits:**
> *Boil 1 cup of pure, good-quality maple syrup down to ¾ cup. Using a pastry brush, paint the top of each cookie with the thickened maple syrup. Top with the optional sprinkle of coarse kosher salt.*

Directions
In a large bowl, cream the butter, shortening, and sugar until light and fluffy. Add the eggs, one at a time, beating well after each addition. Beat in the maple syrup and maple extract. In a medium bowl, whisk together the remaining ingredients. Gradually mix the dry ingredients into the creamed mixture until well combined. Cover and refrigerate for 2 hours or until the mixture is easy to handle. Preheat the oven to 350°F. With a 1-tablespoon cookie scoop, drop the cookie batter onto two parchment covered baking sheets. Flour a flat-bottomed glass and flatten the cookies to a ¼-inch thickness. Bake 3 inches apart at 350°F for 9 to 12 minutes or until golden brown. Remove them to wire racks to cool.
(Yields 3 dozen.)

Chapter 13

SPARTA ROCK HOUSE
STATE HISTORIC SITE

◆━━━━━━━━━━━━━━━━━━━━━━━━━━━━━━━━◆

Built 1835–1839
Sparta, Tennessee

Taproots

Built of Tennessee sandstone between 1835 and 1839, the Sparta Rock House, located in White County, served many purposes. Brothers Barlow and Madison Fiske erected the structure that served as a toll house and a stagecoach inn for travelers who had just crossed (or were about to cross over, depending on their direction) the rough and rugged Cumberland Plateau. It was also a way station for wagons and stagecoaches coming down the Wilderness Trail—with trees tied behind them for brakes! Prior to 1860, the well-traveled Wilderness Trail ran east to Washington, D.C., and Philadelphia, west through Sparta, Lebanon, and into Nashville, where it connected with the Natchez Trace and other westward trails. Over 180 years old, the wooden doors, window frames, ceiling, floor, fireplaces, and mantels of the Rock House remain original.

Upon arrival—and after paying their toll—travelers entered a single but spacious room with two large, open fireplaces at each end. If hungry, visitors were revived by meals simmering within each. Many continued on their arduous journey, while others who arrived at night had the option of a meal and entering the hay and straw-filled attic. The "bedding" wasn't much, but for those who had traveled the trail for six weeks or more, these accommodations must have been welcome comfort.

Still, for others, the joy was not just in finding a place to eat and sleep

Sparta Rock House State Historic Site.

but in the dignitaries who may have stopped along their way from one place to another. Legend says men such as Andrew Jackson, seventh president of the United States, James K. Polk, eleventh president of the United States, Sam Houston, governor of Tennessee and later Texas, were early visitors. Other visitors included senators, congressmen, and governors from Tennessee, Alabama, Texas, and Louisiana who had come up the trail on their way to Washington, D.C.

Today, as you stand outside the Sparta Rock House, imagine the road as it might have been in the early years of this Tennessee landmark. In those days, the road was part of the first paved road that stretched across the state. This well-worn mountain trail from Knoxville through Leba-

Upon entering the small living area, Rock House guests
were likely served a small meal. The "attic" door pulled
down for travelers spending the night.

non and on to Nashville was crowned by North Carolina in 1786 as the
"Broadway of America." It earned this name because of its status as one
of the main east-west thoroughfares of our young nation. By 1828, it was
the most traveled road from East Tennessee to West Tennessee, eventually
earning the nickname "The Gateway." Soldiers were stationed along the
road, posted to prevent robbers and Native Americans from attacking the
men, women, and children who filled the stagecoaches and wagon trains.

The Sparta Rock House State Historic Site also served as a place for
delivering mail and swapping out horses. After the Civil War, the house
was used as a train stop for the mountaintop coal mines. Trains rumbled
and chugged in and out of Sparta to what was, at that time, the long
journey to Chattanooga. Rock House was the first stop on the way down
the mountain, and the railroad ran where Highway 70 runs today. In the
late 1800s and early 1900s, the Rock House was used as a residence, and
later, it was a school simply known as the "Rock House School."

Fireplaces at each end of the Rock House helped
keep visitors warm and filled.

In 1941, the State of Tennessee purchased the Rock House and its
grounds, making it the second building so purchased as a historical site.
Electricity and a back room were added before the Rock House Chapter
of the Tennessee Society Daughters of the American Revolution (TSDAR)
were appointed as "custodians." In 1959, the Sparta Rock House was
placed on the Tennessee Historical Register, and in 1973, it was placed
on the National Register of Historic Places.

The Rock House is located 3.7 miles east of Sparta on Highway 70
and is open every Saturday afternoon from 2:00 p.m. to 4:00 p.m. Visits
can be arranged (in advance) by appointment.

Address and Contact Information

Sparta Rock House
State Historic Site
Highway 70
Sparta, TN 38583
(931) 739-7625

Sparta-White County
Chamber of Commerce
16 W. Bockman Way
Sparta, TN 38583
(931) 836-3552
info@SpartaTNchamber.com

Timeless Recipes

There was usually a pole across the fireplace three
or four feet above the fire from which a pot rack was
hung. There was a hook on the bottom on which a pot
could be hung and swung over the hottest part of the
fire for boiling. Meat was killed, cooled, washed, then
dipped into the hot water over the fire.

—Reverend Monroe Seals, *History of White County, Tennessee* (1935)

For trail-weary travelers arriving at the Rock House on a late afternoon
stagecoach, Conestoga wagon, or by horseback, a hearty meal was welcome fare.

Two open fireplaces at each end of its large single room on the interior of the Rock House would provide ample space for a hanging cauldron or two filled with freshly butchered beef for stew or whatever wild,
small game was caught for food. A long-handled cast-iron skillet with
feet, called a spider, was filled with cornbread batter and set over the
coals on the hearth. Because they had feet, spiders could stand directly
over the hearth, their three legs elevating them over the coals. Potatoes
made into hash would satisfy Rock House guests. Greens could be boiled
or fried, and nuts from nearby shagbark hickory trees could be made
into pies.

Although the flow of commerce through the Rock House was steady
year-round, there are no written records of meals served. But we can
reckon that there was always something cooking at the Rock House. On
any evening in 1836, a slow-cooked meal from the hearth of the Rock
House to the bellies of those hungry sojourners would have been food
for the soul. Dinner, the mid-day and main meal at the Rock House may
have looked like this:

MENU
Biscuits
Poke "Salat" (Salad)
Colcannon
Stewed Beef Shanks
Shagbark Hickory Nut Pie

BISCUITS

Biscuits at the Rock House were essential for travelers on the Wilderness Trail, served hot and fresh from the skillet or, tucked cold into the pockets and knapsacks of hungry wayfarers.

The beauty of this biscuit recipe is that a Rock House cook could count on turning out delicious biscuits even when milk was not available. With four basic ingredients, these biscuits could be made quickly and continually to sate the steady stream of travel-weary, overnight guests.

Tidbits:

Baking powder is made by blending baking soda (sodium bicarbonate) with a starch (such as corn starch) to fend off moisture, and an acidic compound such as cream of tartar. Cream of tartar comes from the lining on the inside of wine caskets. After wine ferments, the white sediment (tartaric acid) is removed, purified, and ground into a fine white powder. Cream of tartar can be found in the spice section of today's grocery stores.

Ingredients

2 cups all-purpose flour
1 level tablespoon baking powder
6 tablespoons soft shortening, butter,
    or cooking oil
1 cup water, milk, or buttermilk

Directions

Preheat the oven to 450°F. In a large mixing bowl, whisk the flour, salt, and baking powder. Add the shortening and work into the flour mixture with your fingertips until it resembles coarse meal. Make a well in the center of the flour and pour in the water (or cold milk or buttermilk). Toss the liquid into the flour until the ingredients are well combined into a dough. Turn the dough out onto a floured surface and knead, folding the dough 5 or 6 times. Roll out into a rectangle to ½-inch thickness and cut with a 2½inch biscuit cutter. Bake in a 10-inch skillet for 10 to 12 minutes.
(Yields 8–10 biscuits.)

POKE "SALAT" (SALAD)

If "Poke 'Salat' Annie" loved these tasty greens enough for Elvis Presley to sing her praises, they must be good. Pokeweed may be referred to as "common," but it's uncommonly delicious when prepared properly. Pokeweed is a native, wild, springtime green that surely pleased the palates of the Rock House guests. "Poke" grows along the edges of fields and orchards and still appears in abundance along trails leading to and from the Rock House. Typically, pokeweed grows from about four to eight feet high. Its edible greens are tender shoots no longer than 6 inches. Tender poke shoots, plucked and gathered in bunches, chopped, boiled in a cauldron until tender, then boiled again, and tossed in a skillet of sizzling bacon grease was considered by some "a dish of majestic proportions."

A Word of Caution: The roots and berries of the pokeweed are poisonous to humans but are a good food source for songbirds, including the catbird, cardinal, brown thrush, and Tennessee's state bird, the mockingbird. One Tennessee aficionado observed that pokeweed arrives every spring "about the time the dogwoods drop their petals."

Ingredients
2 pounds fresh poke greens
1 large sweet onion, diced
4 to 6 slices bacon
Bacon grease
2 hard-boiled eggs, sliced or quartered

Directions
Wash, and rinse well, the fresh, young, tender "poke" shoots. Then, wash and rinse again. Fully immerse the cleaned poke in a large pot of lightly salted, boiling water. Boil for 15 minutes. Drain and rinse with warm water. Chop into bite-sized pieces about the size of a leaf of fresh spinach. In a large pot of fresh water, bring the poke to a rapid, second boil for a few minutes more, until tender. Pour the poke into a colander. Rinse well. Drain well and pat dry. Set aside. Fry bacon crisp enough to crumble. Remove the bacon from the pan. Save the drippings. Fry the onion in the bacon grease drippings until tender. Toss the boiled greens in the frying pan with the bacon drippings and onion. Serve garnished with hard boiled eggs and crumbled bacon.
(Yields 4 servings.)

COLCANNON

Easy to grow and harvest, the potato, one of Tennessee's most copious root vegetables, was likely served at the Rock House in everything from soups to stews to succotash. The potassium-rich white tuber, dubbed "Irish" potato in contrast to the sweet potato, was brought to America by the Scotch-Irish—an American term used to describe immigrants from Northern Ireland, the majority of whom were Presbyterians from the province of Ulster. The potato would not become a popular dietary mainstay in Appalachian valleys and coves until the 1800s, however, because many say religious folk could find no reference to the potato in the Bible. But, as the story goes, once they heard that an Irishman survived for almost an entire year on the lowly spud alone, they jumped on that wagon.

Colcannon is a favorite Irish dish made with potatoes that are boiled and then mashed. They are mixed with a combination of cabbage and kale, flavored with a mixture of onions—all of which were planted on the Tennessee frontier—and combined with milk or cream, then topped with a large knob of butter. Irish immigrants, homesick for the foods of their native culture, introduced colcannon to American palates sometime around 1775, when it is first referenced in the diary of William Bulkely and when a recipe titled "Cabbage and Potatoes" appeared in the 1847 publication of *Mrs. Crowen's American Lady's Cookery Book*.

Overnight guests at the Rock House were in for a treat if one of those Dutch ovens was full of colcannon. Stewed beef shanks, spooned over a heaping helping of colcannon, would keep Rock House guests warmed and filled, with just enough room left for a slice of shagbark hickory nut pie.

Ingredients
4 medium russet potatoes (2 to 2½ pounds),
    peeled and cut into large chunks
1 tablespoon salt
5 to 6 tablespoons unsalted butter (with more butter for serving)
3 lightly packed cups of chopped kale, cabbage, chard, or other leafy green
3 scallions (including the leaves), minced (about ½ cup)
1 cup milk or cream

Directions

Place the potatoes in a medium pot and cover with cold water by at least an inch. Add 1 tablespoon of salt to the water. Bring to a boil. Boil until the potatoes are fork tender (15 to 20 minutes). Drain in a colander. Set aside. Return the empty pot to the stove and set over medium heat. Melt the butter in the pot and when bubbling, add the greens. Stir the greens slowly for 3 to 4 minutes or until they are wilted. Add the green onions and cook 1 minute more. Pour the milk or cream into the pot and continue to stir.

> **Tidbits:**
> *For a variation, substitute half of the potatoes with baked or boiled and mashed parsnips. Additionally, bacon, crisply fried and crumbled, makes a delicious garnish.*

Add the boiled potatoes from the colander. Reduce the heat to medium. Use a potato masher and mash the potatoes, mixing them up with the greens. Add salt to taste and serve hot, with a knob of butter in the center. (Yields 4–6 servings.)

STEWED BEEF SHANKS

Those large Dutch ovens hanging in the fireplaces of the Rock House surely simmered with possum, groundhog, or even squirrel, cooked with whatever seasonal vegetables were on hand. Beef shanks would have been served on important occasions, such as when Andrew Jackson traveled the Wilderness Trail and stopped at the Rock House. Beef, from a locally butchered cow—purchased outright or bought with barter—would have been dished up at the Rock House and enjoyed in its delicious sauce served over hearty colcannon.

Ingredients

4-6 beef shanks (bone-in)
3 tablespoons olive oil or vegetable oil
3 medium carrots, chopped
3 stalks celery, chopped
2 quarts (8 cups) cool water
1 large yellow onion, diced
3 large garlic cloves, smashed, diced
2 heaping tablespoons tomato paste

1 small can tomato sauce
1 can beef broth
Handful fresh parsley, chopped
1 cup red wine (or beef broth)
3 bay leaves
Salt and pepper

Directions

Preheat the oven to 350°F. Chop the carrots, celery, and parsley. Set aside. Dice the onion and mince the garlic. Set aside. Season the shanks with salt and pepper. In a large cast-iron skillet, braise the beef shanks in oil till brown. Remove from the pan. Set aside. Sauté carrots and celery in the remaining olive oil (add a bit more if needed). Add the tomato paste, small can of tomato sauce, garlic, beef broth, parsley, red wine, and 3 bay leaves. Stir and simmer for 15 minutes. Set braised shanks in a Dutch oven or deep baking dish. Pour the sautéed vegetables in liquid over the shanks. Cover and bake in the 350°F oven for 3 hours. Remove the bay leaves before serving. (Yields 6 servings.)

SHAGBARK HICKORY NUT PIE

The shagbark hickory tree, aptly named for its unique "shaggy" bark, grows abundantly in White County. Early settlers would crack the nut open on a rock and painstakingly pick the nutmeat out of its shell. It was tedious work, but worth the prize. Today, machines do the job.

"Hickory" is derived from the word *pawcohiccora,* an Algonquin Indian word describing the tree's oily nutmeat. Andrew Jackson was nicknamed "Old Hickory," a play on the toughness of the hickory nut and the wood. Jackson is said to have stopped at the Rock House on his way up and down the Wilderness Trail.

When the folks at the Rock House got wind that Jackson or other dignitaries were coming up (or down) the trail, they likely pulled out all the stops: a side of beef to stew and a bag of hickory nuts to make a pie.

The Rock House cook was sure to have flour, shortening (lard), and salt on hand. Combining these three simple ingredients with water produced a flaky pie crust, likely made with lard and filled with something tasty for the passenger stepping from the dusty cab of a stagecoach. One can imagine the aroma of a freshly baked pie wafting through the windows of the Rock House. For this hickory nut pie, the pie shell can either be store bought or made using my recipe.

Ingredients
Filling
3 eggs, lightly beaten
¾ cups of white sugar
1 cup light Karo syrup
1 teaspoon of vanilla
2 tablespoons of melted butter (salted)
1 cup of hickory nuts, chopped

Flaky Pastry for Pie Crust
2 cups flour
1 cup shortening
1½ teaspoon salt
ice cold water

Directions
For the Filling: Preheat the oven to 350°F. In a medium-sized bowl, whisk together the eggs, sugar, syrup, vanilla, butter, and chopped nuts. Pour into the pie crust. Bake for 50 minutes, or until knife inserted in the center comes out clean. (Yields 8 servings.)

For the Pie Crust: Whisk together flour and salt. Quickly blend the shortening into the flour until the particles resemble coarse meal. Sprinkle with ice water (1 tablespoon at a time), stirring it with a fork very slowly, just until the dough holds together. Cover the dough and chill for 30 minutes or more. Remove from the refrigerator and let set for about 20 minutes. Roll the dough out

> **Tidbits:**
> To prevent a soggy bottom crust, brush the dough with a lightly beaten egg white or shortening and bake in your preheated oven for at least ten minutes allowing the crust to cool before filling the pie.

on a floured board ¼ to ⅛ inch thick. Place the rolling pin in the center of the dough circle with the ends of the rolling pin at 9 o'clock and 3 o'clock. Drape the bottom half the dough circle (the end closest to you) over the rolling pin Beginning with the loose end of the dough, gently lay the pie crust into an ungreased 9-inch pie plate. Trim the edges and crimp.

Chapter 14

DUCKTOWN BASIN MUSEUM AND BURRA BURRA COPPER MINE STATE HISTORIC SITE

◆————————————————◆

1847–1987
Ducktown, Tennessee

Taproots

You load 16 tons and what do you get?
Another day older and deeper in debt.
St. Peter, don't you call me 'cause I can't go
I owe my soul to the company store.

"Sixteen Tons," words and music by Merle Travis (© 1946)
Recorded by Tennessee Ernie Ford (1955)

Merle Travis wrote the 1946 hit song "Sixteen Tons" based on letters from his father and brother—coal miners in Muhlenberg County, Kentucky. The songs premise could have easily been written about copper miners in southeastern Tennessee who extracted a living from cupriferous veins hidden within the arms of Ducktown's Great Copper Basin.

Ducktown is nestled in the southern Appalachian Mountains, and the Burra Burra Copper Mine covers a portion of Polk County, Tennessee; Fannin, Georgia; and Cherokee County, North Carolina. Unlike the rich farmland to the north and west of Ducktown, this isolated area of Tennessee was once a mass of undulating hills unsuitable for farming. Owned by the Cherokees until President Andrew Jackson's Indian Removal Act was enforced in 1838, the territory is one of the last settled areas of

The boiler house, built in 1901, contained the boilers that
produced steam to power the equipment in the adjacent hoist
house, as well as in other buildings on the site.

southeastern Tennessee. The Act was spurred in part by the 1828
Dahlonega, Georgia, gold strike. Throngs of would-be prospectors rushed
into "them thar hills" of Hiwassee, hoping to uncover the next big strike.

Tennessee's copper mining industry began along the banks of Potato
Creek in 1843 when a prospector named Lemmons discovered what he
thought was gold. Upon closer examination, Lemmons realized he had
uncovered an oxide of copper, but the copper wasn't pure. It was mixed
with pyrite, sometimes called "fool's gold." Lemmons made his discovery

The crane used at the Burra Burra Mine, late 1930s. The purpose of the crane was to lift equipment from the mining company's railroad track, located below this hill, to this level for use in the shops.

where the creek cut into an ore body and exposed the chalcopyrite. It was bright yellow in color with a metallic luster. Lemmons, looking for gold, moved on.

A geologist, however, dug out several casks of the mineral. Noting that the only way in and out of the area was over the mountains by mule or horseback, he loaded his pack animals with the casks and hauled them seventy miles over the old Indian trail to Ellijay, Georgia, for analysis. The analysis revealed that the ground was rich in copper. In mining vernacular, the "boom" was on—and so was the land grab.

Land speculators and early investors bought up nearly all the land in the region. No one knew exactly where all the ore bodies were located. However, because the area was so remote, with no established mode of transportation other than horse or mule, a healthy return on their investment was highly anticipated.

The hoist house, built in 1901, contained the hoisting engines
and a large air compressor. The engines were used to raise and
lower men and equipment into the mine, as well as to raise ore.
The compressor powered pumps, drills, chutes, and loaders.

In 1853, John Caldwell, a hard-working land owner from Jefferson
County, Tennessee, enlisted the help of Cherokee laborers who had es-
caped into the surrounding mountains during the enforcement of Jackson's
Indian Removal Act. They built Copper Road along the nearby Ocoee
River Gorge all the way to Cleveland, Tennessee. Caldwell literally carved
Copper Road out of the wilderness as a way for mules and wagons to
transport ore to the railroad in Cleveland.

The increase in mining brought the need for a means by which to refine
the ore locally. In 1854, the first ore smelter was built at the Hiwassee
Mine. Standing timber, they reasoned, would serve as fuel. Burned in
"roasting yards," timber became charcoal for furnaces that were used as
the primary means of separating minerals.

Hiwassee Town, named after the Hiwassee Mine, became known as
Ducktown in 1900. Ducktown, named after a Cherokee village between

what is now present-day Copper Hill and present-day Ducktown, was known as *Kawa' nah* in Cherokee, which translates as "place of the duck."

Once the mines opened, the entire region became known as the Ducktown Basin. The Ducktown Museum takes its name from the historic name of the region, and the Ducktown Basin Museum at the Burra Burra Copper Mine site was headquarters for the Tennessee Copper Company mining operations from 1899 to 1975.

There were at least a dozen mining companies commercially operating in nine separate ore bodies on the Tennessee side—with three others on the Georgia side. These early mining operations later became the towns of Ducktown, Isabella, Copperhill, and McCaysville (in Georgia). The population of these isolated hamlets went from a dozen families in the 1840s to more than one thousand people working the mines in the 1850s.

Between 1850 and 1920, a significant number of immigrants—mainly Dutch, German, and British—made their way to the Basin. More than two hundred families arrived from England. They were drawn to America by the promise of freedom and President James K. Polk's western expansion. Cornish miners—considered the elite in the mining profession—traveled from Cornwall, England, to work these copper mines after their country's mid-nineteenth-century decline in the tin and copper mining industries.

During the 1850s, the mine employed just four Cornish miners. By 1860, the number of Cornish miners had grown to over one hundred. During the 1960s, the mines employed more than twenty-five hundred people.

The expense of equipping mining operations eventually slowed development of the area, and by 1858, only five mines operated regularly in the Hiwassee area. An acrid air of unrest filtered through the haze of the roasting yards as the impending "War Between the States" hovered like an angry black storm cloud over the country.

In 1860, a group of local businessmen and landowners concluded that consolidating the less productive mines would provide a means to continue operations. As a result, the Burra Burra Copper Company—named after a famous mining operation in Australia—was established. During the first meeting, the board of directors of the newly consolidated company hired a young Julius Eckhardt Raht as "captain" over its mining operations.

In the world of Cornish mining operations, authority was structured as if onboard a ship. During the influx of Cornish miners, Captain Raht, a young German mining engineer, reportedly became the wealthiest man in Tennessee because of his strategic, fair business practices. Raht was an entrepreneurial businessman and American citizen, having long since purchased land and a team of mules for hauling copper.

Money for southern mining operations came mainly from northern investors. This method worked for several years until the outbreak of the Civil War. President Abraham Lincoln understood that to control supply lines to the impending 1863 battle in Chattanooga, Union soldiers must capture and control the railroad in Cleveland, Tennessee—the county seat. Indeed, the Union army captured Cleveland, putting an end to the transport of copper in the region. Consequently, the mines closed, and Captain Raht and his wife, Mathilda, moved to Cincinnati, Ohio, until the war was over.

The mines reopened in 1866 under the direction of Raht and continued to operate until 1878. By this time, hauling copper in and out of the region by wagon had become too expensive, and there were no trees left for fuel. The mines reopened in 1890 when the railroad extended into the Basin and continued to operate until the mines closed in 1987.

Today, a single chimney stands near Ducktown as "captain" over the once culturally vibrant hillside. The hummocks, once desolate and barren from years of acid rain formed by roasting yards and their sulfur dioxide fumes, are being recycled as part of a process to remove mine waste and restore the water in creeks and tributaries. More than 18 million trees planted as part of a reforestation program are supplemented by aerial reseedings of the grasslands.

The mission of the Ducktown Basin Museum and Burra Burra Mine is to preserve and interpret the cultural and industrial heritage of the copper-mining region of southern Appalachia. Much of the local history is preserved at the Ducktown Basin Museum, where visitors can see photos of the once denuded landscape and schedule tours of the grounds to observe reclamation efforts firsthand. Today, much of the region consists of wetlands where reeds and grasses act as nature's filtration process and now cover the once polluted area. Wildlife is slowly returning, even frogs.

The Burra Burra Mine State Historic Site was listed on the National Register of Historic Places on March 17, 1983, and consists of ten historic buildings on seventeen acres.

Address and Contact Information
Ducktown Basin Museum and Burra Burra Mine State Historic Site
212 Burra Burra Hill (off Tennessee Highway 68)
Ducktown, TN 37236
(423) 496-5778

Timeless Recipes

... the picnic grounds, about one mile from Hiwassee, are a lovely spot—well covered with young trees,
forming beautiful shade, which were very acceptable
for a church picnic.

—*Ellijay* (Ga.) *Courier,* June 16, 1877

The company for which coal miners worked owned company stores, which were commissaries for the local miners. In the Great Copper Basin, however, the company store for copper miners was leased to Captain Julius E. Raht, who stocked the store with goods he paid for out of his own pocket and for which he charged the miners a fair price.

Kentucky coal miners, by comparison, were not paid in cash but with "scrip"—that is, nontransferable credit vouchers that could be exchanged for a percentage of cash and were mainly spent on goods sold at the company store. "Deeper in debt," as described in the Merle Travis song, happened in part because coal miners were paid every three months. Unless their "scrip" was budgeted, they could—and usually did—overspend, become mired in debt, and sink into deep depression. Heavy drinking, fighting, and carousing became a means of "entertainment."

But in the Tennessee copper industry, the era of rabblerousing had dissipated by 1860. This was brought about by the dignified, well-organized, fair-minded German mining captain, Julius E. Raht. Brawling and carousing gave way to occasional log-rolling and corn shucking at the yearly church picnic. Women gathered for quilting parties, baptisms, picnics, and all-day singings at their various churches. Picnicking became an art form in Hiwassee.

One man, in his letter to the editor of the *Ellijay Courier,* described the annual church picnic as a "union picnic composed of eleven Sunday schools, each school averaging about one-hundred scholars, making over one-thousand scholars. Band music, refreshments, foot races, 'climb-the-greased-pole,' catch, or rather, 'chase-the-greased-pig,' courting, and even weddings were a part of the annual festivities." Likely, someone barbequed a side of beef and spit-roasted or smoked a whole hog for the crowd.

Picnics and "dinner on the grounds" after church were the order of the day. Hiwassee residents embodied and enjoyed this spirit of moral excellence for the next three decades. Today, Sacred Harp singers sprinkle God's salt and light, peppering the national landscape with all-day singings and dinner on the grounds.

The timeless recipe for the success of the Ducktown and Burra Burra Copper Mine community lies in two secret ingredients: integrity and determination. In this case, it was the integrity and determination of Captain Julius Raht.

Captain Raht was only one of what President John F. Kennedy would, a century later, call "a nation of immigrants; immigrants who value both tradition and the exploration of new frontiers; people who deserve the freedom to build better lives." Families from all over the world came to Ducktown, legally, to labor in and around the Burra Burra mines, not simply to make a living but to make lives for themselves in "the land of the free and the home of the brave."

Many American laborers seeking work in Hiwassee arrived from nearby Georgia. By the middle of the 1850s, the Ocoee Byway, Route 64—the Old Copper Road—made its way through the mountainous wilderness connecting the basin to the railroad in Cleveland, Tennessee. Families came in from across Tennessee looking for work and bringing with them regional recipes and southern Appalachian fare. Cornish, Italian, Dutch, French, German, and Austrian miners, often at odds with each other, flavored this great American melting pot with their traditional recipes and religious customs.

Wagons hauling copper to Cleveland via the Old Copper Road were filled on their return trips with foodstuffs, staples, and supplies for miners and their families, each woman learning to transform recipes from her homeland into delicious meals using available ingredients.

Despite financial difficulties, the diverse influx of these families brought their churches with them. Baptists and Methodists came together once a year for a single, consolidated Sunday school picnic held on picnic grounds near the Southern Methodist Church building.

ONCE UPON A PICNIC TABLE
Soda Crackers
Appalachian Sweet Potato Biscuits
Austrian Verhackert, or Tennessee Bacon Jam
Skillet Fried Corn
Italian Angel Eggs
Roast Duck
Appalachian Shepherd's Pie
Old-Fashioned German Cabbage Rolls
Cornish Rainbow Trout Pie
Sorghum Cake

SODA CRACKERS
With staples available at Julius Raht's company store and milk from her family's cow, a miner's wife could proudly place a platter of her freshly baked soda crackers and fresh cheese as part of her offering at the annual Ducktown church picnic.

Ingredients
4½ cups unbleached all-purpose flour
1 teaspoon baking soda
1 teaspoon salt, plus more for sprinkling
¾ cup (cold) vegetable shortening
1⅔–2 cups whole milk, added gradually
    until dough holds together

Directions
Preheat the oven to 350°F. In a large bowl, sift together the flour, baking soda, and salt. Cut in the vegetable shortening until the mixture resembles small pellets. Make a well in the center of the flour mixture. Add milk.

Toss together with your hands to form a stiff dough. Turn the dough out onto a floured work surface. Roll the dough to ⅛-inch thickness. Cut it into 2-inch squares or scalloped rounds. Pierce the dough with fork tines and sprinkle it lightly with salt. Transfer the squares to a baking sheet. Bake for 30 minutes or until the crackers are brown around the edges. (Yields 8 dozen 2-inch squares.)

APPALACHIAN SWEET POTATO BISCUITS
Bushels of sweet potatoes outnumbered Irish potatoes nearly ten to one, according to Polk County's 1850 agricultural census.

Dug from rich southern Appalachian soil in the fall, these copper-colored gems could be stored in "tater bins" or root cellars and transformed into tasty summer treasures. Slathered with butter or bacon jam, this mountain classic would strike any miner's fancy, as it will yours.

Ingredients
2 cups all-purpose flour
2 tablespoons light brown sugar
¼ teaspoon nutmeg
¼ teaspoon cinnamon
1 tablespoon baking powder
½ teaspoon baking soda
6 tablespoons salted butter (cut in pieces), plus more for skillet or cake pan
¾ cup cooked (peeled and mashed) sweet potato
1 cup buttermilk

Directions
Preheat the oven to 425°F. In a large bowl, whisk together the flour, brown sugar, baking powder, baking soda, and salt. Add butter with your fingers until the mixture resembles coarse meal, with some pea-sized lumps of butter remaining. In a small bowl, whisk together the sweet potato and buttermilk. Stir the sweet potato mixture into the flour mixture until just combined. Turn out the dough onto a lightly floured surface, kneading gently 5 or 6 times until the dough comes together. Shape the dough into a disk and pat to a 1-inch thickness. Refrigerate for one hour. Using a floured, 2-inch biscuit cutter, cut out the biscuits. Gather the scraps and

repeat the process. Butter a 10-inch cast-iron skillet. Place the biscuits snugly in the pan. Brush their tops with melted butter. Bake on the middle oven rack for 20 minutes until they are golden brown.
(Yields 12 biscuits.)

AUSTRIAN VERHACKERT, OR TENNESSEE BACON JAM

The rugged wilderness surrounding the Great Smoky Mountains must have reminded Austrian copper miners of their homeland. In many respects, their animal husbandry was similar: pork is a staple on Austrian tables as well as Tennessee's.

Austrian cuisine was influenced by neighboring Hungary. The Mangalica (meaning "hog with a lot of lard") is a Hungarian breed of domestic pig developed in the 1830s by cross-breeding pigs from Szalonta and Bakony with European wild boar and the Serbian Sumadija. Austrian miners could make up a batch of bacon jam from Tennessee hogs.

Verhackert is kin to Tennessee's bacon jam. Both are "bread spreads." Verhackert is made up of minced bacon, garlic, and salt; after a two-day method of freezing and thawing, the meat is served cold with crusty bread as an appetizer.

Tennessee bacon jam is made by slow cooking a combination of crisp bacon, onions, brown sugar, and a liquid—sherry, apple juice, bourbon, or vinegar—blending the mixture and pouring it into small jars. Maple sugar, listed on Tennessee's 1850 census, is added for an extra dimension of sweet.

Ingredients
1½ pounds smoked bacon, chopped into 1-inch pieces
2 teaspoons salted butter
3 medium yellow onions, diced
½ teaspoon salt
¼ cup brown sugar, packed
¼ cup apple juice
1½ teaspoons fresh lemon thyme leaves, divided
    (or one medium lemon thyme stem)
1 teaspoon freshly cracked black pepper
Pinch of cayenne pepper

½ cup water
2 teaspoons apple cider vinegar
2 teaspoons maple syrup
2 teaspoons extra-virgin olive oil

Directions
Spread the bacon pieces evenly across the bottom of a large cast-iron skillet and cook over medium-high heat until the bacon is crisp and the rendered fat is foaming (about 10 minutes). Into a wire strainer placed over a bowl, pour the crispy bacon pieces and rendered fat. When the bacon has cooled and the fat has completely drained, remove the bacon to a clean work surface and chop finely. Return the skillet to medium-high heat; add 2 teaspoons of the reserved bacon fat and the butter. Sauté the onions until translucent (about 10 minutes). Stir the brown sugar, apple juice, thyme leaves, black pepper, and cayenne into the onion mixture; add the finely chopped bacon. Stir the water and apple cider vinegar into the bacon-onion mixture and simmer until the jam is a reddish-copper color and has a jam-like consistency (about 15 minutes). Remove the mixture from the heat and stir in the maple syrup and olive oil until heated through. Pour into sterilized mason jars with lids while hot.
(Yields 12 servings.)

SKILLET FRIED CORN
Miners' wives fried corn in cast-iron skillets with butter and bacon fat, a sprinkle of salt, and a shake or two of pepper—the perfect side dish for the annual Ducktown picnic. Today, canned, bagged, or even "steam-in-the-bag" corn from the freezer is convenient. But corn—cut fresh from the cob—is a beautiful thing.

Ingredients
8 ears fresh corn, kernels removed from the cob
2 tablespoons salted butter
1 tablespoon bacon grease
Salt and pepper to taste

Directions

In a large cast-iron skillet over medium-high heat, melt the butter and bacon fat to bubbling. Add the fresh corn kernels. Fry for 4 minutes until the corn begins to brown. Toss and cook for 1 additional minute. Add salt and pepper. Serve hot.

(Yields 8 cups.)

ITALIAN ANGEL EGGS

The origin of stuffed or "deviled" eggs can be traced back to Rome, Italy, sometime between the fourth and fifth centuries A.D. Fast-forward to the 1800s in America, when "deviling" became a verb to describe the process of making food spicy.

This popular picnic fare was eventually referred to as "salad eggs" or "dressed eggs" to avoid any hint of impropriety or unseemly association with Satan when served at church functions. I, therefore, omit the hot sauce. And the name has been changed to protect the innocent.

Ingredients

6 hard-boiled eggs, shells removed

2 tablespoons mayonnaise (I prefer Duke's)

1 teaspoon white vinegar

1 teaspoon prepared mustard

½ teaspoon salt

Sprinkle of paprika

> **Tidbits:**
> *Adding one tablespoon of pickle relish and a grind of freshly cracked pepper lends sweetness to acidity.*

Directions

Slice the eggs in half lengthwise; remove the yolks and set the whites aside. Place the whites on an egg platter or plate, cover with foil, and place in the refrigerator to chill. Place the yolks in a small bowl and mash with a fork. Add the mayonnaise, vinegar, mustard, and salt; mix well. Use a spoon to fill each egg white. Sprinkle each egg with a dash of paprika. Serve immediately or chill until ready to serve.

(Yields 12 eggs.)

ROAST DUCK

The Cherokees named this portion of God's green garden "Ducktown" or *Kawa' nah,* place of the duck." Therefore, we can safely assume the heavens and earth were, at one time, filled with these water fowl in Hiwassee, a Cherokee word meaning *meadow.*

Whether oven-roasted or pan-fried, duck is a symphony of succulence, a testimony to taste.

Ingredients
1 five-pound duck, rinsed thoroughly
Salt and freshly ground pepper to taste
¼ teaspoon ground thyme
5 small onions, peeled
1 seven-inch (medium) carrot, scraped and cut into ¼-inch rounds

Tidbits:

Duck breast is considered red meat and is best served medium or medium rare. After roasting the duck for the initial fifteen minutes, carve out the breast and return the remainder of the duck to the pan to continue roasting. Just before removing the duck from the oven, slice the duck breast in half and sear in a skillet with duck fat from the roasting pan. Slice and serve alongside the roast duck.

Directions
Preheat the oven to 450°F. Sprinkle the duck inside and out with salt and pepper. Sprinkle the cavity with the thyme and insert one of the onions. Truss the duck (bind together the legs of the fowl with kitchen twine) and place it, breast side up, in a roasting pan. Arrange the carrot rounds and remaining onions around duck. Roast for 15 minutes; there's no need to baste. Reduce the oven heat to 350°F. Turn the duck over on its side and roast for 30 minutes. Remove most of the fat from the pan. Turn the duck on its other side and roast for 15 minutes, then turn the breast side up again. Roast for 15 minutes longer. Lift the duck so that the cavity juices run into the pan. When the thigh is pricked and the juices run pale yellow, the duck is done. Slice and serve as you would one whole chicken.

APPALACHIAN SHEPHERD'S PIE

What better way to celebrate a pastor than baking a shepherd's pie in his honor and bringing it to the annual Ducktown church picnic! Typically served as a hearty fall dish, many of these ingredients could be dried or stored in root cellars for use in spring and summer meals.

Ingredients

Mashed Potato Crust

6 large russet potatoes, peeled and quartered, boiled, and mashed
¾ cup whole fat buttermilk, more if needed
4 tablespoons butter

Gravy

½ cup dried tomatoes
½ cup chicken stock
2 teaspoons olive oil
1 medium onion, peeled and sliced
1 large green pepper, cored, halved, and sliced
1 small red bell pepper, sliced
2 large cloves garlic, minced
1 teaspoon dried basil
½ teaspoon ground cumin
½ teaspoon dried oregano
1 tablespoon Worcestershire sauce

Hash

1 teaspoon olive oil
1 large yellow onion, chopped
2 medium carrots, sliced
2 to 4 tablespoons chicken stock
2 cups cooked lentils
2 cloves garlic, minced
1 tablespoon Worcestershire sauce

Directions

For the Mashed Potato Crust:

Peel, and quarter the potatoes. Place the quartered potatoes in a 3-quart saucepan; add enough water to cover them. Cover the pan and heat water to boiling; reduce heat and simmer for 30 to 35 minutes until potatoes are tender when pierced with a fork. Drain well. Add the butter and mash the potatoes using a potato masher. Pour in the buttermilk and continue mashing until achieving the desired consistency.

For the Gravy: Place the dried tomatoes in a small saucepan with ⅔ cup water. Cover and simmer for 5 minutes or until softened. Remove the tomatoes from the liquid and chop them up, reserving the cooking liquid. In a medium saucepan, heat two teaspoons of oil over medium-high heat. Sauté the medium onions, peppers, and two garlic cloves until lightly brown, stirring in the spices during cooking. Add the tomatoes, their cooking liquid, and Worcestershire sauce. Cover and simmer for about 15 minutes.

For the Hash: In a medium skillet, heat 1 teaspoon of oil over medium-high heat. Sauté the remaining onion until translucent (about 1 minute). Add carrots and 2 tablespoons water. Sauté until the carrots are tender; about 8 minutes. Stir in the lentils, remaining garlic, oregano, and Worcestershire sauce. Cook a minute or two until heated through.

To Assemble: Lightly butter a 2-quart baking dish. Turn out half of the mashed potatoes into the buttered baking dish. Make a well in the center of the potatoes. Spoon the hash into the center of the well. Spoon the gravy over the hash. Add the rest of the potatoes, smoothing the top and making slight dips with the back of a spoon. Sprinkle the potatoes with grated cheddar cheese, if desired. Bake for 30 minutes, until bubbly and the potato topping has slightly browned.

(Yields 6–8 servings.)

OLD-FASHIONED GERMAN CABBAGE ROLLS

A small store, situated on the picnic grounds sold candy, oysters, oranges, figs, nuts, canned goods, and other items to benefit the Sunday schools.

Surely Mathilda Raht, Captain Raht's wife, whom he married shortly before moving from Germany to the United States, made one of her husband's favorite traditional German foods.

While cabbage is generally considered a fall garden vegetable, it is actually a "cool-season" vegetable. Cabbage can be grown as a spring *and* fall crop. If the weather is right, green cabbage can be planted as early as late February and harvested sixty to seventy-five days later—just in time for a June picnic.

Ingredients
1 medium head of cabbage (about 3 pounds)
½ pound uncooked ground beef
½ pound uncooked ground pork
1 fifteen-ounce can tomato sauce, divided
1 medium onion, diced
½ cup uncooked white rice
1 tablespoon dried parsley
½ teaspoon salt
½ teaspoon dried dill weed
½ teaspoon garlic powder
Pinch of cayenne pepper
1 fifteen-ounce can diced tomatoes, undrained
½ teaspoon sugar

Directions
Preheat the oven to 350°F. Cook the cabbage in boiling water just until the outer leaves pull away easily from the head (about 10 minutes). Gently pull 12 leaves from the head of cabbage. Set aside to use as rolls. In a small bowl, mix together the beef and pork until well combined. Add ½ cup tomato sauce, onion, rice, parsley, salt, dill weed, garlic powder, and cayenne; mix well. Cut out the thick vein from the bottom of each cabbage leaf, making a V-shaped cut. Place ¼ cup of the meat mixture on a cabbage leaf, overlapping the cut ends of the leaf. Fold in the sides and—beginning from the cut end—roll up. Repeat until all the cabbage leaves are rolled. Slice the remaining cabbage and lay it across the bottom of an oven-proof 9x13x2-inch baking dish. Place the cabbage rolls

on top of the sliced cabbage. Pour the remaining tomato mixture over the rolls. Cover with aluminum foil. Bake for 1½ hours until the cabbage rolls are tender.
(Yields 12 servings.)

CORNISH RAINBOW TROUT PIE

The waters of the Ocoee and Hiwassee Rivers in Polk County were fairly teeming with rainbow trout. In his book *Ducktown: Back in Raht's Time*, Robert E. Barclay shares his poem about the habits and an occasional food source for miners who came all the way from Cornwall, England, to work in the copper mines:

> Where the trout had anchored in silence
> Where the Indian lolled at rest
> Where the pioneers swarmed in a frenzy
> For the spot that might prove best
> They wielded their picks and shovels
> They panned the streams up and down
> And out of their vision and labor
> Was molded the famed Ducktown.

Tidbits:
Removing the skin of the trout, and completely deboning the fish is crucial to the success of this recipe. Cod may be used as a substitute.

Ingredients
2 pounds fresh rainbow trout, filleted (skin removed and deboned)
4 large russet potatoes, peeled, boiled, and mashed
4 tablespoons butter
½ cup green peas
¼ cup whole milk
Cheddar cheese (to be grated on top of potato "crust")
Chives, dill, and parsley
Salt and pepper to taste

Directions
Preheat the oven to 350°F. Cut the trout fillets into bite-sized chunks and place them in a medium saucepan with the milk and peas. Add the chives,

dill, and parsley. Cover and bring the mixture to a simmer on medium heat for about 5 minutes. Allow it to cool in the pan. Pour the slightly thickened mixture into a 9-inch pie pan. Add the butter to the mashed potatoes and mix until well combined. Spread the mashed potato mixture over the fish mixture. Sprinkle grated cheddar cheese on top of the potato crust. Bake for 25 to 30 minutes until the crust is slightly brown. (Yields 8 servings)

SORGHUM CAKE

One of the first permanent settlers south of the Ocoee River was Joseph Pierce from Epworth, Georgia, near Newtown, Tennessee. It was Pierce who built a grist mill near Newtown and introduced sorghum cane to the area.

Ingredients
Cake Mixture
3 cups all-purpose flour
1 teaspoon baking soda
1 teaspoon baking powder
1 teaspoon ground cinnamon
1 cup buttermilk, chilled
1 cup raisins
1 cup chopped dates
1 cup chopped pecans, toasted

Sugar Mixture
1 cup sugar
1 cup shortening
1 cup sorghum syrup
3 large eggs, room temperature

Coffee Glaze
1 cup powdered sugar
1½ tablespoons strongly brewed coffee

Directions
Preheat the oven to 325°F. In a small mixing bowl, whisk together the flour, baking soda, baking powder, ground ginger, and cinnamon. Set

aside. In a separate bowl, beat the sugar and shortening at medium speed with a hand mixer until fluffy. Add the sorghum; beat until just blended. Add the eggs, one at a time, beating each until just blended. Gradually add the flour mixture to the sugar mixture alternately with the buttermilk and ending with the flour mixture. Beat on low speed until just blended. Fold in the dates, raisins, and pecans. Spoon the mixture into 2 greased and floured 8×8-inch pans. Bake for 35 minutes or until a toothpick inserted into the center of the cake comes out clean. Remove from the pans. Place the cakes on a wire rack to cool. While the cakes are baking, whisk together the powdered sugar and coffee. Set aside. Allow the cakes to completely cool (one hour). Drizzle each cake with the coffee glaze. (Yields two 8-inch square cakes.)

BLACKBERRY MINT LEMONADE

In addition to canned goods and incidentals, the Hiwassee Sunday school store sold quarts of lemonade, much to the delight of picnickers.

Blackberries and mint still grow prolifically in Tennessee. When "muddled" together, these teammates beget a trinity of taste, excellent for sipping on a Sunday-after-church, picnic-blanket kind of day 'neath the shade of a sycamore tree.

Ingredients
3 cups water
1 cup sugar
18 mint leaves torn into small pieces
2 cups fresh or frozen blackberries
Ice
3 mint sprigs
4 cups (1 quart) natural store-bought lemonade
Extra mint sprigs, to be used as a garnish

Directions
Pour the water and sugar into a small pot and bring to a boil. Stir the water and sugar together until the sugar is completely dissolved. Turn off the heat and remove the pot from the hot burner. Add the torn mint leaves to the pot and give the mixture a stir. Allow the mixture to cool.

Add the blackberries to a blender. Place a strainer over the mouth of the blender and pour the sugar-water-mint mixture into the blender. Discard the mint leaves. Blend the blackberry mixture on low speed for just a few seconds until the berries break up. Do not puree. Fill a pitcher halfway with ice and the remaining mint sprigs. Pour the lemonade and blackberry mixture over the ice and stir to combine. Strain the blackberry lemonade into iced-tea glasses. Garnish with a mint sprig.

(Serves 6-8 Sunday picnickers.)

Chapter 15

SAM DAVIS MONUMENT
STATE HISTORIC SITE

◆————————————————————————————◆

Built 1906
Pulaski, Tennessee

Taproots

If I had a thousand lives, I would lose them
all here before I would betray a friend
or the confidence of my informer.

—Private Sam Davis,
Confederate scout, 1st Tennessee Infantry, 1863

The Sam Davis Monument is prominently displayed on the south side of the Giles County Court House in Pulaski's public square.

Captured on November 20, 1863, carrying classified information on Union army movements from Middle Tennessee to Chattanooga, the story of twenty-one-year-old Sam Davis— known to his admirers as the "Boy Hero of the Confederacy"—reads like a Civil War version of David and Goliath: a man of youthful innocence, believing in a cause greater than himself, bursting with integrity and hope for the future, and unafraid of the wiles of the devil. In the words of his biographer, Edythe Whitley, Davis was "a man who learned as a boy and as a soldier to fear nothing and to obey orders."

Sam Davis was born to Charles Lewis and Jane Simmons Davis on October 6, 1842, in Rutherford County. The Davises moved from their small farmhouse to a beautiful Greek Revival–style antebellum home on 168 acres of farmland in Smyrna, Tennessee. Built in about 1810 by

A meticulously sculpted marble monument of young Sam Davis
graces the grounds of the Pulaski Courthouse.

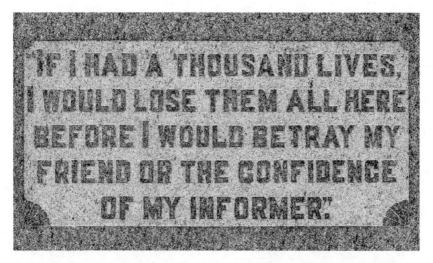

Sam Davis's famous last words before his execution by hanging
are etched on the marble pedestal bearing his likeness.

Moses Ridley, the home was renovated in 1850 by the Davis family.
Charles and Jane Davis gave their promising, responsible young son, Sam,
the best education possible. While attending Western Military Institute
in Nashville, he met his favorite teachers—and soon-to-be generals in the
Confederate army—Bushrod Rust Johnson and Edmund Kirby Smith.

On April 12, 1861, as Sam's first year of college ended, news of shots
fired on Fort Sumpter, in Charleston Harbor, South Carolina by Confederate general Pierre Gustave Toulan (P. G. T.) Beauregard spread rapidly.
The Civil War had begun.

As the Western Military Institute dismissed its students, Sam knew in
his heart that it was a man's duty and honor to fight for the South—the
land he loved. He enlisted in the Rutherford Rifles, renamed Company I of
the Tennessee Infantry, Confederate States of America (CSA). Tennessee,
the last state in the Union to secede, was now fully engaged in the war.
Sam Davis and his company were sent to Virginia to serve in the opening
campaigns. There, Sam proved to be an able marksman and soldier.

Less than a year after enlisting, Sam had served under four of the
most renowned generals in the Confederacy: Robert E. Lee, Thomas

The Sam Davis Memorial Museum is located
in the historic section of Pulaski.

"Stonewall" Jackson, Bushrod Rust Johnson, and P. G. T. Beauregard,
"hero" of the Battle of Bull Run.

General Braxton Bragg, a West Point graduate and career army officer,
was promoted and placed in command of the Army of Tennessee after
the death of General Albert Sidney Johnston at the Battle of Shiloh in
West Tennessee. It was Bragg who determined that a company of scouts
was needed to serve as the "eyes and ears" of the Confederate army. Sam
Davis, and his older brother, John, were among the chosen few to serve
in this elite group.

One of Sam's former high school teachers, Henry B. Shaw, alias "E. Coleman," was in charge of Bragg's new army taskforce, dubbing it the "Coleman Scouts." These scouts would be key players in uncovering and transporting information about secret Union army operations to leaders of the Confederate military campaign—with Shaw often wandering between battle lines posing as a disheveled herb doctor.

As one version of the story goes, during dinner at the St. Cloud Hotel, located at the corner of 5th Avenue and Church Street, in downtown Union-held Nashville, Davis and his friends dressed in civilian clothing and dined at the same large dining room table with General William Starke Rosecrans, a Union strategist. Davis dined and listened as Rosecrans unveiled the plans of his scouts and their missions—Union troop movements in Tennessee. The scouts' discovery of these secrets led to the surprising Confederate victory at the Battle of Chickamauga. Learning that the Coleman Scouts had somehow uncovered this information, Union officials put a price on the heads of the scouts and their leader, E. Coleman.

The night before his capture, Sam reportedly spent the night in Campbellsville, Tennessee, at the home of Robert and Susannah English. The Englishes were wealthy Southern sympathizers who frequently opened their home to the Coleman Scouts. Sam's mission the next morning was to carry important written information—the location and number of Union troops making their way from Middle Tennessee to Chattanooga—to the principal commander in the Western Theater of the Civil War, General Braxton Bragg.

As Sam made his way to northern Alabama to regroup with the Coleman Scouts, he stopped to rest beneath the branches of an old plum tree near Lamb's Ferry Road in Minor Hill, Tennessee. Two men dressed in Confederate uniforms riding out of the evening fog approached Sam. Presenting his pass, which indicated that he, too, was a Confederate soldier, Sam came to the realization that the men were, in fact, Union soldiers in disguise.

Davis was routed eleven miles to Pulaski, the county seat, now occupied by the Union army. Searching his haversack and boots, the Union soldiers discovered maps and information, as well as papers given to him by Captain E. Coleman, for delivery to General Braxton Bragg who was camped in Chattanooga.

Arrested and confined to a jail cell on the northwest corner of the Pulaski public square, Sam awaited interrogation from the Union commanding officer, General Grenville Mellen Dodge. The exact military information Sam carried cannot be verified. It's reasonable to believe, however, that crucial information regarding Nashville's reinforcements and the numerical strength of the Union army was entrusted to him. General Dodge, aware that secret information was being delivered into the hands of his enemies, was anxious to capture Davis's informant.

When Sam was brought before General Dodge, the general made several attempts to frighten him into revealing the name of his commanding officer and his whereabouts. Dodge threatened court-martial and death by hanging. Sam Davis said nothing. Dodge assigned the Union army's chief of scouts, Levi "Chickasaw" Naron, to interogate Sam. He offered Sam his life for the names of his commanders. Sam held his peace.

Ironically, on the way back to his cell, two captured prisoners sat in a jail cell adjacent to Sam's. As one version of the story goes, Sam glanced at the two men and kept walking. In that cell sat his friends Henry Shaw (E. Coleman) and fellow scout Joshua Brown—the very men whose names General Dodge was seeking.

Less than a year after Davis was chosen as part of the Coleman Scouts, he stood before General G. M. Dodge, who, unable to elicit any information from Sam regarding his informant, court-martialed Sam. He sentenced him to hang by the neck until dead on November 27, 1863. The general gave Davis several chances throughout his week of captivity to reveal his source, but Sam refused, saying he would die a thousand deaths before he would betray a friend.

During his brief incarceration, Sam became well-liked and admired by Confederate and Union soldiers alike. Dodge, finding Davis an exasperating prisoner, sent Union soldiers into the jail to beseech him to reveal the name of the person who had given him the secret information. Sam remained silent.

The night before his death, Sam, with the stub of a pencil, wrote the following letter to his mother:

Pulaski Giles County, Tennessee
November 26, 1863

Dear Mother: O how painful it is to write to you! I have got to die to-morrow—to be hanged by the Federals. Mother, do not grieve for me. I must bid you good-bye for evermore. Mother, I do not fear to die. Give my love to all.

Your dear son

Mother: Tell the children all to be good. I wish I could see you all of you once more, but I never will anymore.

Mother and Father: Do not grieve for me; it will not do any good. Father: you can send after my remains if you want to do so. They will be at Pulaski Tennessee. I will leave some things, too, with the hotel keeper for you. Pulaski is in Giles County, south of Columbia.

G. W. Petway, a leading citizen of Giles County, visited Davis in his jail cell during his last hours. Sam is reported to have said to him, "I do not fear death, but it makes me mad to think I am to die as a spy."

International law, used by the United States Army as a textbook, defines "spy" as "a person who enters the lines of an army in disguise or under false pretense for the purpose of securing information." Sam Davis, having not been among those who had obtained information by crossing enemy lines, who was dressed in proper Confederate attire at the time of his capture, and having presented his written, official "army pass," could not legally be deemed a spy.

On November 27, 1863, the day of his execution, Sam was instructed to sit on top of his coffin in the back of a buckboard as it drove through the streets of Pulaski on the way to the gallows. Escorted by an entourage of Union soldiers, a mob of local sympathizers and curious onlookers watched Sam pass by the courthouse. Looking up, he observed Henry Shaw watching the processional from the windows on the second floor. Sam Davis, his hands cuffed behind him, bowed his head toward his friend and commander in a gesture of solidarity, his lips sealed for eternity.

The consequences of Sam's decision still echo through the ages like the chorus of his favorite hymn, "On Jordan's Stormy Banks." Chaplain James Young, with the Eighty-First Ohio Infantry, stood at Sam's side the night before his execution. At Sam's request, they sang:

I am bound for the promised land,
I am bound for the promised land;

Oh, who will come and go with me?
I am bound for the promised land.

Engraved on the base of the Sam Davis Monument in Pulaski's public square, a Bible verse from the Book of John holds true to this day: "Greater love hath no man, than this; that a man lay down his life for his friends" (John 15:13).

Address
Sam Davis Monument
Madison Street between 1st Street and 2nd Street Courthouse Square
Pulaski, TN 38478

Timeless Recipes

It was the women of the Confederacy who watched by
the wounded on the battlefields and nursed the sick,
who lifted the men up to the highest standard
of chivalry. At home, the women kept the fires
burning; they planted the crops, they sowed the
seed and reaped the grain for food.

—Edythe Johns Rucker Whitley,
author, historian, and genealogist

The Coleman Scouts could neither visit nor stay in their families' homes for fear of reprisal from the Federals. Southern sympathizers often opened their homes to Confederate soldiers for shelter and sustenance. Among these civilians, the families of Squire Peter and Susannah Shuler and Robert and Margaret English of Campbellsville, Tennessee, in Giles County, offered soldiers invaluable hospitality, in many cases helping prevent their capture.

Campbellsville is a stone's throw from Pulaski. With acres of rich, undulating farmland, Campbellsville is as charmingly spacious and secluded today as it was in 1863. According to the Shulers' grandson, Clyde Shuler, Sam Davis spent many a night taking shelter in his grandparents' attic.

Southern farmers like the Schulers and Englishes barely remained self-sufficient, struggling to retain their farm-to-table lifestyle. Margaret English and Susannah Shuler, as was commonplace for women of their day, still baked biscuits in wood stoves and fried, stewed, or roasted whatever meat and vegetables were available in their kitchen fireplaces.

As the Union army seized railroad systems, captured more seaports, and set up road blockades, however, folks in the South experienced the ravages of war in every aspect of their daily lives.

BREAKFAST MENU
Fried Pork Chops in Southern Cream Gravy
Margaret's Sweet Potato Skillet Hash with Fried Eggs
Cornmeal Mush, or "Coosh"
Plum Cobbler

FRIED PORK CHOPS IN SOUTHERN CREAM GRAVY
Hogs, sweet potatoes, and corn were primary food sources in Giles County, according to the Tennessee Agricultural Census of 1860.

In 1862, when the Union army captured Pulaski, Major General William Tecumseh Sherman, known for his "scorched earth" policy—"to target food sources, transportation, communication, and anything deemed useful to the enemy while advancing or withdrawing from an area"—wrote the following dispatch to General G. M. Dodge: "While at Pulaski, let your mounted men hunt out the pests that infest the country. Show them no mercy. If the people don't suppress guerillas, tell them that your orders are to treat the community as enemies. If they keep order and quiet, then pay them for corn, hogs, etc., or give vouchers, but eat up all the supplies, grain, hogs, and cattle." In the Campbellsville countryside, fifteen miles north of Pulaski, however, Robert and Margaret English could still provide a warm breakfast for their overnight guest.

Before Sam set out on that fateful morning—the day of his capture—he may have tucked a pork chop–stuffed biscuit from Margaret's breakfast table and a can of Van Camp's Pork and Beans in the pocket of his waterproof haversack, as well as those papers meant for General Bragg in his boot.

Ingredients
Pork Chops
4 four-ounce boneless, center-cut pork chops (about one-inch thick)
1 teaspoon salt, divided

Cream Gravy
3 tablespoons all-purpose flour
¼ teaspoon ground thyme
¼ teaspoon black pepper
2 tablespoons butter
1½ cups milk

Tidbits:

During the Civil War in Giles County, chickens were needed for eggs and considered a luxury to eat. Today, cream gravy spooned over pork chops or fried chicken is considered southern cuisine.

Directions
Sprinkle ½ teaspoon salt over both sides of the chops. Set aside. Over medium-high heat, melt the butter in a 10-inch cast-iron skillet. Add the pork chops. Simmer three minutes per side. Remove the chops from the skillet. Set them aside and keep them warm. In a small bowl, whisk together the milk and flour until well combined. Add the milk and flour mixture to the skillet, whisking constantly. Stir in the remaining salt, pepper, and thyme. Return the chops to the pan of gravy. Cover. Reduce the heat and simmer for 10 minutes, until the gravy has thickened and the chops are cooked through.
(Yields 4 servings.)

MARGARET'S SWEET POTATO SKILLET HASH WITH FRIED EGGS

Margaret English likely plucked sweet potatoes from the family's large garden plot as part of a "stick-to-the-ribs" breakfast for her husband and their overnight guest, young Sam Davis. Sweet potatoes provide a nutritional source of calcium, potassium, vitamins A, B-6, and C, and manganese—fortifying Sam for his long day's journey south to General

Bragg's Chattanooga camp. The Englishes' lone cow and few chickens provided the occasional butter, cream, and eggs.

Ingredients
2 tablespoons salted butter
3 medium sweet potatoes, washed, peeled, quartered, and cubed
2 small red or yellow onions, peeled and diced
¾ cup chicken or vegetable broth
4 large eggs
Salt and pepper, to taste

Directions
In a 10-inch cast-iron skillet, melt the butter over medium-low heat. Add the diced onion, stirring occasionally, allowing it to caramelize (about 20 to 30 minutes). Fold the diced sweet potato into the onion mixture and add ½ cup of the broth. Cover the skillet with the lid and allow the sweet potato mixture to simmer on medium heat, untouched, for about 15 minutes. Pierce the potatoes with a knife to determine if they're cooked through. If not, let them simmer for another 5 minutes, adding the ¼ cup of liquid. If there is liquid left in the pan, remove the lid and allow the liquid to cook away. Using a metal spatula, turn the sweet potato hash over, leaving the crusty, cooked side up. With the back of a spoon, make 4 small indentions in the hash mixture. Crack one egg into each indention. Place the lid back on the pan. Allow the eggs to simmer for about 3 to 5 minutes, allowing the whites of the egg to set but leaving the yolks runny. Salt and pepper to taste. Serve the sweet potato hash with egg immediately. Pierce the yolk to coat the hash.
(Yields 4 servings.)

> *Tidbits:*
> Spices were not readily available because of shortages in the South brought on by the Civil War. Today, garlic, cinnamon, nutmeg, and seasoned salt are basic, palate-pleasing options. Consider adding red and green pepper when sautéing the onions.

CORNMEAL MUSH, OR "COOSH"

Sam Davis, as part of the elite company of Coleman Scouts, could find refuge and a home-cooked meal with southern sympathizers. These meals were a welcomed reprieve from Confederate army rations—overly salted pork, cornmeal, hardtack, and what soldiers called "desecrated," or dried, vegetables. Yet, cornmeal became a staple in homes and on the field for soldiers—both Blue and Gray. An army camp "cook" fried salt pork or bacon, then added water and cornmeal to the grease to make a cornmeal mush dubbed "coosh" or "cush."

Ingredients
4 slices bacon
1½ cups water, divided
½ cup cornmeal
½ teaspoon salt

Directions
In a 10-inch cast-iron skillet, fry the bacon until crisp. Remove the bacon from the pan and allow the bacon grease to cool. In a small bowl, combine the cornmeal and salt. Over medium-high heat, warm the bacon grease and add 1 cup of water. Stir ½ cup of water into the cornmeal and salt mixture. Add the cornmeal to the skillet of heated bacon grease and water. Cook over medium-high heat, stirring continuously until thickened. Top with crumbled bacon, if desired.
(Yields 4 servings.)

ROASTED CARROTS WRAPPED IN MAPLE GLAZED BACON

Campbellsville's hospitable terrain hosts a reasonable amount of Giles County rainfall. In 1863, this small town just outside of Pulaski, produced acres of homegrown produce around homegrown husbandry. Sugar maple trees like the well-drained soil of the flat to easy-rolling countryside of Campbellsville. A healthy, orange-colored tuber wrapped in hickory-smoked bacon basted in sweet, liquid gold from a sugar maple tree became more than just a rudimentary root when dressed in this finery for Sam Davis.

Ingredients
6 medium carrots, peeled
6 strips hickory smoked bacon
¼ cup pure maple syrup
Freshly cracked black pepper

Directions
Preheat the oven to 400°F. Wrapping each carrot in one strip of bacon, place each carrot on a rimmed baking sheet. Liberally baste each carrot with the maple syrup. Season with black pepper. Bake the carrots for 10 minutes. Remove the carrots from the oven and baste them again with the remaining syrup. Bake for 15 minutes more, or until the carrots are tender and the bacon is crisp. Serve immediately.
(Yields 6 servings.)

PLUM COBBLER
One of three sites erected in Giles County along the Sam Davis Trail Stops is in Minor Hill, Tennessee. This site is said to be in the proximity of where Sam was captured as he rested beneath a plum tree.

Perhaps Margaret English served her supply of precious plums, stashed away from a fall harvest, in a warm, cobbler—sweet sustenance for her husband, Robert, and their overnight guest.

Ingredients
Plum Mixture
¾ cup sugar
3 tablespoons cornstarch (non-GMO)
½ teaspoon ground cinnamon
4 cups fresh, unpeeled purple plums, seeded and sliced
1 teaspoon fresh lemon juice

Biscuit Dough
2 cups all-purpose flour
6 tablespoons butter, chilled
1 tablespoon sugar
1 tablespoon baking powder

½ teaspoon salt
1 cup heavy cream

Directions
For the plum mixture: Combine the sugar, cornstarch, and cinnamon in a 2-quart saucepan. Add the plums and lemon juice, stirring until well combined. Over medium-high heat, simmer until the mixture thickens and boils. Boil for 1 minute, stirring constantly. Pour the hot plum mixture into an ungreased 2-quart casserole dish (or 8-inch square baking dish). Cover with foil to keep warm.

For the biscuits: Preheat the oven to 425°F. Combine the flour, sugar, baking powder, and salt in a medium bowl. Cut the cold butter into pieces and work it into the flour until the mixture resembles small peas. Make a well in the center of the mixture and pour in the heavy cream. Combine the cream and flour mixture until a soft dough forms. Turn the dough out onto a floured surface and roll out to ½-inch thickness. Cut out biscuits using a 2-inch biscuit cutter. Place the biscuits on top of the plum mixture. Bake for 25 minutes or until the biscuits are golden brown and the plum mixture is bubbling. Serve warm.
(Yields 6–8 servings.)

Chapter 16

THE CLEMENT RAILROAD MUSEUM AND HOTEL HALBROOK STATE HISTORIC SITE

◆————————————————————————◆

Built 1913
Dickson, Tennessee

Taproots

We must solemnly, but with sharp and vigorous determination, raise our hands toward heaven and say
as Cordell Hull of Tennessee, the young "David,"
the shepherd lad who came to lead world Democ-
racy toward peace and understanding said when
he led 106 neighbor boys of a mountain section of
Tennessee into the fight against the Spanish king's
denial of rights and liberty in the Southern seas,
"We are ready, sir, ready to fight." So must we, as
loyal Americans and lovers of freedom. . . .
You shall not press down upon the brow of
the small businessman monopoly's crown of thorns.

—Governor Frank Goad Clement
Keynote Speech, Democratic National Convention, Chicago, 1956

Hotel Halbrook is the birthplace of Governor Frank Goad Clement, Tennessee's forty-first and forty-third governor (1953–59, 1963–67), and home
of the Clement Railroad Museum. Often described by Dickson County
residents as "our biggest artifact," the museum—preserved inside historic
Hotel Halbrook—celebrates the heyday of railroading within one of the
few enduring examples of a railroad hotel in a small Tennessee town.

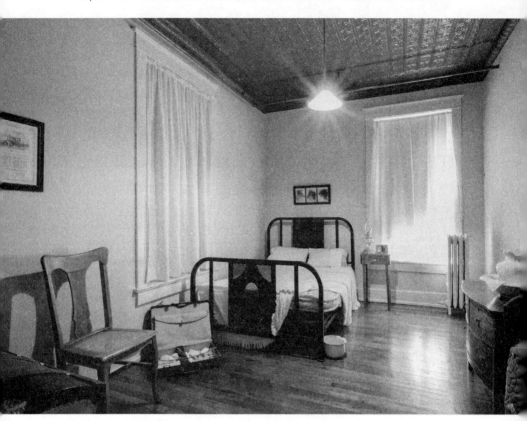

Governor Frank Goad Clement was born in room #5 on June 2, 1920. He became the longest serving modern Tennessee governor (1953–59, 1963–67) and, at age thirty-two when he was first elected, the nation's youngest.

The first child of Robert S. and Maybelle Goad Clement, Frank G. Clement was born in room #5 amid the bustle and commotion of passenger trains. Mile post #42 was just off Main Street in Dickson, and trains screeched and rumbled in and out of the station during Clement's birth. Maybelle gave birth to their baby boy even as her family checked in guests, changed bed linens, and took care of business.

Great individuals often arise from humble beginnings. In 1916, Belle Goad and her daughter Maybelle traveled to the home of relatives in West

The second floor of the museum traces Governor Clement's
high school, college, and early career days and allows
visitors to follow his gubernatorial campaigns.

Tennessee shortly after the sudden death of Belle's husband, attorney William Goad. Stepping off the train in Dickson, Belle Goad noticed a "For Rent" sign in the front window of Hotel Halbrook.

Having gained experience running a boardinghouse out of her family's Scottsville, Kentucky, home, Belle Goad became the proprietress of the two-story brick train stop named for Jack Halbrook, its builder and owner. This would give her a place to raise her five children and earn an income. Hotel Halbrook—with its enormous kitchen and accompanying dining room—became home to the Goad family. The family lived in rooms on the first floor while Maybelle, who was in her early twenties, helped her mother run the hotel.

Maybelle married Robert S. Clement in Dickson on August 10, 1919, and through sixty-plus years of marriage, they produced three remarkable children—Frank Goad Clement, governor of Tennessee for nine years; Senator Anna Belle Clement O'Brien; and Emma Gene Clement Perry— along with a notable heritage.

Frank G. Clement became part of a large political family who cared as much for the people and the state of Tennessee as they did for each other. Known for his "evangelical" style of oratory, Frank Clement, pontificating on politics, brought state and national audiences to their feet in rousing applause.

The property on which Hotel Halbrook stands was the Dickson Hotel, a building purchased in 1880 by A. J. Alexander and renamed the Alexander Hotel. After several owners and names changes, local businessman J. T. Halbrook bought the property for $2,800. He razed the building and hired R. F. Ridings, an architect and contractor, to build his new hotel in 1913.

The historic building was restored in June 1990 to its original 1913 facade. The first floor of the Hotel Halbrook Railroad Museum displays a folk-art model of a train engine and "tender" (or coal) car. It also features miniature examples of the North Charlotte & St. Louis train engine and Vanderbilt tender displayed in a 1920 photograph of Dickson. Period maps, lanterns, whistle markers, postcards, and books are tangible reminders of the dynamic heritage of railroading throughout Tennessee's nineteenth century. The large, original front desk stands just off the lobby.

Halbrook's hotel was designed with the latest in modern technology;

this included radiator heating, indoor plumbing, and electric lighting known as "knob-and-tube." This type of lighting consists of copper conductors with porcelain knob insulators and porcelain insulating tubes.

Uniquely stamped tin ceilings have been meticulously restored as have the original wood floors. Intricately carved cornices were designed to lend an air of elegance to this working man's train stop—which continued as such until 1954.

Room #5 looks much like it did when the Clements occupied Hotel Halbrook, and it is furnished with several pieces of Goad-Clement memorabilia. The second floor follows Governor Clement through his high school days, college days, and early political career. His governor's desk and phone—even his famous white hat—are displayed as they might have been when he was in office.

The Governor Frank G. Clement Railroad Museum and Hotel Halbrook joined the National Register of Historic Places in 1990.

Timeless Recipes

The prices back then you just wouldn't believe; a
whole fancy meal for 75 cents or something like that.
It included dessert and all the coffee you could drink.

—Jack Halbrook, grandson of J. T. Halbrook

Belle Goad and the Clements rented Hotel Halbrook from around 1917 through 1923. The cook and staff were local African Americans; therefore, the menu at Hotel Halbrook would have offered a variety of southern cuisine prepared with local agriculture and what was brought into Dickson by rail. As part of the hotel's restoration, the dining room was renovated to its 1920s-period design, including a refurbished kitchen in the location of the previous kitchen, which housed a huge wood-burning stove.

In its prime, Hotel Halbrook thrived, as traveling salesmen, called "drummers," filled the front room with long tables for displaying their wares. The dining room held a large number of small tables for diners, and there were chairs and benches in the lobby. Rocking chairs on the front porch provided comfort and relaxation on a warm summer's evening as locals and guests swapped stories for entertainment and watched the trains roll in and out of Dickson at Milepost #42.

HOTEL HALBROOK DINNER MENU
Cornbread Sticks
Southern Fried Chicken with Old School Tomato Gravy
Fresh Green Beans
Strawberry Shortcake
Peach Preserves
Tennessee Strawberry Sheet Cake

CORNBREAD STICKS
Cornbread sticks were in high demand at Hotel Halbrook. Store-bought bread—called "boughten" bread—was never served, according to Jack Halbrook. "You either had cornbread sticks, or, once in a while, you would have the cornbread cut into squares—and that would be baked in pans in these huge ovens," he explained. "These sticks were about six inches long and about one and a half inches around and baked to a golden brown. And then you always had country butter. They would never serve anything but country butter. Even when the creamery came into Dickson and they started having creamery butter; that was not the thing to do because most folks looked down on creamery butter. . . . It just didn't have the flavor of country butter." He continued: "You know, back in those days, if you were around a while in a territory, you could look at somebody's butter dish and tell who they got their butter from because each one of them had their own mold . . . and it had a little gal or a frog, or I don't know what on it."

I use two Lodge preseasoned cast-iron corn stick pans—seven impressions each—for this recipe.

Ingredients
3¼ tablespoons bacon grease
2 cups white cornmeal
1 teaspoon baking soda
1 teaspoon salt
2 medium eggs, lightly beaten
1 cup buttermilk
6 tablespoons butter, salted

Directions

Preheat the oven to 400°F. Using a pastry brush, generously coat each cast-iron corn stick impression with ½ teaspoon of melted bacon grease. Place in the oven. In a large bowl, whisk together the dry ingredients: cornmeal, baking soda, and salt. In a smaller bowl, beat the egg and buttermilk until well combined. Stir the egg mixture into the dry ingredients until well combined. Fold in the melted butter. When the oven is preheated, remove the corn stick pan from the oven. Fill each impression with 2 tablespoons of batter (the batter will sizzle). Bake for about 15 minutes or until golden brown and an inserted tooth pick comes out clean. With a small, shape knife, remove the sticks from their impressions carefully to a wire rack. Serve hot. Butter them generously.

(Yields 14 cornbread sticks.)

SOUTHERN FRIED CHICKEN WITH OLD SCHOOL TOMATO GRAVY

According to Jack Halbrook, grandson of J. T. "Pappy" Halbrook, there was a huge cage at the hotel that held "twenty to thirty frying chickens and a couple of hens for baking." At least once during the week—and twice on Sunday—fried chicken was served to the "drummers" and folks coming in after church for dinner or an early supper. It was a dish that went especially well with an old-school tomato gravy.

The Sunbright Canning Company canned tomatoes in a Dickson factory for many years. Located on East Broad Street, the factory was founded by D. E. "Dan" Beasley, who served as Dickson's mayor from October 1918 through October 1920.

Ronni Lundy, in her cookbook *Victuals,* offers a tangy tomato gravy recipe using my favorite canned tomatoes, Glen Muir Fire Roasted Organic Tomatoes. Tomato gravy spooned over crispy fried chicken must have made those drummers march back for more.

Ingredients
Fried Chicken
1 cup whole-fat buttermilk
1 tablespoon garlic salt
1 teaspoon kosher salt
2 teaspoons freshly ground black pepper

1 four-pound whole fryer (preferably skin-on), cut into 8 pieces
3 cups all-purpose flour
3 tablespoons cornstarch
1 teaspoon baking powder
2 teaspoons cayenne pepper, or to taste
2 teaspoons paprika
1½ teaspoons freshly ground black pepper, or to taste
24 ounces vegetable shortening (I prefer nonhydrogenated shortening such as Spectrum Naturals, All Organic Vegetable Oil, and Nutiva Organic Shortening)

Tomato Gravy
2 tablespoons bacon drippings
½ medium yellow onion, finely diced
1 tablespoon all-purpose flour
One 14½-ounce can (2 cups) diced tomatoes, with their juices
½ tablespoon sorghum syrup
Salt and freshly cracked black pepper, to taste

Directions
For the Chicken: Whisk together the buttermilk, garlic salt, kosher salt, and black pepper. Place the chicken in the buttermilk mixture and completely submerge; cover with plastic wrap, and place in the refrigerator to "brine" for at least 6 hours or overnight. Whisk together the flour, cornstarch, baking powder, cayenne, paprika, and black pepper; place in a large paper bag. Lift a piece of chicken out of the buttermilk mixture, allowing the excess buttermilk to drain off. *(Don't drain off too much buttermilk, or you will not achieve a crispy coating.)* Add one piece of chicken at a time to the bag of flour mixture and shake to thoroughly coat the chicken. Place each piece of chicken on a wire rack set over a baking sheet to rest until they are ready to fry. Spoon the shortening into a large cast-iron frying pan or Dutch oven; place over medium-high heat until the melted shortening registers 360°F on a deep-fry thermometer. The oil should come about halfway up the side of the pan. (The oil temperature is the key to the success of this recipe. Never allow the temperature of the oil to drop below 350°F.) Once the deep-fry thermometer indicates 360°F,

fry the chicken in batches, skin-side down, until golden brown and cooked through (about 6 to 8 minutes per side); use tongs, not a fork, to turn the chicken. Crowding the pan causes the chicken to cook unevenly. Between batches, use a skimmer to remove all the crispy pieces of batter from the oil. Cook the chicken to an internal temperature of 165°F or use a fork to

Tidbits:
Salt acts as a brine. Salt combined with buttermilk produces tender, flavorful chicken.

pierce the skin making sure the juices run clear. (Dark meat takes longer to cook than white meat.) Using tongs, transfer the fried chicken to a paper-lined platter or wire rack on a baking sheet.
(Yields 8 pieces.)

For the Gravy: In a large, heavy cast-iron skillet or saucepan, melt the bacon grease over medium-high heat. Add the onions and sauté until almost translucent (about 2 minutes). Sprinkle the flour over the onions and cook for 1 to 2 minutes, stirring constantly, until flecks of flour begin to turn golden. Add the tomatoes and the sorghum syrup until it dissolves. Reduce the heat and simmer the mixture for 20 to 30 minutes. When the tomatoes have disintegrated, remove the pan from the heat and add salt and cracked pepper. Spoon over the southern fried chicken.
(Yields 1⅓ cup)

STEAMED FRESHLY PICKED GREEN BEANS

There was no shortage of garden truck in rural Dickson. Cooks at the hotel knew that one pound of trimmed green beans would yield about three cups raw and almost two cups cooked, and they adjusted the recipe accordingly. Cooks likely picked the beans fresh and brought them to the kitchen by the bushel basket.

Tidbits:
Sliced sweet white onion on top of cooked beans adds a smoky tang.

Ingredients
1-pound garden-fresh green beans, washed and drained

Directions
Trim off the ends of the beans using a small sharp knife. Cut the beans into 1- to 3-inch sections. Place the bean sections in a steamer basket over a pot containing an inch or two of boiling water. Steam time can vary but when the beans turn bright green they are done (4 to 5 minutes). Serve hot with a pat of butter on top. Salt and pepper to taste.
(Yields 2 cups.)

STRAWBERRY SHORTCAKE
Shortcake, with its biscuit-like quality, offers a crumblier texture more suitable for moist fruit fillings. Split in half, filled with local fresh strawberries, and topped with freshly whipped cream, this shortcake was a Sunday after-dinner delight.

Ingredients
Shortcakes
2 cups all-purpose flour
1 tablespoon baking powder
¾ teaspoon salt
1 tablespoon sugar
2 tablespoons butter
1 cup milk
Whipped cream or ice cream

Strawberry Mixture
4 pints fresh strawberries, lightly rinsed, hulled and sliced
1 tablespoon fresh lemon juice
1 tablespoon sugar

Directions
For the shortcakes: Preheat the oven to 450°F. In a large mixing bowl, combine the flour, baking powder, salt, and sugar. Cut in the butter until the mixture resembles coarse meal. Stir in the milk until just combined. Drop by large spoonfuls onto a lightly greased baking sheet. Bake for 12 to 15 minutes or until golden brown. Cool, split, and fill with the straw-

berry mixture (directions below). Top with whipped cream or ice cream and more strawberries, if desired.
(Yields 12 medium shortcakes.)

For the strawberry mixture: Mix hulled, sliced strawberries with the sugar and lemon. Let sit, to combine. Spoon over the shortcake. Add a dollop of whipped cream.

PEACH PRESERVES
Peach orchards in the north district of Dickson County produced loads of luscious, amber fruit, so much so that air-conditioned railroad cars packed with baskets of these succulent drupes departed Mile Post #42 from June through September and headed north to market.

Spreading this Tennessee treat on breakfast biscuits (or shortcakes) was one sweet way to start the day at Hotel Halbrook.

Ingredients
2½ pounds ripe peaches (about 7 medium-sized)
3 cups sugar
2 tablespoons fresh lemon juice
2 tablespoons orange juice

Directions
Lightly score the bottom of each peach with an "X." With a slotted spoon and working in batches of 3 or 4, add the peaches to a pot of boiling water for 2 to 3 minutes. Using a slotted spoon, transfer the peaches to an ice bath to stop the cooking. Remove the skin with a paring knife. Slice and pit the peaches. Put the peaches into a heavy-bottomed sauce pan; stir in the sugar and juices. Cook on medium heat, stirring occasionally until the mixture thickens and gels on the back of a spoon. Remove from the heat and allow to cool. Store the cooked fruit in four sterilized Ball ½ pint canning jars. Seal the jars with the sterilized lids and store in a pantry, cupboard, or refrigerator.
(Yields 1 quart.)

TENNESSEE STRAWBERRY SHEET CAKE

Tennessee is noted for two kinds of strawberries: Sweet Charlies and the ever-popular Chandlers. Dickson farmers sowed their strawberry seeds in September to reap a ruby red reward come May. Desserts at Hotel Halbrook were the talk of the rails.

Ingredients
Sheet Cake
4 eggs, lightly beaten
2 cups sugar
¾ cup vegetable oil
¾ cup milk
2 cups self-rising flour
¼ cup fresh strawberries, mashed and drained

Strawberry Icing
4 tablespoons butter, softened
1 cup confectioner's sugar
¼ cup strawberries, mashed and drained well

> **Tidbits:**
> *Add more confectioner's sugar, if needed, for a thicker, more spreadable icing.*

> **Tidbits, Too:**
> *For more strawberry flavor, stir a box of strawberry Jell-O into the sheet cake mixture.*

Directions
For the Sheet Cake: Preheat the oven to 350°F. In a large mixing bowl, whisk together the eggs, sugar, oil, and milk. Slowly add the flour until well combined. Fold in the mashed, drained strawberries. Pour the ingredients into a 9x13x2-inch sheet pan. Bake for 25 to 30 minutes or until a toothpick inserted into the center of the cake comes out clean.

For the Strawberry Icing: Rinse the fresh strawberries well. Pat dry. Combine the butter, confectioner's sugar, and mashed strawberries until well-combined and smooth. Spread over the cooled cake. Store the finished (iced) cake in the refrigerator for at least 2 hours before serving. (Yields 15–20 servings.)

Chapter 17

ALEX HALEY HOME MUSEUM AND INTERPRETIVE CENTER STATE HISTORIC SITE

Built 1919
Henning, Tennessee

Taproots

Believe me, my roots are right here in Henning. One
of the nicest things that ever happened to me was
growing up in a little town in the South, in Henning,
Tennessee.

—Alex Haley

Alexander Murray Palmer "Alex" Haley is a Pulitzer Prize–winning American writer best known for his 1976 book and television miniseries *Roots: The Saga of an American Family.* He was born in Ithaca, New York, on August 11, 1921, to Simon Alexander Haley and Bertha George Palmer Haley.

Simon and Bertha were married in 1920 at New Hope Methodist Church in Henning—the same church in which Bertha's parents married. They honeymooned in Ithaca and decided to stay because of the higher educational opportunities afforded African Americans. Simon studied at Cornell University, working toward his master's degree in agricultural science while Bertha pursued a music degree in piano at the Ithaca Conservatory of Music.

Six weeks after Alex was born, Simon and Bertha Haley traveled back to Tennessee and presented their baby boy to his maternal grandparents, William and Cynthia Palmer, as a surprise. The Palmers were overjoyed—Will having always wanted a son—and helped rear Alex in Henning, which enabled Simon to finish his studies in New York.

The boyhood home of Alex
Haley, who is buried on
the grounds.

The Palmer house, known today as the Alex Haley Home Museum
State Historic Site, was built in 1918 by four African American master
carpenters from Covington, a small town just south of Henning, at the
edge of an all-white neighborhood. Will Palmer, having purchased the
local lumber mill from its white owner (unheard of in this era), paid only

A replica of Grandmother Cynthia Palmer's cast-iron,
coal-burning kitchen stove.

for the workmanship. He constructed his home according to plans he acquired through business relationships with builders of upscale residences
along the Eastern seaboard.

When Palmer began construction on the ten-room, Craftsman
bungalow-style home, folks were curious. By Henning standards, the
house was palatial. Across the street, members of the small community
kept watch over the modern construction from the bare backs of horses
and atop buckboards.

The Palmer house is a classic turn-of-the-century residence, with period wallpaper and draperies adorning the front parlor, reproduced according to Will and Cynthia Palmer's tastes. The surprisingly spacious
interior of the home boasts seven rooms on the first floor. The second-floor
rooms are reached by a narrow staircase in the center of the northwestern
end of the house, and the parlor, located in the south corner of the main
section, has a fireplace and two sets of French doors. The oak floors are
original. A front porch was unheard of in Henning, and high ceilings
were considered extravagant. The Palmers' home had both.

There would be no "goin' to the creek" for the Palmers, as Will Palmer

The Palmers' well-appointed living room flows into the dining room, where Sunday after-church lunch was served.

built his home near Henning's water supply. They had their own pump, which sits on the back porch. Two original galvanized pails and a large, cast-iron cauldron, once used in melting down animal fat for making lye soap, squat stubbornly, as if awaiting gainful employment. The kitchen icebox—a rare and prized commodity in Henning—stands as a silent witness to Will Palmer's financial success.

The family ate three meals a day in a sunlit breakfast room, saving their dining room, in all its splendor, for Sunday dinner with the pastor or bishop. The delicate, hand-painted, porcelain-and-brass lighting fixture in the living room, above the dining room table is original.

Will Palmer knew that "society folks" held music performances in their homes for guests, so he built a music room on the first floor for Bertha and bought her a piano, in part to encourage their gifted child. When Bertha played the piano, neighbors would gather across the street, on the Palmers' lawn, and even their front porch. They often squeezed into the parlor to bask in the presence of such refinement and culture.

In 1926, Will Palmer fell gravely ill. Grandmother Cynthia, generally loving and even-tempered, shooed five-year-old Alex out of the way and, often, out of the house. He took refuge inside the honeysuckle vines under his grandfather's bedroom window. "Here," he said, "I could hear him and come quickly, if he asked for me."

In his hiding place, he watched hummingbirds dive for nectar and wondered if they were "like the angels described in Sunday school—the angels who would flutter about when they came to take grandfather to heaven." The death of Alex's grandfather—his best friend—had a profound impact on him; one he carried into adulthood.

After Will Palmer's lumber mill was sold in 1929, the Haleys moved to Normal, Alabama, where Simon held his longest teaching tenure at Alabama Agricultural and Mechanical College. Bertha began teaching in one of the local grammar schools. The Haleys now had three sons—Alex, George, and Julius—and the boys spent summers with Grandmother Cynthia in Henning. Here, the seeds of his West African heritage began taking root.

When young Alex wriggled in beside his grandmother on the front porch swing or sat on the floor behind her, he listened and dreamed as Grandmother Cynthia, her sister Elizabeth, and their church friend, Sister Scrap, regaled him with stories of a West African ancestor, Kunte Kinte. They also recounted tales of Cynthia's grandfather "Chicken George," known as "the best cock fighter in Caswell County, North Carolina." Chicken George won tens of thousands of dollars in prize money for his plantation owner and master, finally gaining his freedom after the Civil War. Chicken George told his son, Tom Murray, about the small town in Tennessee "where white people were waiting for ex-slaves to help in building a community," according to scholar Mary Seibert McCauley in her PhD dissertation, "Alex Haley, a Southern Griot." So, Tom Murray, Alex's great-grandfather, brought his family to Henning in 1874.

On the Palmer's front porch, Alex listened to Grandmother Cynthia recount the family tradition of oral history being passed down from an African *griot* (pronounced "gree-oh."). The *Collins English Dictionary* defines *griot* as "in Western Africa, a member of a caste responsible for maintaining an oral record of tribal history in the form of music, poetry, and storytelling." Years later, Alex located his family's African griot during an amazing journey to Gambia, West Africa, and he became a masterful southern griot in his own right through his blockbuster novel, *Roots: The Saga of an American Family.*

In *Roots,* Alex Haley tells the story of a seventeen-year-old West African named Kunte Kinte, who left his village of Juffure in Gambia one afternoon to chop wood and never returned. Captured by slave traders, Kunte Kinte's nightmarish voyage across the ocean in the bowels of the slave ship *Lord Ligonier* delivered him to a wharf in Annapolis, Maryland. There, he was put on the auction block and sold into slavery. Ironically, Haley, as a thirty-year veteran in the United States Coast Guard, stood on that very dock in Annapolis where the real-life *Lord Ligonier* docked. It was during his enlistment as a mess attendant aboard the 250-foot cutter *Mendota* that Haley began his writing career, penning letters home for his shipmates.

The Interpretive Center annexed behind the Alex Haley Home Museum houses an extension that details the life of Alex Haley. It includes family photographs, his life in the Coast Guard, and displays a built-to-scale slave ship demonstrating Kunte Kinte's journey as an African American sold into slavery.

Alex Haley died of cardiac arrest on February 10, 1992, ending an illustrious career as a writer and personality. His final request was to be buried on the front lawn of his grandparents' home in Henning, where he is, in fact, interred.

Address and Contact Information
The Alex Haley Home Museum and Interpretive Center
200 Church Street
Henning, TN 38041
(731) 738-2240
www.alexhaleymuseum.org

Timeless Recipes

The kitchen is one of the most precious places to me.
My seat was the window ledge. I sat with my back
to the window facing the work table upon which
grandmother prepared foods.

—Alex Haley

Will Palmer was known to invite the bishop or local pastor over for dinner after their Sunday morning church service. In those early days, at New Hope Colored Methodist Episcopal Church (or CME), pastoring was not a salaried position. Palmer started this church and, as chairman of the board, wanted to express his appreciation for the men of God who occupied its pulpit.

"Mrs. Palmer and her 'sisters' have prepared lunch, bishop," Palmer would say. "Would you care to join us?" The bishop would smile. "Why, thank you, Brother Palmer; I believe I will."

Preparation always began the night before the meal. And Alex Haley's favorite spot was on that window ledge in his grandmother's kitchen. She snapped beans there. She kneaded and cut out biscuits. She beat cake batter at that work table. And every so often, when there was a morsel fit to eat, she handed it to Alex. He'd gobble it up as they continued talking.

The kitchen is where Alex Haley could ask questions about Chicken George and that African griot. It was on the front porch and in this kitchen the images of his African heritage began taking shape in his mind.

Alex described Sunday's dining room table as being so loaded with food it fairly sagged in the middle. There were always ten to twelve vegetables on the table for friends and family: crowder peas, purple hull peas, black-eyed peas, white beans, sweet potatoes, okra, collard greens, turnip greens, mustard greens, and corn. And there were usually at least four meats: pork, beef, fowl, guinea hen, a selection of fish—crappie or sun perch—and maybe some wild game. And there were always—yes, *always*—plenty of freshly baked butter biscuits.

SUNDAY DINNER AT THE PALMER HOUSE
Sweet Tea
Butter Biscuits
Pot Roast with Vegetables
Pan-Fried Crappie with Homemade Tartar Sauce
Slow-Cooked Southern Greens
Snap Beans
Pan Fried Okra Cakes
Field Peas
Candied Sweet Potatoes
Stewed Tomatoes
Pecan Pie
Pecan Pie Bread Pudding

SWEET TEA
Cynthia Palmer made her Sunday-after-church tea on Saturday afternoon and kept it chilled in the icebox. This southern elixir needs nothing more than the sugary glory of "simple syrup" to convert a thirsty soul into a confirmed teetotaler.

Ingredients
2 quarts (8 cups) cool water
2 family-size tea bags
1 cup simple syrup

Directions
Pour 2 quarts of water in a stock pot over medium heat and slowly bring to a boil. Remove from the heat and add the 2 tea bags. Cover and let steep for 5 minutes. Make a simple syrup of 1 cup of sugar dissolved in 1 cup of boiling water. Remove the tea bags and pour the warm tea into a half-gallon glass or ceramic pitcher. Add the simple syrup and stir until dissolved. Refrigerate. Serve with a sprig of fresh mint and a wedge of lemon. (Yields 9 cups.)

BUTTER BISCUITS

Sunday biscuits patted out by Grandmother Cynthia could not be prepared the night before. Her made-from-scratch dough created high-rising, pillow-soft biscuits that graced the Palmer's Sunday table.

Ingredients
2 cups all-purpose flour
¼ teaspoon baking soda
1 tablespoon baking powder
1¼ teaspoon salt
6 tablespoons salted butter, cut into small pieces (plus 2 tablespoons, melted, for brushing the tops of the biscuits)
1 cup buttermilk, cold

Tidbits:
Traditional buttermilk refers to "the liquid left behind after churning butter out of cultured cream." A barn on the Palmer property indicates they likely had a milk cow, and it's reasonable to assume Cynthia Palmer used real buttermilk in her biscuits rather than adding baking soda to soured milk.

Directions
Preheat the oven to 425°F. Adjust the oven rack slightly below the middle shelf. In a large bowl, whisk together flour, baking soda, baking powder, and salt. Work the butter into the flour mixture with a pastry cutter, or use your fingers, until it resembles coarse meal. Make a well in the center of the flour mixture and add the buttermilk. Stir the mixture with a rubber spatula until just combined. Do not overmix. Turn the sticky dough out onto a floured surface. With floured hands, gently pat the dough out to ½-inch thickness. Sprinkle flour over the dough and fold it over itself 5 times, gently pressing down and forward as you turn. Press the dough out with the palms of your hands into a rectangle about a 1-inch thickness. Flour a 2½-inch round biscuit cutter. Push the biscuit cutter straight down and through the dough. Do not twist. Twisting the biscuit cutter causes the edge of the biscuit to seal and prevents the biscuit from rising well. Beginning with one biscuit in the center of a 10-inch

cast-iron skillet, place the rest of the biscuits around the outside of the pan pressing the biscuits together so that they rise and don't spread. There will be space left in the pan. Bake for 18 to 20 or until the tops are golden brown Brush the tops of the biscuits with melted butter.
(Yields 8 biscuits.)

POT ROAST WITH VEGETABLES
What would a Sunday meal be for a distinguished pastor or bishop without Grandmother Cynthia's melt-in-your-mouth pot roast? Some folks said the aroma coming from her kitchen was good enough to eat.

The Palmers' home and kitchen was always open to their small community. As Alex recalled, "If neighborhood children were playing in the backyard around supper time, Grandmother would shout, 'All y'all come in and eat!'"

Cynthia Palmer would never have added wine in her Sunday afternoon offering to the bishop or pastor, but one cup of dry red wine may be substituted for one cup of beef broth in this recipe, if you prefer.

Ingredients
Spice Rub
2 teaspoons fresh thyme, chopped
2 teaspoons sweet paprika
2 teaspoons kosher or sea salt
2 teaspoons freshly ground black pepper
2 teaspoons dry mustard
1 tablespoon (packed) light brown sugar

Roast
¼ cup flour
2 tablespoons vegetable oil
1 four-pound boneless beef chuck roast, tied
2 cups beef broth
¾ cup chicken stock
2 large yellow onions, thinly sliced
12 garlic cloves, peeled
3 bay leaves

4 large carrots (about 1 pound), peeled and cut into 1-inch pieces
4 medium parsnips (about 1 pound), peeled and cut into 1-inch pieces
1 small celery rib, with leaves, peeled and cut into 1-inch pieces

Directions

Preheat the oven to 350°F. Mix together the six ingredients for the spice rub in a small bowl and rub the spices all over the beef. Set a large, cast-iron Dutch oven over medium heat and add the vegetable oil. Dredge the beef in flour and shake off any excess so that the beef is only lightly coated. Cook the beef until each side is deeply browned and crisp. Set the beef aside, and add beef broth to the Dutch oven. Bring to a boil while scraping up brown bits from the bottom of the pan. Boil until the liquid is reduced to ½ cup (about 15 minutes). Add chicken broth, and return the beef to the Dutch oven along with the onions, garlic, and bay leaves. Cover the Dutch oven and place in the oven to roast for 1 hour. After 1 hour, turn the beef over and stir the onion mixture, and then return to the oven to roast for an additional hour. Add chicken stock by the ½ cup if the beef becomes dry. Remove the beef and add the carrots, parsley, and celery to the onion mixture. Place the beef so that it sits atop the vegetables and roast until the carrots are tender (about 45 minutes). Transfer the beef to a platter and spoon the sauce over beef. Serve over vegetables.
(Yields eight ½-pound servings.)

PAN-FRIED CRAPPIE WITH HOMEMADE TARTAR SAUCE

In his 1965 American classic *The Autobiography of Malcolm X,* Alex Haley quotes Malcolm's description of southern hospitality and the food women enjoyed serving their guests: "She was the kind of cook who would heap up your plate with such as ham hock, greens, black eyed peas, fried fish, cabbage, sweet potatoes, grits and gravy, and cornbread. And the more you put away, the better she felt." Grandmother Cynthia was a member of this fine assemblage.

Ingredients

For the Crappie

12 fresh-caught crappie, scaled and gutted (perch filets
    from the grocery store are a delicious substitute)

½ cup cornmeal
½ cup flour
Peanut oil for frying
Lawry's Seasoned Salt and pepper to taste
Wedges of lemons, if desired

For the Tartar Sauce
2 eggs, room temperature
1 cup light oil (grapeseed or olive oil works well)
2 teaspoons sweet pickle relish
¼ teaspoon garlic powder
1 tablespoon finely diced yellow onion
1 teaspoon lemon juice
Salt and pepper, to taste

Directions
For the Crappie: Liberally season the fish with Lawry's Seasoned Salt and pepper. Mix together the cornmeal and flour and dredge the fish in the mixture. In a large cast-iron skillet, heat the oil to 360°F and fry the fish in peanut oil until golden (about 4 minutes per side). Serve immediately with a squeeze of lemon and tartar sauce, if desired.
(Yields 12 servings.)

> **Tidbits:**
> *Using a cup of store-bought mayo (I prefer Duke's) and mixing together all the ingredients is a time-saving yet delicious short cut.*

For the Tartar Sauce: Separate the eggs yolks from the egg whites and add the yolks to a medium sized bowl. Whisk the yolks until smooth, add the lemon juice, and slowly add the oil while continuing to whisk. Add all remaining ingredients and mix well. Refrigerate.
(Yields 8 servings or about 2 tablespoons per person.)

SLOW-COOKED SOUTHERN GREENS
Grandmother Cynthia kept her well-tended garden on the southwest side of their backyard. In it, she grew everything from corn to crowder peas to cabbage, collard greens, and kale. Whether serving pot roast, fish,

possum, or squirrel, there was generally a mess of silky greens steeped in plenty of delicious pot "likker" on the Palmer dining room table come Sunday after church.

Ingredients
2 pounds collard greens
2 smoked ham hocks, scored (slashed) with a sharp knife
1 medium white or yellow onion, finely diced
2½ teaspoons kosher salt
1½ teaspoons freshly ground black pepper
2 large garlic cloves, peeled and minced
½ teaspoon crushed red pepper flakes
4 cups chicken stock or broth
1 tablespoon apple cider vinegar
2 teaspoons granulated sugar

Directions
Vigorously plunge the greens 4 or 5 times into a sink filled with lukewarm water. Pull the greens out and hold to drain. Rinse the silt from the sink. Remove the leafy outer leaves from the stem and discard the tough center rib (stem) from the greens. Stack the leaves one on top of the other and roll into a cylinder. Using a sharp knife, crosscut the cylinder into thin strips. Refill the sink with lukewarm water and wash the chopped greens again by swishing them around. Lift the greens out of the water and drain in a colander, repeating the process if they still appear dirty. Place a large sauce pot or Dutch oven over medium heat. Add the chicken stock along with the scored ham hocks. Bring the stock to just a boil and then continue simmering the hocks until they are tender and falling off the bone (about 2 hours). Stir in the onions and cook until translucent. Season with salt and pepper and add the garlic and red pepper flakes and cook 1 minute more. Add the greens in batches to the simmering broth, cooking them until wilted (about 20 minutes). Before serving the greens, remove the ham hocks, dice the meat, and add back to the greens.
(Yields 4 servings.)

SNAP BEANS

Cynthia Palmer learned that picking garden truck "while the dew is still on the roses" is the best time to gather greens for Sunday after-church luncheons. She snapped the beans and boiled them to a bright emerald green, adding a lump of butter just in time for guests.

Ingredients
1 ham bone, cooked
2 pounds snap beans (4 cups, cooked)
1 teaspoon sugar, brown or granulated
Pinch of red pepper flakes
2 tablespoons butter
Salt to taste

Directions
Place the ham bone in a pot and add enough water to completely cover the beans. Bring to a boil. "String" the beans (remove the center vertical string) and snap or cut into desired lengths. Add to the pot along with the sugar and pepper flakes. Cook over medium heat for 1 hour. Drain in a colander and turn out into a serving bowl. Add two tablespoons of butter and salt to taste. Serve hot.
(Yields eight ½-cup servings.)

PAN-FRIED OKRA CAKES

Produce was homegrown—planted and tended, picked, cooked, and enjoyed from the Palmer's backyard garden. Will and Cynthia kept a small cornfield out back and likely dried the kernels, grinding them into fresh cornmeal, or they picked up a box of cornmeal at Henning's only grocery store. Okra was a prized pod, whether fried whole, stewed with tomatoes, or chopped and patted into crispy cakes.

Ingredients
1 pound fresh okra, washed, sliced thinly, and diced
½ cup chopped yellow or white onion, finely diced
1 teaspoon salt

¼ teaspoon pepper
1 large egg
½ cup chicken broth
1 teaspoon baking powder
¼ teaspoon garlic powder (optional)
½ cup flour
½ cup cornmeal
¼ cup vegetable oil, for frying

Directions
In a large bowl, combine the chopped okra and onion, salt, pepper, chicken broth, and egg. Mix well. In another bowl, combine the flour, baking powder, cornmeal, and garlic powder. Add dry ingredients to the okra mixture, stirring well. In a cast-iron skillet, drop ¼-cup portions of the okra mixture into the hot oil. Fry over medium-low heat until cooked through and crisply browned (about 5 minutes per side).
(Yields ten to twelve ¼-cup patties.)

FRESH FIELD PEAS
Field peas such as the crowder, whippoorwill, Dixie Lee, and even lady peas such as white acre peas and cream peas were planted in the backyard garden of the Palmer house.

Grandmother Cynthia planted black-eyed, purple hull, and pink-eye peas, adding color as she sprinkled these lowly legumes across their backyard corn field to return valuable nitrogen back to the soil.

But field peas aren't just for corn fields anymore. The humble pea is a featured menu item in today's fine-dining cuisine.

Ingredients
1 pound (3 cups) fresh field peas,
5 cups chicken stock or broth
2 slices hickory smoked bacon, crisply fried
1 tablespoon butter, melted
2 medium garlic cloves, peeled and minced
1 sprig, lemon thyme
1 large bay leaf

1 medium yellow onion, diced
1 medium carrot, rough chopped
1 stalk celery, rough chopped
Salt and pepper to taste

Directions
Rinse the peas thoroughly. Fry the bacon until crisp. Remove the bacon from the pan and add the butter. Sauté the onion and garlic in the bacon grease and melted butter mixture. Add the onion and garlic mixture to the peas. In a large sauce pan or Dutch oven, bring 5 cups of chicken broth to a boil. Add peas, onion and garlic mixture, carrots, celery, thyme, and bay leaf. Adjust the chicken broth to submerge the peas to a depth of 1½ inches. Bring the pea mixture to a boil. Skim off the foam. Reduce the heat, cover, and simmer gently for 30 to 45 minutes, until the peas are tender. Taste the peas and broth and add salt, if needed. Remove the bay leaf, carrots, and celery. Store the peas in cooled liquid or drain. Refrigerate or serve immediately.
(Yields 3 cups.)

CANDIED SWEET POTATOES
Nothing says "southern" like sweet potatoes. Whether this root vegetable was served fresh from the garden, or fashioned into a casserole, cake, or pie, Sunday lunch at the Palmer house wouldn't have been complete without these golden sweet spuds.

Ingredients
6 medium-sized raw sweet potatoes
⅓ cup softened butter
¼ cup brown sugar
Pinch of salt

Directions
Preheat the oven to 350°F. Peel and slice the raw sweet potatoes into ¼-inch rounds. In a 12-inch, cast-iron skillet, layer the potato slices with brown sugar, salt and melted butter Cover with aluminum foil. Place the skillet in the preheated oven and bake for 30 minutes. Remove the skillet

from the oven. Lift the foil and baste the potatoes with the melted butter/
brown sugar syrup in the bottom of the skillet. Cover and place the skillet back in the oven. Bake for 25 minutes. Uncover and bake a few more
minutes to lightly brown the top layer.
(Yields twelve ½-cup servings.)

STEWED TOMATOES
Red, ripe, and rich in heart-healthy nutrients, the Palmers' homegrown
tomatoes were sliced for sandwiches, sectioned for salads, and stewed
for Sunday gatherings.

Ingredients
12 medium-sized, vine-ripened tomatoes
1 medium yellow onion, diced
¼ cup bread crumbs
2 tablespoons butter
¼ teaspoon sugar
Large bowl of ice water

Directions
On your stovetop, in a large Dutch oven, boil enough water to cover the
tomatoes. With a large slotted spoon, carefully lower the tomatoes into
the simmering water. Allow the tomatoes to simmer for 30 seconds to 1
minute. When the skins begin cracking, gently lift each tomato out of the
water with the slotted spoon. Place the tomatoes in ice water and leave
for 1 minute. Remove the tomatoes from the ice bath. Let sit. Slip the
skins from the tomatoes. Drain the water from the Dutch oven, and place
the tomatoes back inside the pot. Add the onion, salt, sugar, and bread
crumbs. Gently crush the tomatoes with a fork or potato masher and stew
over low heat for 45 minutes. Stir frequently. Stir in the butter and serve.
(Yields 8 servings.)

PECAN PIE
The Palmers' backyard was teeming with pecan trees. Today, American
Heritage Trees, a nonprofit organization based in Lebanon, Tennessee,
collects seeds and saplings from these remaining hardwoods.

Pecan pies were more than a Sunday favorite. They were perfection baked in buttery, flaky goodness, ruling and reigning on Grandmother Cynthia's dining room table.

Ingredients
3 eggs, lightly beaten
1 cup sugar
3 tablespoons flour
1 cup white corn syrup
1 cup shelled pecans
3 tablespoons butter, melted
2 teaspoons vanilla
1 nine-inch, buttery, flaky pie shell

Directions
Preheat the oven to 350°F. In a medium bowl, combine the beaten eggs, sugar, flour, and syrup gradually until well combined. Add pecans, butter, and then vanilla. Pour the mixture into the unbaked pie pastry. Bake at 350°F for approximately 50 minutes or until a knife inserted halfway into the pie comes out clean.
(Yields 8 servings.)

PECAN PIE BREAD PUDDING
Cynthia Palmer was resourceful. Her well-stocked pantry provided the means by which she put together a family meal, Sunday feast, or lunch for friends. Their cow provided fresh milk and cream. Chickens scratched and pecked nearby, providing her family—and often a neighbor in need—with fresh eggs. And with the abundance of pecans and some day-old bread, she could whip up this simple recipe.

Ingredients
1 sixteen-ounce (8 cups) loaf of French bread, cubed
2½ cups milk
1 cup heavy cream
1 tablespoon vanilla
4 eggs, lightly beaten

1 cup granulated sugar
Generous pinch of salt
½ cup butter, softened
1½ cups brown sugar, firmly packed
1 cup pecans, chopped

Tidbits:
The butter, brown sugar, and pecan mixture measures 1½ cups. Use a ¾-cup portion each for the middle and top layers of the bread mixture.

Directions
Preheat the oven to 350°F. Cut the loaf of bread into ½ inch strips with a serrated bread knife. Then cut the strips of bread into ½-inch cubes. Arrange the bread cubes in a single layer on a cookie sheet and place the cookie sheet in the preheated oven. Allow the bread cubes to bake for 10 minutes. Remove the bread cubes from the oven and place them in a large bowl. In a second large bowl, beat the eggs and add the milk, cream, sugar, salt, and vanilla. Whisk the mixture until combined. Pour the mixture over the bread cubes. Press the bread cubes into the mixture with the back of a large spoon, or spatula until submerged. Allow the bread to soak for 10 to 15 minutes. In a smaller bowl, combine the softened butter, brown sugar, and pecans. The mixture should resemble wet sand. Pour half of the bread mixture into a 2-quart oblong baking dish (8×11×2-inch.) Press the mixture down into pan. Top the bread mixture with half of the pecan mixture. Spoon in the remaining bread mixture and top it with the remaining pecan mixture. Place the pan on a rimmed baking sheet to catch any mixture that may boil over. Bake for 1 hour or until a toothpick inserted into the center of the bread pudding comes out clean.

(Yields twelve ¼-cup servings.)